It's A Disaster

The Money and Politics that Follow Earthquakes, Hurricanes and Other Catastrophic Losses

David T. Russell

Silver Lake Publishing

It's A Disaster
The Money and Politics that Follow Earthquakes, Hurricanes
and Other Catastrophic Losses
First edition, 1999

Silver Lake Publishing
2025 Hyperion Avenue
Los Angeles, CA 90027

For a list of other publications or for more information from Silver Lake Publishing, please call (888) 663-3091.

Library of Congress Catalog Number: pending

Russell, David T.
It's A Disaster
The Money and Politics that Follow Earthquakes, Huricances
and Other Catastrophic Losses
Includes index
Pages: 308

ISBN: 1-56343-172-6
Printed in the United States of America.

ACKNOWLEDGMENTS

It's A Disaster began as a concept for a college course at Illinois Wesleyan University about catastrophes and the insurance market. From those first discussions in 1995 came the realization that there is no compendium of information on disasters and disaster-related insurance coverages. This book is designed to fill that gap for both the general interest market and the college course market.

I want to thank the staff at Silver Lake Publishing, without whose efforts I could not have completed this book. In particular, I want to acknowledge the efforts of Christina Blackett Schlank, Megan Thorpe and Jamie MacKinnon Walsh. Thanks also go out to Dan Carrigan, Catastrophe Consultant at State Farm for his help.

Editor and Publisher Jim Walsh deserves special credit for his willingness to take a chance on the book's concept. His wisdom and work are apparent throughout this work as well as many of my other projects. I am especially grateful for his perseverance and, more important, his friendship.

Finally, I would like to dedicate this work to my maternal ancestors, the Treadways and the Popes. I am so proud of all that they have accomplished and I hope that my achievements make them proud as well.

David Treadway Russell
Normal, Illinois
November 1998

TABLE OF CONTENTS

INTRODUCTION

In early September 1998, a warm wind blew from the western Sahara desert toward the Atlantic coast of northern Africa. When it reached the coast, the wind crashed into some rain clouds loitering over the water. It pushed the clouds into a rotating pattern. The rotation pulled air up in the middle and pushed it out toward the edge of what was fast shaping into a circle.

The up-and-out motion created a point of low air pressure in the middle of the circle—and a tropical depression was born. The system began its methodical march across the Atlantic, gathering strength as it moved toward the Caribbean and the Florida Keys.

As the depression grew into a storm and then a hurricane, weather watchers in the United States followed their normal practice and gave the thing a name. The U.S. Weather Service uses the names—coming in alphabetical order during a given year and alternating gender to avoid the appearance of sexism—to keep track of them and to identify the paths and lifecycles of storms that often develop in close bunches.

The September storm heading for Florida was called Georges. Millions of Americans tracked its progress through the media and stayed glued to reports from the National Hurricane Center in Miami and The Weather Channel on television.

An anthropologist observing the reaction might wonder why people showed so much interest in a storm thousands of miles away. An economist would probably offer the truest answer. Those millions of people weren't watching satellite images of pinwheel-shaped storms because of ancient tribal impulses. They were watching because the pinwheels represent one of the few truly uncontrollable influences on their material well being.

As advanced as modern technology has grown, it can't influence weather. And, as sophisticated as financial markets have become, they—like humans—still respond with more fear than reason to things they can't influence. The result: For all of our money and data processing capacity, we still treat natural disasters with a superstition that would make the anthropologist feel at home. While the economist is left to shake his head ruefully at the inefficiency and waste generated by that superstition.

In the meantime, Georges worked his way across the Atlantic, gaining power from the significant differences in temperature and barometric pressure. As his winds grew to velocities of 125 miles per hour, Hurricane Georges hit the southeastern Caribbean islands hard—leveling thousands of buildings and leaving tens of thousands of people homeless. On islands like Cuba, where crude design and poor constrution make structures that aren't up to the task of withstanding high winds, the impact was particularly devestating.

As it moved from the deep Atlantic toward continental North America, Georges arched slightly to the north from its east-west path. This turn suggested the storm would pass over the southern tip of Florida and draw even more power from the warm water of the Gulf of Mexico. This path is so common for Atlantic storms that it has a name—Hurricane Alley.

In the Florida Keys, 90 mile-per-hour winds were reported for over 10 hours during storm passage. The wind and high water caused heavy structural damage, according to the Florida Division of Emergency Management: More than 900 homes suffered minor damage, 500 suffered major damage, and more than 150 were completely destroyed—including 75 houseboats on so-called "Houseboat Row" near Key West.

People living on the islands lost electrical power and were warned to boil water to avoid sickness from viral and bacterial contaminates. Full restoration of utilities would take more than a week. Of all of the Keys, Big Pine Key and Kudjoe Key were hardest hit, including severe flooding from the high water associated with a hurricane.

Since the highest land elevation in the Keys is about 14 feet above sea level, high water quickly swept into homes and businesses. The Key West Airport was closed to all but relief flights for several days. Still, the worst of the storm had stayed out over the water to the south of Key West.

The bigger problems looked like they were going to come farther to the north and west. Having glanced past the Keys, Georges was heading toward the most heavily populated part of the northern Gulf Coast—New Orleans.

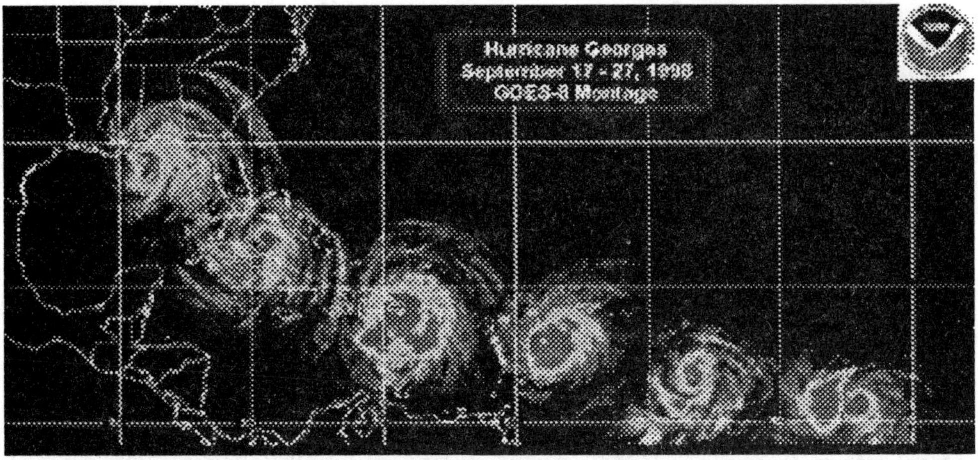

Hurricane Georges on its path from the Atlantic to the Gulf Coast

Once in the shallow, warm water of the Gulf of Mexico, Georges regained some of the intensity he'd lost passing over the islands. A hurricane acts like a vacuum cleaner when it moves over water, sucking water up and depositing it into the rotating clouds. Calm, shallow, warm water—like the water in the Gulf of Mexico—is the perfect incubating place for hurricanes.

Hundreds of thousands of people in and around New Orleans were glued to their televisions and radios, waiting for the storm to plod its way up the Gulf. And *plod* was the word. Georges was in no hurry, he slowed down over the Gulf, as if biding his time to choose where to come ashore.

People in coastal cities from Florida to Texas went through familiar rituals—making sure their house insurance was paid up and their valuables were stored up high out of reach of flood waters. Business people and homeowners covered their windows with plywood so that they'd be protected from debris kicked up by hurricane winds. Local officials secured levees and canals in low-lying areas with sand bags and mounds of dirt. Rising water precedes a hurricane like an advance man moving ahead of a fat-cat politician.

And, speaking of fat-cat politicians, the governmental apparatus of disaster response prepared to deal with the consequences. The Federal Emergency Management Agency (FEMA), the National Guard, various congressmen, staffers from the governor's office and local potentates got their paperwork and speeches ready for the federal gravy train which would invariably follow the storm. Insurance companies scrambled an army of claims adjusters to handle the onslaught of claims that would arrive alongside the gravy train.

In New Orleans, with brownish clouds circling overhead, the mayor opened the Superdome as an emergency shelter. Hundreds of thousands of residents simply evacuated ahead of the storm. In Biloxi, riverboat casinos begrudgingly closed their doors.

Georges inched ashore near Biloxi and—even though it wasn't quite as powerful as some people had feared—still managed to damage or destroy thousands of homes and vehicles in the Gulf States. Several people were killed in the flukey ways that people usually are during hurricanes...hit by doors torn off their hinges, or electricuted by down power lines.

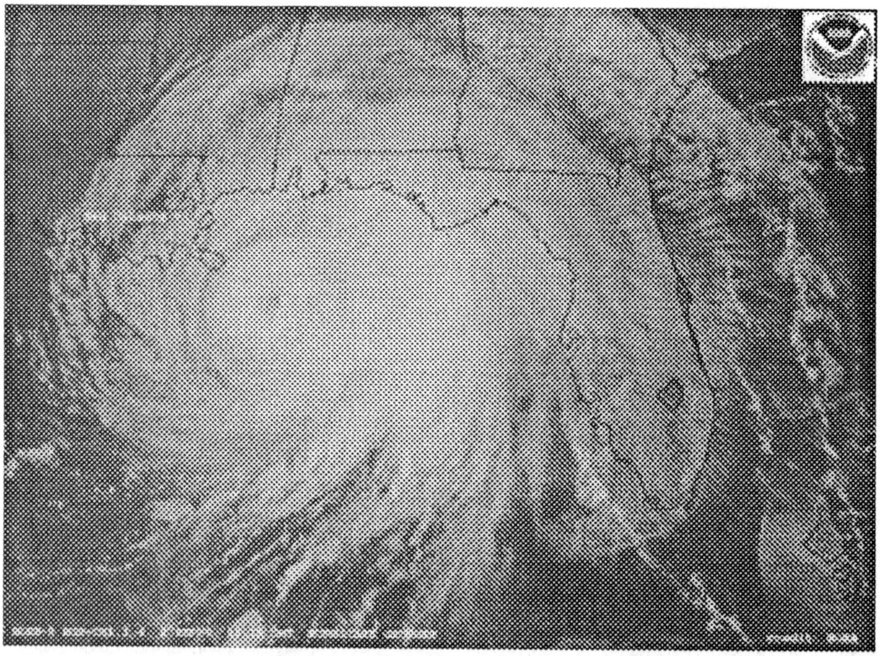

Hurricane Georges as it looked when it reached land near Biloxi, Mississippi

New Orleans was largely spared the brunt of the hurricane's wind and water, but not before causing panic that Georges would inundate an already flood-prone area.

In the days after the storm, most of the insurance claims appeared to come from water damage to walls and personal property, rather than the wind damage usually associated with tropical storms.

According to estimates from the Insurance Services Office's Property Claims Services (PCS) unit, insurance claims from Hurricane Georges would total about $2.5 billion in the United States and its territories—not to mention billions in non-U.S. damage and uninsured damage as well.

Equally impressive was the sheer volume of an estimated $685,000 in policyholder claims associated with the storm system. The American Red Cross appealed to citizens for help in replacing over $100 million spent on aid to disaster victims. That figure was its highest total ever.

Damage estimates from Georges total well over $1 billion in Puerto Rico alone. Extreme flooding was reported with rainfall amounts of 20 to 30 inches along portions of the southern Gulf Coast. Mobile, Alabama, received 13.0 inches of rain from the storm, which boosted the monthly total to 23.0 inches, breaking the September record of 16 inches set 100 years earlier. The highest individual storm total reported was Munson, Florida, which reported 25.0 inches of rain from Georges.

Even the Chicago Cubs' home run star Sammy Sosa committed his own funds and raised money from others to help disaster victims in his home country of the Dominican Republic, which was hit extremely hard by Georges. In that country alone, estimates included at least 210 dead, more than 500 missing and about 100,000 homeless. Georges left approximately 70 percent of all bridges damaged or out, 90 percent of all plantation crops destroyed, and total damages estimated at more than $1 billion.

It Can't Happen to Me

A disaster is an event that affects many people or a wide geographical area all at one time. It can be natural or man-made. It can be expected and managed to minimize damage—or come as a surprise and be devastating.

Although only a small part of the U.S. population has suffered badly enough from a natural disaster to need financial help, most of us know that bad things can happen to ordinary people. And we like watching disasters unfold. If for no other reason, the electronic and print media love disasters because the immediacy of the things make news essential.

People find entertainment in watching others cope with adversity. The string of disaster movies of the 1970s (Earthquake, The Towering Inferno and others) and more recent box office hits about asteroids with global effects (Deep Impact and Armageddon) point to a society that enjoys the excitement of surviving a threatening situation. But we take comfort in the belief that these risks are largely fictional, and that we don't really have to cope with such issues ourselves.

For our own personal risks, we carry basic auto, homeowners, health, and life insurance to protect against the isolated events that can affect our family's lives—car accidents, burglaries, house fires, illness, or even unexpected death. In addition to the financial support of insurance, we rely on the emotional and financial support of our family to carry on through personal tragedies. And government agencies such as FEMA and non-profit organizations like the American Red Cross can assist in a time of crisis.

But, natural disasters such as hurricanes and earthquakes severely test the support of family, insurance and even the government upon which we have come to rely. By their very nature, catastrophes affect hundreds or thousands of people all at once. This type of event can stretch society's resources to the breaking point in the short run—and can have lasting emotional and financial reprecussions for years into the future.

Still, most of us cling to some fearful version of the refrain "it can't happen to me." Living under that illusion, people aren't fully prepared for disasters when they do strike. And, perhaps more importantly, the illusion prevents us from thinking critically about the financial tools that are available for dealing with disasters. This is unfortunate. We need to understand the programs and products that follow disasters. Some are not as effective as we may think they are.

Disaster Trends

Both practical home and financial preparedness usually prove inadequate when widespread disasters occur. This is a problem because the evidence—both anecdotal and scientific—shows that virtually anyone could experience a serious catastrophe. A surprisingly diverse mix of areas of the country actually has suffered tremendous losses in disasters.

The 10 Most Costly U.S. Catastrophes

Date	Catastrophe	Est. Insured Loss (Mil)
August 1992	Hurricane Andrew (Florida)	$15,500
January 1994	Northridge Earthquake (California)	12,500
Sept. 1989	Hurricane Hugo (Mid-Atlantic states)	4,195
Sept. 1998	Hurricane Georges (Florida, Gulf Coast)	2,500
October 1995	Hurricane Opal (Florida)	2,100
March 1993	20-State Winter Storm (Midwest)	1,750
October 1991	Oakland/Berkeley Fires (California)	1,700
Sept. 1996	Hurricane Fran (Eastern Seaboard)	1,600
Sept. 1992	Hurricane Iniki (Hawaii)	1,600
May 1995	Flood/Wind/Hail (Texas, New Mexico)	1,135

Source: Property Claims Services, a unit of AISG, Inc.

Recent Events

According to a report from American Insurance Services Group (AISG), economic losses from 25 catastrophic events in 1997 caused $2.6 billion in insured damage in the United States—a 65 percent drop from the $7.4 billion in 1996. (The figures from AISG's Property Claim Services division exclude personal injury claims.) Events in 1997 were the fewest since 1987, when AISG recorded 24 catastrophes. The total losses were the lowest since 1988, which saw $1.4 billion in insured losses. Insurance experts define a catastrophe as an event that causes more than $25 million in damage. In 1997, the AISG raised its catastrophe threshold to claims over $25 million from $5 million.

"[1997] was the first year since 1990 without a single $1 billion catastrophe," said AISG spokesman Gary R. Kerney. Furthermore, "Catastrophe frequency fell off significantly in the second half of [1997]," he said.

"Seventeen of the 25 events occurred in the first six months of the year and caused $1.8 of the $2.6 billion in damage.... An important factor in the reduced number and cost of catastrophes was below normal hurricane activity," Kerney added.

Estimated Losses from US Catastrophes

Year	Number of Catastrophes	Payments (Billions)
1982	33	$1.5
1983	33	2.3
1984	26	1.6
1985	34	2.8
1986	26	0.9
1987	24	0.9
1988	32	1.4
1989	34	7.6
1990	32	2.8
1991	36	4.7
1992	36	23.0
1993	36	5.6
1994	38	17.0
1995	34	8.3
1996	41	7.4
1997	25	2.6

(These loss estimates represent anticipated insured loss on an industry-wide basis. Each estimate reflects the total pure loss insurance payment for personal and commercial property lines of insurance. The estimate does not include loss involving uninsured property, including uninsured publicly owned property and utilities, agriculture, aircraft and property insured under the National Flood Insurance Program or Write-Your-Own Program. The estimates also exclude loss adjustment expense.)

Source: American Insurance Services Group, Property Claims Services Division

David DeSantis, the executive director of the Natural Disaster Coalition concurred. “There were virtually no major storms,” he said. “That is probably the biggest single factor this year.”

DeSantis, whose organization is funded by insurers and educates consumers about reducing loss, said the National Flood Insurance Program (NFIP) cuts losses for private companies.

DeSantis said claims were lower in part because insurers have been teaching consumers about ways to lower property losses and have increased deductibles to lower their insurance premiums.

In early 1997, PCS's Kerney looked back at the disasters that had occurred during1996:

> The [insurance] industry has a tendency to plan for a repeat of something like Hurricane Andrew or an event even worse. But for those involved in catastrophe claim handling on a day-to-day basis, and for insurers and reinsurers trying to gauge the risk of their catastrophe coverages, the fact is we are seeing a continual increase in the number of smaller events that cost the industry heavily because of the demographic shift of people to catastrophe-prone areas.

These areas include California and Florida.

Ninety percent of all natural disasters are floods, but few people appreciate the frequency or severity of floods. Rising water damages or destroys virtually everything in its path: cars, houses, livestock, farmland, businesses and everything else that doesn't react well to being underwater.

What's worse is that many people don't understand that most insurance policies do not cover flood damage. Although automobiles damaged by flood are covered by the comprehensive portion of the auto insurance policy, homeowners must purchase the optional flood insurance contract to collect any flood related claims.

Furthermore, many people mistakenly believe that the Federal government will bail them out (no pun intended) from flood related damage. This is one of the most dangerous illusions surrounding disaster response.

A group of appeals court decisions made in August 1993 shows how foolish some people's notions of disaster assistance can be. The four cases—*Robert Powers et al. v. United States*, *Joe Glenn et al. v. United States*, *Johnny Childs et al. v. United States* and *Big/Little Stores et al. v. United States*—were combined into a single trial that considered charges that the government negligently failed to publicize NFIP.

The groups of angry property owners pushing the suits were all residents of Alabama who fell victim to a series of flash floods that occurred in 1990. Because none of them had purchased flood insurance, their losses weren't covered. And because they made foolish assumptions about

FEMA bailing them out with loans, etc., they were stuck with water damaged houses and ruined personal effects. And little chance of being compensated.

The groups invoked provisions of the Federal Tort Claims Act (FTCA). They alleged that:

- the National Flood Insurance Act placed a mandatory duty upon the Director of FEMA to publicize the availability of federally subsidized flood insurance;
- the Director had "totally failed" to perform this duty; and
- as a result, they were unaware of the availability of such flood insurance and were uninsured when they suffered flood losses.

FEMA countered that these claims were barred by provisions of the FTCA and that the United States was immune from suit for any liability associated with flood control. Specifically, the law states that "[n]o liability of any kind shall attach to or rest upon the United States for any damage from or by floods or flood waters at any place."

At the preliminary hearing stage, the district court dismissed the combined cases, citing federal law that provided sovereign immunity enacted by Congress in connection with the government's construction of flood control projects. The angry Alabamans appealed.

The appeals court focused on one issue: whether the discretionary function exception to the FTCA bars suit against the United States for the alleged failure to publicize federally subsidized flood insurance.

The statute establishing FEMA authorizes the Director to "from time to time take such action as may be necessary in order to make information and data available to the public." The agency argued that this language was a clear statutory grant of discretion and therefore protected by the discretionary function exception to the FTCA.

The angry Alabamans countered that the discretionary function exception did not apply to their claim because they had alleged that the FEMA Director "totally failed" to comply with a mandatory statutory duty.

The FTCA allows lawsuits against the United States for injury or loss of property, or personal injury or death caused by the negligent or wrongful act or omission of any employee of the Government while acting within the scope of his office or employment.

However, Congress did protect the government from some claims. Under FTCA, sovereign immunity *does* prohibit "[a]ny claim...based upon the exercise or performance or the failure to exercise or perform a discretionary function or duty on the part of a federal agency or an employee of the Government...."

The Alabamans sought damages for the alleged failure of the Director of FEMA "to take necessary actions to make information and data available to the public and to publicize widely the availability of the flood insurance program, its coverage and objectives."

They cited the law establishing FEMA, which states:

> The Director shall from time to time take such action as may be necessary in order to make information and data available to the public, and to any State or local agency or official, with regard to—(1) the flood insurance program, its coverage and objectives, and (2) estimated and chargeable flood insurance premium rates, including the basis for and differences between such rates....

Emphasizing Congress's use of the word "shall," the Alabamans argued that the law imposed a "specific mandatory legislative directive" upon the Director of FEMA to publicize federally subsidized flood insurance.

The appeals court didn't agree. It pointed out that the law followed this "shall" with "from time to time take such action as may be necessary." So, Congress had not specifically prescribed a course of action for the Director to follow. Rather, it had given the Director discretion to decide when and how best to make information and data available to the public regarding federally subsidized flood insurance.

"The Director must then make these decisions and act without reliance upon a fixed or readily ascertainable standard," the appeals court wrote. "The Director's decision clearly involves an element of judgment or choice and therefore involves the exercise of discretion."

The Alabamans made a big deal about the alleged "total failure" of the Director to publicize NFIP. But the appeals court pointed out several examples—albeit technical ones—of how FEMA had legally publicizied NFIP. Specifically, it noted:

> The Code of Federal Regulations contains a detailed description of the National Flood Insurance Program...and notice is provided in the Federal Register when a county enters the program and insurance becomes available in that county.... Further, the FEMA Publications Catalog indicates that pamphlets concerning the National Flood Insurance Program were available throughout the 1980s.

So, the Alabamans were wrong about FEMA not publicizing NFIP. Really, what they were doing was criticizing the manner in which the agency promoted the plan—and, so doing, challenged the exercise of a discretionary function.

Because the homeowners didn't like the way FEMA publicized NFIP, they argued that they should be made whole on uninsured losses. This was a weak—and surprisingly childish—claim.

The appeals court concluded:

> We hold that the conduct challenged here falls within the discretionary function exception to the FTCA. Congress has authorized the Director of FEMA to use discretion in making available information regarding federally subsidized flood insurance. Such discretion is of the type Congress sought to protect with the discretionary function exception to the FTCA. Accordingly, we affirm the judgment of the district court dismissing this action....

Catastrophes Galore

While California and the coastal areas of the Southeastern U.S. seem to bear the brunt of catastrophic losses, other parts of the country experience extensive disaster activity, including flooding, hail storms, severe winter weather and tornadoes. Texas and the Midwestern U.S. are home to some of the world's most severe storms. During the summer, colliding masses of warm and cool air spawn hail—producing squall lines and tornadoes.

While late afternoon thunderstorms often come and go in a matter or hours, and may affect only a very localized area, their intensity and unpredictability make up for what they lack in size. They can also dump large amounts of water in a short period of time. Unusual weather activity in the Central U.S. can turn a drought into a flooded area in a matter of days.

The Northern portions of the U.S. frequently experience costly winter weather that collapses buildings, snaps power lines, and interrupts the flow of goods and services for days at a time over areas that extend hundreds of miles. "Nor'easters," as they're often called, because they blow in from the Northeast, can have significant costs that defy typical measurement since much of their impact arises out of lost worker productivity and opportunity costs.

The concentration of buildings and population near the earthquake zones in San Francisco and Los Angeles accounts for the severity of losses when a serious earthquake occurs, though building codes and loss mitigation efforts can reduce losses significantly. While California receives plenty of earthquake publicity, earth movement exposure is not limited to the West Coast.

The New Madrid, Missouri area is where a series of devastating earthquakes struck in 1811-1812. These quakes were felt as far away as Boston. Geological conditions in the New Madrid region favor an eventual repeat of the early Nineteenth Century event. And the rock and soil formations of this region will carry the energy released during such an event for hundreds of miles. In both California and the Midwest, forecasters expect that the next "Big One" could cost upwards of $100 billion.

Some sections of the U.S. face the risk of wildfires that can consume thousands of acres, acres that include residences big and small. Coastal sections of California, in particular, accumulate a dry brush that serves as tender for arsonists and carelessly flicked cigarettes. Other parts of the country also can become ripe for fires after long dry spells. Sections of Florida and the Appalachian Mountains have been known to catch fire from lightning strikes and poorly attended campsites.

Some disasters have origins in the creations of man. With the Twentieth Century in its twilight, technological innovations such as nuclear power and the microprocessor have improved work productivity and reduced airborne pollution. But these "advancements" have brought about problems of their own that have potentially devastating results. When control is lost, nuclear power possesses the potential to kill millions of people and render large sections of land uninhabitable.

The experiences of Three Mile Island in Pennsylvania and Chernobyl in the Ukraine prove that the unthinkable can happen.

Societal reliance on the computer has proven risky since the usefulness of a programming convention is coming to a potentially catastrophic end. The Y2K problem has been anticipated and programmers have spent millions of man-hours correcting the bug. Unfortunately, the installed base of software using the two-digit year abbreviation is so large that it is impossible to predict the consequences when the year 2000 arrives.

So, It Could Happen to Me. What Can I Do About It?

Since no person is immune to the consequences of disasters (natural or man-made), responsible citizens should understand the risks of their locale and make reasonable preparations to limit the negative impact.

Sadly enough, a May 1997 National Science Foundation-funded study of risky behavior found that most people are reluctant to purchase insurance against natural disasters because they believe such events will not happen to them. The findings essentially duplicated the findings in a similar study twenty years prior.

According to Professor Howard Kunreuther, who conducted the 1997 study, factors such as the cost of insurance and perceived likelihood of disaster are not the primary drivers of most people's decisions to insure or not to insure against floods, tornadoes, earthquakes, hurricanes and other disasters. Unfortunately, insurance purchases tend to be impulse buys made after people have seen shocking new clips.

Following a flood or earthquake, the study found that residents often show an active interest in purchasing insurance—even though subsequent purchases do not solve problems after the fact. Unfortunately, people usually cancel these policies after several years without claims. Kunreuther, Paul Kleindorfer and Neil Doherty, all economists at the University of Pennsylvania's Wharton School, believe that insurance companies, government, financial institutions, real estate brokers and property owners each have a role in minimizing property damage. Their research found property owners ill-informed about the frequency of disaster and about the extent of government assistance available for recovery.

Pursuing "Free" Federal Money

On August 24, 1992, Hurricane Andrew swept through the southern tip of Florida. It cut a 30 mile-wide path, destroying many residential neighborhoods and leaving thousands of people homeless. Many of these people were forced to evacuate their homes and ask the government for shelter. And many expected that the government would roll into town with money for everyone who got wet during the storm.

They were about to find out how tough it can be to get free money. In a familiar exercise, President George Bush declared certain South Florida counties as disaster areas, thus invoking the provisions of the Stafford Disaster Relief Act—which meant that the hurricane victims could receive various kinds of relief, including temporary housing assistance benefits.

FEMA stepped into motion.

Among the victims seeking aid: Rita Marie Lockett, Clemene Pierre, Bertha Cross, and Ralph Leamy. Their homes in the Miami area had been destroyed and they wanted financial support from the government. They all had problems getting as much of it as they wanted. Their problems would raise questions about FEMA's ability to enact emergency relief programs at its discretion.

Rita Marie Lockett was living with her children in a one room travel trailer set up in one of the so-called "tent cities" which housed people after Andrew had smashed through. She wanted federal disaster housing assistance to get back into a reasonable apartment.

But FEMA denied her application because someone else in her pre-disaster household had already received insurance payments—even though Lockett had not received any portion of the payments.

Clemene Pierre was also living with her children in a one-room mobile home. She had applied for federal disaster housing assistance and had been found eligible to receive assistance. However, FEMA failed to provide her with housing.

Bertha Cross had been living in the tent city, too. She had applied for temporary housing assistance; FEMA had found her eligible for benefits. However, she alleged that FEMA had refused to provide her with actual housing until after they received notice that the tent city in which she was living was due to close. She also claimed that FEMA was threatening—illegally—her with dispossession of her mobile home because of her inability to repay the cash assistance she had received.

Ralph Leamy had applied for temporary housing assistance and been found eligible for benefits by FEMA. He received cash assistance—but FEMA provided him with actual housing only after he'd been hospitalized for a stress-related condition. And, after that, FEMA was seeking repayment of the monetary assistance it had given to him.

Lockett and the others found Miami-based Legal Aid lawyers and sued FEMA. In their lawsuit, they claimed that the agency failed to provide them with actual housing, failed to notify them of all types of housing assistance available, and implemented the statutes and regulations in an arbitrary and illegal manner.

Specifically, they claimed that FEMA's policies and practices had systematically prevented South Florida disaster victims—especially poor ones—from obtaining information and receiving housing assistance. Instead, they claimed, FEMA tried to convince poor people to take a little bit of pocket money...and go away.

The lawyers for Lockett and the others sought class action status to include "all persons residing in Dade, Broward, Monroe and Collier counties, Florida, on August 24, 1992, who have applied for, or will apply for disaster housing assistance under the Stafford Act."

The class could also be divided into two parts. The first included all victims otherwise eligible for temporary housing assistance who received only cash rental assistance pursuant to FEMA's "cash-assistance rule." This was a problem because in the aftermath of the storm, housing had become very expensive in the Dade County area.

The second included victims otherwise eligible for temporary housing assistance but who were denied—or were asked to return—assistance based solely upon a finding that another person in their pre-disaster housing unit had already received assistance. This "single-household rule" was intended to prevent double-dipping—especially among unmarried couples.

The Legal Aid sharpies asked the federal court in south Florida for declaratory and injunctive relief on behalf of their clients and all others similarly situated. In short, they wanted FEMA to abide by rules they considered were the requirements of the Stafford Act.

Lockett's lawyers also alleged that, by failing to provide temporary housing assistance to otherwise eligible disaster victims as specifically stated in the Stafford Act, FEMA violated the Due Process Clause of the Fifth Amendment. The theory: By arbitrarily depriving plaintiffs of their entitlement to assistance, FEMA had acted unconstitutionally. This claim would later prove the most significant.

FEMA moved to dismiss the Lockett lawsuit on various technical grounds, arguing that people seeking aid needed to go through all of the agency's bureaucratic process before suing.

In August 1993, the United States District Court for the southern district of Florida issued its ruling on whether to dismiss the case.

The federal judge hearing the case reiterated mechanics of the dispute:

> [Lockett's lawyers] claim that FEMA cannot or will not grant the requested relief and any challenge at the administrative level would be fruitless. Therefore, they contend that there is no need to exhaust administrative remedies. Also, [they] maintain that exhaustion of administrative remedies is unnecessary because FEMA is clearly acting in violation of its authorizing statute.

On the material issues of the dispute, FEMA claimed that it had the authority to waive the cash-assistance rule...and offer pocket money if it decided to do so. FEMA also argued that it could enforce its single-household determinations because it had the discretion to decide whether "the size of the household requires that more than one residence be provided."

The court pointed out that the Stafford Act states:

> An applicant declared ineligible for temporary housing assistance, an applicant whose application has been canceled for cause, an applicant whose application has been refused because of late filing, and an occupant who received a direct housing payment but is not eligible for continued assistance...[may] dispute such a determination within 60 calendar days following notification of such action.

However, this point didn't mean as much for the Lockett group as its members had hoped. The fact that they could appeal didn't mean that their appeal would hold up.

FEMA had broad discretion to handle financial aid as its people deemed necessary. In fact, the agency only had authority to provide certain forms of assistance "when existing rental resources are not available and repairs to the home will not make it livable in a reasonable period of time, or when the eligible applicant is unable to physically leave the home due to the need to tend crops or livestock."

What's more, FEMA pointed out that Lockett already had appealed the decision and won a partial adjustment in her favor. Doing so, it argued, she eliminated her right to dispute its administrative conclusion.

The court concluded:

> The appeal procedures adopted by FEMA fulfill neither of the...criteria. Under the provision, only certain applicants have the right to dispute particular adverse determination on assistance. The Stafford Act only authorizes appeal of administrative decisions regarding eligibility, ineligibility, cancellation and refusal. The regulation is silent regarding an appeal where a recipient disputes the type of temporary housing assistance offered.

FEMA had also argued that the Disaster Relief Act specifically provided that administrative actions taken by the agency were exempt from judicial review. Additionally, it suggested that "agency action is committed to agency discretion by law."

In response, Lockett's lawyers argued that the Stafford Act did not preclude review of FEMA's decision to provide cash assistance instead of unoccupied habitable dwellings, "suitable rental housing, mobile homes, or other readily fabricated dwellings to" otherwise eligible disaster victims.

So, the court had to determine whether any of the actions set forth in the complaint were discretionary...and dismiss those that were. It ruled that, even where discretionary acts are precluded from judicial review, "[t]here is no reason to believe that Congress ever intended to commit to an agency's discretion the question of whether or not to act constitutionally. The law now...is that adherence to constitutional guidelines is not discretionary, it is mandatory."

Therefore, the court had jurisdiction over the claims alleging constitutional violations. The issue it had to consider: FEMA was required under the Stafford Act to provide temporary housing to all eligible disaster victims;

however, the President—and, through him, FEMA—clearly had discretion to choose how and when to implement the temporary housing assistance program...or not.

At what point did the President's discretion end?

Lockett's lawyers argued that, once a disaster had been declared, the President did not have discretionary authority to deny the entitlement to housing aid once an individual had been found eligible according to stated criteria.

The court concluded that Lockett's position "is not entirely true. The plain language of the regulation provides that '[t]emporary housing assistance may be provided only when both of the following conditions are met....' This clearly shows that assistance is discretionary, not mandatory."

It ruled that, even when an applicant met the requirements of eligibility, the language, by including the term "may," signified that FEMA had the discretion to award that assistance.

Lockett's lawyers argued several other constitutional points against FEMA. First, they claimed that the practice of denying temporary housing assistance to otherwise eligible hurricane victims, based on a finding that another person in the pre-disaster housing unit received assistance, was inequitable and had the effect of discriminating against persons based on their economic status.

The Stafford Act provided that "the processing of applications, and other relief and assistance activities shall be accomplished in an equitable and impartial manner, without discrimination on the grounds of...economic status." And FEMA's own regulations stated that "[a]ll personnel carrying out Federal major disaster or emergency assistance functions, including...the processing of applications...shall perform their work in an equitable and impartial manner, without discrimination on the grounds of...economic status."

Lockett's lawyers also argued that FEMA violated their clients' Due Process rights guaranteed under the Fifth Amendment. The Stafford Act and federal regulations required that "[e]ach person who applies for assistance...shall be notified regarding the type and amount of any assistance for which such person qualifies."

The information that must be provided includes:

- all forms of such assistance available;
- any specific criteria which must be met to qualify for each type of assistance that is available;
- any limitations which apply to each type of assistance; and
- the address and telephone number of offices responsible for responding.

Lockett's lawyers argued that because the hurricane decimated much of the local rental properties in south Dade County, temporary housing assistance made in the form of money payments violated FEMA regulations because "existing rental resources [were] not available" after the hurricane.

But the court ruled that FEMA's decision to disperse monetary assistance was exactly the kind of decision that Congress intended to be beyond the jurisdiction of the federal courts.

This, the court held, was particularly true in the absence of guidelines for determining which form of temporary housing FEMA and other agencies have to provide to hurricane victims.

The court went on to decide that FEMA's practice of denying housing assistance to otherwise eligible hurricane victims, based on a finding that another person in the pre-disaster housing unit received assistance—even without proof that the applicant actually received such assistance—was within its discretionary jurisdiction.

In their claim, Lockett's lawyers mistakenly characterized the Stafford Act as *requiring* that temporary housing assistance be provided to "persons who, as a result of a major disaster, require temporary housing."

More correctly, the Act stated that the "President *may*... provide ...temporary housing...or other dwellings."

The court allowed a few of Lockett's claims to go forward. But the overwhelming impact of its ruling was that FEMA had the discretion to enforce its policies as it saw fit. This point is very important for people who want to bounce back financially from the next disaster...without relying on the government's "discretion."

Summary

The purpose of this book is to educate you about the past, present and future of natural and man-made disasters, as well as disaster recovery and financing services available through a host of private and public sources.

Armed with this knowledge, you should make better informed decisions about the risks you are prepared to accept and those risks you would prefer to transfer to an insurance company or a government entity.

Also, we will examine the larger issues created by catastrophes including questions of government preparedness, taxpayer subsidies, insurance company solvency, and catastrophe protection financing. So, you'll have a good idea of what you *can* and *cannot* transfer to an insurance company or government agency and what you have to bear on your own.

"Any time you allow development in high-hazard areas for fires or floods, you are setting yourself up for major losses...or even loss of life," said Scott Bollens, a professor of political science at the University of California, Irvine. "It's not just about environmental concerns. It has to do with public safety and major economic loss."

The best time to prepare for a disaster, big or small, is before it happens, not when everything around you is in a state of chaos. The challenge is to leave behind the "I'll cross that bridge when I come to it" mentality and take steps today to protect yourself.

PART ONE

Weather Phenomena

The Weather Channel slipped, seemingly effortlessly, into American consciousness in 1982. The channel's programming—a somewhat dry and steadily repetitive cycle of temperatures, forecasts, satellite images and outside shots from remote locations—draws a cult-like audience during most of the year. But its audience size explodes whenever a storm or other weather event occurs.

And all of those people see a lot of commercials, pushing everything from insurance to hardware to household staples. In fact, the Weather Channel runs more advertisements than any other network on television.

Bad weather and money are an intense—and familiar—combination. Despite mankind's best efforts in war and commerce, most catastrophic disasters are caused by nature. Of the top ten insured-loss disasters in United States history, weather has accounted for eight...and certainly contributed to nine...of the ten.

Most natural disasters trace their origins to extreme weather events. And most weather events are created by the same combination of factors: excessive wind, heat, cold or rainfall. These factors are usually caused by the interaction between bodies of water and the uneven heating of the Earth by the Sun. Because the Sun's radiation carries much more energy than any earthly power, it shouldn't be so surprising that weather possesses the strength to impact the physical state of the earth.

Understanding the factors that influence weather allows people to respond to it in a general way. We can minimize the damage caused by weather events with practical preparations as simple as boarding up windows or sand-bagging levees and with financial preparations as complex as developing specialized catastrophe insurance. But, despite our best brains and plainest common sense, we can't do anything to control weather events. They come when...and how...they will.

An ominous corollary: The best-laid plans may not have much effect in the face of overwhelming forces of nature. And that may be why people find natural disasters so interesting—precisely because we can't control them. In fact, we can't even predict them.

Disasters are, by their nature, exceptions to rules and trends. They're what statisticians call outlier events. They're useful in developing trends, but they don't conform to the parameters of trends. For this reason, insurance companies usually exclude disasters from standard policies—or minimize the coverage they do offer so much that consumers are fairly tempted to avoid the insurance and take their chances.

When people take their chances with disasters, they're often assuming someone—read: the government—will support them if things turn out badly. Understandably, most governments would rather not have to face this exposure (and, as the taxpayers who support the government, most of us agree with this resistance). So, they instruct their regulators to force insurance companies to sell the disaster coverage.

As a result, large amounts of money are moving through a system in which history—while educational, in general terms of what to do when a disaster is approaching—doesn't help model future outcomes. There are bound to be inefficiencies: Too much money dedicated to certain activities; not enough money to others.

So, weather experts take full advantage of ever-more capable computer technology that allows better modeling...for the partial measure that it provides. Insurance companies use this modeling as a basis for doing what they can to predict trends in severe weather insurance claims. And then they wait, hoping that they've priced policies accurately. But even these state-of-the-art tactics can't get past the basic fact that weather is unpredictable.

The whole process seems steeped in frustration and irony. The more technology mankind devotes to predicting the weather, the less predictable it seems to be. The storm watch that followed Hurricane Georges through the Caribbean reflects this frustration. We can take pictures with satellites, measure the clouds and air pressure with million-dollar weather planes and extrapolate its path based on a hundred years of data. But will Georges cross into the Gulf of Mexico? Will he land at Galveston or New Orleans? No one knows.

Your grandmother's aching bunion is as reliable a weather prognosticator as the National Weather Center's data crunching mainframes. In fact, with natural disasters, our technological advances may make things even less predictable. Some risk theorists talk about ways in which technology warps people's responses to potential loss. In layman's terms, this means that the satellites and computer models do their best work distinguishing average outcomes—in this case, storms—from exceptional ones. This is helpful, because it means you don't need to board up your windows every time you see dark clouds.

However, the isolation of exceptional outcomes increases their impact...on a psychological level, if no other. And even if the effect is mostly psychological, it can still be a major influence on the decisions people make.

So, our better technology lets us psych ourselves up about natural disasters. Hardware stores get to sell a few extra panels of plywood and flashlight batteries. What's the harm in too much preparedness?

The harm comes from the fact that preparedness is only one of the ways that people deal with the threat of catastrophic disasters. They spend money on insurance and other financial products. And, most ominously, they pressure the government to take care of disaster aftermath.

That last response has led to some of the most inefficient activities and expenditures that the government takes. In the following several chapters that make up this part, we'll consider some of the most basic kinds of natural disasters—weather phenomena—and the impact they have on victims who experience them directly and the public policies that force us all to experience them indirectly.

CHAPTER ONE

Hurricanes

Before Hurricane Andrew hit southern Florida in 1992, insurance experts didn't think that insured losses from a hurricane could exceed $8 billion.

They were wrong. Andrew's collision with the area just south of Miami led to some $15.5 billion in insurance claims. Big insurance companies like State Farm and Allstate had such large shares of the property insurance market in Florida that their losses from Andrew ran into the billions of dollars.

Most insurance companies reacted in one of two ways. They either tried to get out of the Florida market entirely; or they tried to raise the price of their coverage to correct their flawed estimates.

Recognizing the dire consequences for property prices if owners were unable to get insurance, Florida lawmakers scrambled to do damage control. They passed a moratorium—emergency legislation that prevented insurance companies from non-renewing more than five percent of their policyholders statewide in any given year.

To provide insurance for new or non-renewed policyholders, Florida expanded its Joint Underwriting Association (JUA). The JUA allowed homeowners unable to buy coverage elsewhere to buy basic insurance. Insurance companies doing business in the state contributed money and expertise to the JUA.

The moratorium and the JUA slowed the exodus of panicky insurance companies. But the state still had to allow the imprisoned insurance companies to raise their rates. The result was an upward spike in the price of insurance and related financial instruments.

Perhaps most importantly, insurance companies implemented "exposure management" plans that called for writing fewer policies on waterfront properties. This did a couple things. First, it pushed the price of insurance on waterfront real estate up even higher than the rest of the market. And as a result, it forced the state to face the hard reality that its insurance regulations had kept coverage of waterfront real estate artificially cheap.

It's an irony that will repeat throughout this book. The fact is that, the combined efforts of Florida insurance regulators and the companies they watch had subsidized financial protection for the wealthy living in South Beach mansions—at the expense of everyone else.

The Mechanics of the Big Storms

Hurricanes do damage to real estate in two ways. They kick up vicious winds that can toss around cars, trees and anything else that is above ground. They also bring a lot of water with them—both in the form of rain and the so-called "storm surge," extremely high tides that usually occur to the north and east of the storm.

Most people can protect their houses or apartments from the wind by covering windows with plywood or masking tape. And by moving anything under 100 pounds indoors.

The water damage is harder to prevent. You can move valuables up—to high shelves or second floors. But rain can seep into a house from all points. And, when it happens, flood damage defies prevention efforts.

The 1994 federal court decision *Daniel Holtz v. Omaha Property and Casualty Insurance Co.* considered some of the finer mechanical points of how insurance—especially federal flood insurance—works in the wake of a hurricane.

Holtz owned a house in Miami and was the named insured under an Omaha flood policy on that house. In August 1992, the house was damaged by flooding that resulted from Hurricane Andrew. At the time of the damage, the policy was in full force and effect. So, Holtz filed a claim for losses caused by the flooding.

Omaha refused payment on the claim, citing an exclusion in the policy for flood damages occurring "below the lowest elevated floor of the [house]." The house was described in the policy as an "elevated, single-family residence consisting of three or more floors with a garage and enclosed area at the ground floor." However, like most houses in south Florida, it had no basement. But there was a twist here. Holtz had converted part of his ground-floor entryway into an enclosed living space. For the purposes of the policy, this was a basement.

And, like most flood policies on houses in south Florida, the Omaha contract was based on some fairly detailed and, at times, confusing language.

Its declaration page described the base elevation of the residence at 15.0 feet—which represented the elevation of the first elevated floor. The ground floor of the property, including the garage and an enclosed area, contained Holtz's "hot water heater, air conditioning equipment, clothes washer and dryer, and certain other equipment."

These ground-floor items were described in Holtz's application—but the policy excluded coverage for the following:

> Enclosures, contents, machinery, building components, equipment and fixtures located at an elevation lower than the lowest elevated floor (except for the required utility connections and the footing, foundation, posts, pilings, piers or other foundation walls and anchorage system as required for the support of the...building), including...finished basement walls, floors, ceiling and other improvements...and contents, machines, building equipment and fixtures in such basement areas.

However, making things even more complicated, there was an exception to this exclusion. The Omaha policy did provide coverage:

> in basement areas and in areas below the lowest elevated floor of an elevated...building for sump pumps, well-water tanks, well-water tank pumps, oil tanks and the oil in them, cisterns and the water in them, pumps and/or tanks used in conjunction with solar energy systems, furnaces, hot water heaters, clothes washers and dryers, food freezers and the food in them, air conditioners, heat pumps and electrical junction and circuit breaker boxes; and coverage is also provided in basement areas and in areas below the lowest elevated floor...for stairways and staircases attached to the building which are not separated from the building by elevated walkways and for elevators and relevant equipment....

At stake was Holtz's personal property and certain improvements that fell outside of the listed basement coverage or essential appliances and, therefore, would not be covered under the policy.

The insurance company—which only offered the flood insurance because Florida law and FEMA guidelines said it had to—based its denial on the exclusion. Holtz—who bought the policy because Omaha had a reputation for not jerking people around—based his claim on the exception to the exclusion. A heavy dispute was brewing.

Omaha insisted that Holtz's losses weren't covered because the area of damage was an "enclosure...at an elevation lower than the lowest elevated floor" which was above ground and, therefore, not covered by the "basement" provision in the policy. The company interpreted its policy to provide coverage "in areas below the lowest elevated floor" (but not in the basement) only for sump pumps, well-water tanks, oil tanks, cisterns...and the rest of the items mentioned in the exception to the exclusion.

Holtz insisted that Omaha's policy was ambiguous at best and could not be read to exclude coverage for the ground level of the insured property including the garage and the enclosed area. He argued—in a savvy nod to public policy issues—the broad purpose of NFIP was to alleviate economic stress caused by flood disasters. Therefore, the spirit of the law under which the Omaha policy was begrudgingly written suggested his losses should be covered.

His lawsuit against Omaha was one the court seemed almost eager to consider.

Holtz and Omaha were both so confident of their positions that they asked the court to make a summary judgment. One side was going to be sorely disappointed.

The court concentrated on the exception-to-the-exclusion language. Omaha correctly pointed out that, according to other federal court decisions, insurance policies issued under NFIP are supposed to be "interpreted as insurance contracts and not as public benefits." This is an important issue for insurance companies, because they are nervous about issuing insurance policies whose terms are actually controlled by federal bureaucrats.

The federal court hearing the case did its part to calm Omaha's nerves. It assured: "FEMA's administration of the insurance program under which insurance policies are written does nothing to alter the status of the policies as insurance contracts."

That said, the rest of the decision fell against the insurance company. The court ruled:

> Any ambiguity in an insurance policy must be strictly construed against the insurer and in favor of the insured. ...Here, the policy at issue is a flood insurance policy issued by FEMA under the National Flood Insurance Program. The purpose of this program is to promote public interest by providing appropriate protection against the perils of flood losses....

Congress, in enacting this legislation, found that "it is in the public interest of people already living in flood-prone areas to have both opportunity to purchase flood insurance and access to more adequate limits of coverage, so that they will be indemnified for their losses in the event of future flood disasters."

The insurance company couldn't claim the exclusion because:

> upon close scrutiny of [the exclusion] in its entirety, [the court] finds a significant ambiguity in this provision and some doubt as to whether it should exclude the ground floor. On the one hand, the provision excludes from coverage enclosures "lower than the lowest elevated floor" which can be read to define a first floor enclosure below the lowest elevated floor which is not a basement as defined in the policy. On the other hand, the use by Congress of the phrase "basement areas and in areas below the lowest elevated floor" in two separate places...can be interpreted as congressional intent to provide the same coverage for areas below the lowest elevated floor whether such areas are basements or first floor "enclosures."

The court concluded that Holtz's argument was strengthened when realizing that FEMA's policy was "a standard policy used throughout the United States which provides coverage for flood losses for homes with or without basements."

Finding an ambiguity, the court had to construe the policy strictly against the insurer and in favor of coverage. It concluded:

> Clearly, the purpose of this policy was to afford flood protection for

> the insured property. Adopting an interpretation against coverage, based on a distinction between basements and first floor enclosures, would frustrate the obvious purpose of that policy.

So the court issued the summary judgment for Holtz—and ordered Omaha to make him whole for the his damages in the flood.

Business Claims Are a Problem

The Holtz claim was a personal residence dispute. Of course, the biggest claims that come in after a hurricane smashes through any population center are commercial claims. Businesses tend to have more property and income at stake than individuals.

The June 1997 federal court case *Southern Hotels v. Lloyd's Underwriters et al.* considered in some detail how insurance companies deal with business claims—among the most complex under normal circumstances—resulting from a hurricane.

Southern Hotels Limited Partners (SHLP) owned and operated a Travelodge Hotel in Harvey, Louisiana, a suburb of New Orleans located on the west bank of the Mississippi River.

After wreaking havoc on south Florida, Hurricane Andrew followed Hurricane Alley north through the Gulf of Mexico. It hit the Louisiana Gulf Coast with winds gusting up to 54 miles per hour and heavy rain. While this was nothing like the power the storm had when it first came ashore in Homestead, it was still strong enough do some harm.

The SHLP Travelodge sustained wind, rain and flood damage. SHLP had an all risk insurance policy with a Lloyd's syndicate that covered wind and water damage to the building and its contents. As most do, the policy excluded damage caused by normal wear and tear and faulty, inadequate or defective maintenance. It also included a $200,000 deductible for flood damage. SHLP also had a flood insurance policy with the National Flood Insurance Program (NFIP), with a limit of $200,000 and a deductible of $500. Taken together, the two policies were designed to give SHLP a fairly complete level of flood coverage.

After the hurricane damage had been assessed, SHLP submitted a proof of loss to its NFIP flood insurer for $19,114; it was eventually paid $15,806 for flood damages. SHLP also sought the following damages from Lloyd's:

a. Sign Damage $ 4,000.00
b. Canopy Repairs & Replacement $2,280.00
c. Home Depot (Item unidentified) $19.44
d. Glass Replacement $54.00
e. Roof Inspection $ 220.00
f. Pool Service $222.40
g. Power supply $2,158.92
h. Light rental $546.78
i. Taylor rental $144.44
j. R's Professional Cleaning $793.80
k. Interior Damage $3,141.60

These various items totaled $13,561.38 in damages. Of this amount, Lloyd's determined that items f. through k., totaling $7,007.94, were not covered under the policy. After deducting these and the normal policy deductibles, Lloyd's paid SHLP $5,326.46.

After receiving the payment, SHLP sought additional damages totaling $165,713.43 for: building damages, including permanent repairs to the roof; contents damage; and loss of revenue. At a hefty $121,407.80, the cost to replace and repair damage to the roof was the largest item claimed under the policy.

SHLP claimed that Andrew's high winds had caused gas pipelines, attached to wooden blocks imbedded in pitch pockets on the hotel's roof, to move. This caused cracks in the roof tar. SHLP claimed that rain water then entered through these fine cracks and dripped down the walls, wetting the ceilings, sheetrock and insulation, and carpet. This caused damage to various rooms, which made trouble for the hotel's business.

After subtracting the deductible of $1,250 and the $5,326.46 already paid by Lloyd's, SHLP sought $159,136.97. The insurance companies saw things differently. They refused to pay the claim. SHLP filed suit, seeking property damages and business interruption losses.

Lloyd's argued that the damage to the roof and, therefore, various leaks that led to the loss of business were not the result of Hurricane Andrew. The insurance company insisted that the poor condition of the roof resulted in leaks before the hurricane. Lloyds argued that SHLP was trying to fix some long-standing problems by means of the hurricane. It bolstered its argument by pointing out that SHLP had already submitted a claim to the NFIP.

After reviewing all of the evidence and considering the arguments of both sides, the Court found that neither position was tenable. It said:

> [SHLP] is seeking the cost of replacing the entire roof, which is aged and which had pre-existing [*sic*] problems which were temporarily repaired. [Lloyd's] is seeking to escape all liability, instead of agreeing to pay for the portion of the roof repairs due to the high winds. While it is difficult to segregate the repairs necessitated by the storm damage from the complete roof replacement actually performed, the Court finds a logical starting point for this task in the cost of the roof repairs which were done immediately after the SHLP purchased the hotel in order to remedy leaks and prevent future leaks, which is $15,000. Certainly, as a result of the storm, this work would have been necessary to ensure that the roof membranes were sound and would have placed the roof back in the condition in which it was prior to the storm damage, in addition to emergency repairs. [SHLP] sought $13,001.16 for emergency repairs, so adding these two figures, the Court finds that the plaintiff sustained damages to the roof in the amount of $28,001.16 as a result of a covered cause of loss, i.e., wind and wind-driven rain damage.

Then the court turned to SHLP's claim of $32,877.57 for contents. It determined that the water damage to the furniture and other items occurred either due to flood, which has a $200,000 limit, or to sewer back up as a result of a power outage originating off of the premises, which was excluded under the policy. So, SHLP could not recover for any of the damage to contents.

The court determined that 35 percent of the interior repairs claimed by SHLP were caused by a covered loss—namely wind-driven rain—and the remaining 65 percent were caused by flood. Of the total amount sought by SHLP under the policy, the court found that it had sustained insured damages to the hotel roof in the amount of $28,001.16 and interior damages of $1,533.01.

The court—which was federal, but had to show that its decision was consistent with local law—explained the rationale behind its ruling:

> Louisiana jurisprudence mandates the courts to give legal effect to insurance policy provisions in accordance with the true intent of the parties.... Any doubt, however, in interpretation must be construed in favor of coverage for the insured. Furthermore, the policy language should be read broadly in favor of coverage.

The federal court cited other local guidelines—and these references suggest the general approach courts take to ruling on such insurance cases. When assessing and quantifying property damages, the following general rules apply: If property is damaged as a result of a covered cause of loss, the primary goal is to restore the property, as nearly as possible, to the state it was in immediately prior to the damage. Three tests usually determine property damage:

- cost of restoration if the damaged item can be adequately repaired;
- value differential, the difference in value prior to and after the damage; and
- cost of replacement, less depreciation, if the value before and after the damage cannot be reasonably determined or if the cost of repair is more than the value of the damaged item. (i.e., the insured is entitled only to the amount it will cost to place the item in the same condition it was in before the loss.)

So, SHLP was only entitled to have the property replaced in the condition it was in before the loss. Before Hurricane Andrew, the roof was a number of years old and had experienced some leaks. Lloyd's only had to pay enough to return it to that shaky state.

The moral of this story: If you own real estate, keep it in the best condition you can. If you think you can slip some sly improvements into a disaster claim, you stand a good chance of being discovered. Insurance companies are looking for that kind of claim.

Real estate is not the only kind of property exposed to hurricane loss. Businesses can also lose hard assets and profitability when in the wake of a hurricane. They often need weeks to recover from a disaster—and their doors are shut in the meantime.

The 1997 federal court decision *Dictiomatic, Inc., et al. v. United States Fidelity & Guaranty* highlighted a rare but important issue of commercial property insurance. In the case, a Florida-based developer of consumer electronic products sued its insurance company for breach of contract in connection with a claim for business interruption coverage.

From 1989 to 1991, Dictiomatic made money from the development and sale of a hand-held device that translated commonplace words into any of six different languages. In those early years, the company sold over 120,000 of these devices through various distributors.

However, at a consumer electronics show in late 1991, Dictiomatic president Domingo Linale started hearing complaints from the marketplace. His distributors were unhappy with the product. The translation devices—which seemed like they'd sell well—were starting to drop off in sales. Dictiomatic was sitting on a lot of inventory...and the market was indicating it didn't want the product.

The problems didn't take long to impact the company's finances. By mid-1992, Dictiomatic's debt exceeded $1 million.

Then, in August 1992, Hurricane Andrew came ashore not far from Dictiomatic's South Miami headquarters. The company's facility was damaged—fairly seriously. As a result, Dictiomatic didn't have access to its offices for several weeks. A delicate balance of business factors started to crash. Inventory still built up...and the company wasn't doing the things it should have to shore up its dwindling sales.

By the middle of September, Dictiomatic was back in business. But, the problems had ballooned. The company sold only a few of its devices through the end of the year.

Dictiomatic's original business interruption claim included alleged lost sales from August 24 through December 31, 1992. The company claimed that, if not for Hurricane Andrew, it would have sold more than 7,250 translation devices for sales of $1,266,791 during those four months.

In October 1992, Dictiomatic submitted a written claim to United States Fidelity & Guaranty (USF&G) for business interruption loss of $1,360,747 for lost profits and expenses incurred from August 24 through December 31, 1992.

Before the end of September, USF&G paid Dictiomatic its business personal property limit of $50,000. But it hesitated to pay any more.

There were some problems with the rest of the claim. Dictiomatic's products were actually manufactured in Singapore. Its inventory was—for the largest part—spread among various distributors. So, although the South Miami building had been damaged, it wasn't so clear how much of its manufacturing facility or inventory had been.

Dictiomatic later supplemented its claim to account for loss of business

income through June 1993, when it went out of business. At that point, the claims with USF&G became one of the company's biggest assets. USF&G delayed as long as it could. Dictiomatic sued.
The company's lawsuit was as bizarre as its claim had been. It contended that damage to inventory and other hard assets actually exceeded $100,000. However, it admitted at trial that it never repaired or replaced any of the property for which the insurance contract limits were intended. So, that part of its suit collapsed.

The business interruption (that is, lost income) part of its claim remained problematic. During the processing of the claim, Dictiomatic hadn't provided USF&G with reliable information to support its claim for loss of business income. Therefore, the court hearing the case found that USF&G had acted reasonably when it decided to deny Dictiomatic's claim in June 1993.

To support its decision, the court cited the insurance contract between the parties, which stated:

> We will pay the actual loss of "business income" you sustain due to the necessary suspension of your "operations" during the "period of restoration." We will also pay for loss of "business income" sustained immediately after the "period of restoration" but not to exceed 30 consecutive days. We will only pay for loss of "business income" that occurs within 12 consecutive months after the date of direct physical loss or damage.
>
> We will not pay for loss or damages caused by or resulting from any of the following: consequential loss; delay; loss of use; or loss of market.

This language seemed to anticipate the Dictiomatic situation. Under the terms of the policy, Dictiomatic was entitled to recover its actual loss of business income during the period of time necessary to restore the business operation. The insurance policy defined the period of restoration as beginning on the date that the physical damage to the business premises occurred and ending on the date when the business premises should have been repaired, rebuilt or replaced.

Therefore, Dictiomatic was only entitled to its loss of business income for the period beginning August 24, 1992 and ending no later than September 14, 1992.

Florida's law on recovery of anticipated profits was first stated by the state supreme court in 1936. The gist of rule was that the anticipated profits of a business are too speculative to be measured. There is an exception to the rule, however. The loss of profit from the interruption of a business may be recovered if the policyholder can prove with reasonable certainty what the amount of his actual loss was. To recover under its business interruption policy, Dictiomatic had to prove that:

- it sustained damage to property that is covered under the policy and that the damage was caused by a covered cause of loss;
- there was an interruption to the business which was caused by the property damage;
- there was an actual loss of business income during the period of time necessary to restore the business; and
- the loss of income was caused by the interruption of the business and not by some other factor or factors.

It actually had a hard time proving *any* of these things. The court wrote: Dictiomatic has not made it reasonably certain from competent proof that it would have realized profits from the sale of its products and, therefore, has not established that it was entitled to payment from USF&G for lost profits under the business interruption policy.

Most importantly, the court ruled that Dictiomatic's failure to sell products after August 24, 1992, was not the result of Hurricane Andrew.

The court also noted that business interruption insurance isn't supposed to be used to put the insured company in a better financial position than it would have been without the interruption. Instead, business interruption insurance is intended to return to the insured business the amount of profit it would have earned had there been no interruption of the business.

Dictiomatic proved that it sustained property damage from Andrew, and that the damage caused it to close its offices for 20 days. However, it failed to prove that beyond the 20 day suspension of operations it sustained an actual loss of business income caused solely by the hurricane.

The court dismissed the company's claims against USF&G.

Tracking Hurricane Damage

There's no question that insurance companies—and the risk management experts with whom they consult—track hurricane losses closely. There's a competitive market for this intelligence.

Saffir-Simpson Hurricane Intensity Scale

Category 1	Winds of 74 to 95 m.p.h. Minimal damage.
Category 2	Winds of 96 to 110 m.p.h. Moderate damage.
Category 3	Winds of 111 to 130 m.p.h. Extensive damage.
Category 4	Winds 131 to 155 m.p.h. Extreme damage.
Category 5	Winds of 156 m.p.h. and up. Catastrophic damage.

In September 1998, while Hurricane Georges was still bearing down on the Gulf Coast, one risk consulting group was already announcing that its projected insured losses in the Caribbean would exceed $1 billion. This figure was drawn from loss reports between the island of Puerto Rico, the U.S. Virgin Islands, Antigua and other Leeward Islands, and the Dominican Republic.

Hurricanes are classified according to the Saffir-Simpson intensity scale, which makes distinctions based on peak wind velocity.

The estimate—from Risk Management Solutions Inc., which builds computer models for projecting insurance losses—placed Georges as one of the worst Caribbean basin hurricane losses to date.

RMS compared Georges to other Caribbean hurricanes.

Hurricane	Year	Intensity	Damage ($bill.)
Georges	1998	Category 2/3	1.0
Marilyn	1995	Category 3	0.8
Luis	1995	Category 4	1.0
Hugo	1989	Category 4	1.2

RMS warned that:

> While significant losses are modeled to occur across a number of Caribbean islands, the relatively high levels of insured exposures in Puerto Rico will make this island the focus of insured loss.

While Hurricane Georges was less intense than other top loss-producing storms, its path resulted in significant levels of damage to the islands along the northern margin of the Caribbean basin and caused an accumulation of loss across multiple territories.

In 1989, Hurricane Hugo had gone on from its Caribbean debut to produce a significant loss in North Carolina and South Carolina, resulting in an additional $3 billion in insured loss on the U.S. mainland.

When it came to Georges' damages, RMS estimated that the value of insured property in Puerto Rico totaled $50 billion. But people on that island understood the storms. According to RMS:

> Due to the 'bunker' style construction of single family residential building stock, the drivers of hurricane risk in Puerto Rico are the commercial and industrial exposures. Since Hugo, only limited improvements have been made to mitigate the vulnerability of these exposures, and the growth in values since 1989 has only been partially offset by the industry's widespread application of 2 percent wind-deductibles.

Reliable wind-speeds recorded for Hugo at two sites around San Juan, Puerto Rico, had indicated peak gusts up to 120 miles per hour. Initial recordings from Georges indicated similar levels of wind.

But the paths of the storms held much different fates for Puerto Rico. Hugo had barely clipped the northeast corner of the island, traveling with a northwest orientation, which placed the concentrations around San Juan. Georges, on the other hand, traveled the full length of the island from east to west, exposing the entire length of the southern coast to damaging wind—and exposing the northern coast to the more damaging right-hand side of the hurricane. But, because Georges did not pack as much force as Hugo, the results were comparable.

Summary

Insurance companies, state governments and various risk management think tanks have all contributed to a situation in which certain imbalances dominate the way that hurricanes result in insured claims. A relatively few affluent consumers and businesses carry full coverage against the big storms, while the rest of the population buys limited insurance, prays for big storms to stay away and foolishly hopes the government will subsidize them if disaster strikes.

In 1996, when Florida was fine-tuning its state-run hurricane insurance program, one member of the state legislature's financial services committee came away unsatisfied with the compromise solution that the committee had reached.

Sooner or later, he said, people who live in the coastal areas most prone to hurricane damage would have to pay higher rates and stop being subsidized by others elsewhere in the state. "We have devised a system over decades that politically camouflages the true cost of insurance in Florida," he said, "and no commissioner in recent memory has had the courage or gumption to tell the truth."

While the specific legislation has been modified since, that statement holds—generally—as a fair criticism of how people and insurance companies in the U.S. spread the financial losses of hurricanes.

CHAPTER TWO

Floods

Hurricanes may get more press. Tornadoes may seem more dramatic. But, of all natural disasters, floods do most of the damage. They dominate all other weather events, accounting for nine out of ten of the disasters which occur in a given year.

One of the most memorable examples in recent times of the utter destructive force of flood waters and the resulting staggering losses in human lives and possessions is hurricane Mitch, which devastated parts of the Central American countries of Honduras and Nicaragua in late-October and early November 1998.

Floods can result from numerous specific causes—which accounts for their frequency. Rain, melting snow or even blocked waterways can cause streams and rivers to run over their banks or lakes to overflow.

Coastal regions can experience wind-driven surf or unusually high tides which are part of the so-called "storm surge" that comes with hurricanes or north Atlantic storms.

Whatever the cause, floods can damage homes and personal property more effectively than any other disaster. Homes hit by a tornado may usually have some salvageable property left; the few possessions not swept away by flood waters are often unusable.

To make matters worse, flooding is often accompanied by other storm conditions—heavy rain and high wind.

Many people buy their first homes blissfully unaware that flood damage isn't covered by standard homeowners policies. To get insurance coverage against flood damage, you have to buy optional flood insurance coverage.

For the second-largest item most people buy—a car—flood insurance is actually easier to get. For cars, flood coverage is usually part of the comprehensive portion of an auto insurance policy. So, if you're worried about your '65 Rambler getting soaked, make sure you've bought the comprehensive coverage.

The National Flood Insurance Program

The National Flood Insurance Program (NFIP) was created by Congress under the National Flood Insurance Act of 1968. Congress passed NFIP in response to "concern over the enormous personal hardship and economic distress caused by flood disasters." The purpose of the program was to enable the public to "overcome the devastation accompanying floods by providing a reasonable method of sharing the risk of flood losses... through a program of flood insurance which can complement and encourage preventive and protective measures."

Congress found that "many factors have made it uneconomic for the private insurance industry alone to make flood insurance available to those in need of such protection on reasonable terms and conditions" and, therefore, authorized the creation of NFIP "with large-scale participation of the Federal Government and carried out to the maximum extent practicable by the private insurance industry."

So, the NFIP is a federally-subsidized program that makes affordable flood insurance available to the public at or below actuarial rates. NFIP is overseen by the Federal Emergency Management Agency (FEMA). The specific policies are sold by private companies through the "Write Your Own" program—but the policies have the same prices and coverages, and all flood risk is borne by the NFIP.

Although the NFIP is generally available to the public, Congress granted FEMA authority to define and limit the nature and scope of coverage provided under the Standard Flood Insurance Policy (SFIP). Among other things, the SFIP requires a claimant to submit a signed and sworn proof of loss in order to qualify for flood insurance benefits.

FEMA uses the NFIP as a tool for controlling local bureaucracies as much as for helping needy people obtain insurance coverage. Because flood damage can be reduced through proper flood plain management, FEMA requires that communities in which it offers the SFIP adhere to certain guidelines to limit development in flood prone areas.

Some 19,000 cities, towns and other communities in the U.S. are part of the NFIP. Although it has not been strictly enforced in the past, federal law directs lenders to require flood insurance on properties located in so-called "Special Flood Hazard Areas" before granting any mortgage that carries Federal guarantees—such as Veterans Administration and Federal Housing Administration loans.

The resulting problem: You may need flood insurance even if you don't live in an area you believe is at risk. About 10 percent of American households are in federally designated flood plains. If yours is one of them, you need flood insurance. (Your bank will require you to have it to qualify for a federally backed mortgage.)

To find out if you live in a high-risk area, call the zoning department of your local or county government. If the answer is yes, get out your wallet.

Even if you're in a moderate- to minimal-risk area, you should consider flood protection. "Nearly 30 percent of our claims come from outside the high-risk areas," says Mark Stevens, a spokesman for the FEMA.

Since flooding takes on many different forms, the SFIP must first define under what conditions its coverage will take effect. Flooding is defined as:

> ...a general and temporary condition during which the surface of normally dry land is partially or completely inundated with water.

The term "general condition" is understood to mean that either two acres of land are inundated or two adjacent properties are affected.

While floods tend to strike high-risk areas with regularity and frequency, FEMA reports that between 25 percent and 30 percent of claims originate outside areas designated as high risk. Low-risk areas carry lower premiums to account for their lower claims experience, but the possibility of flood damage to any given property almost always exists.

The SFIP is a "single-risk" insurance policy, which means it only provides coverage for "direct physical loss by or from flood." The term "flood," is defined in the SFIP as:

> (a) A general and temporary condition of partial or complete inundation of normally dry land areas from:
>
> 1) The overflow of inland or tidal waters.

2) The unusual and rapid accumulation or runoff of surface waters from any source.
3) Mudslides (i.e. mudflows) which are proximately caused by flooding as defined in subparagraph A-2 above and are akin to a river of liquid and flowing mud on the surfaces of normally dry land areas, as when earth carried by a current of water and deposited along the path of the current.
(b) The collapse or subsidence of land along the shore of a lake or other body of water as a result of erosion or undermining caused by waves or currents of water exceeding the cyclical levels which result in flooding as defined in A-1 above.

"Direct Physical Loss By or From Flood" is defined in the SFIP to be "any loss in the nature of actual loss of or physical damage, evidenced by physical changes, to the insured property ... which is directly and proximately caused by a 'flood'..."

Flood Insurance Coverage and its Limitations

If rising inland or coastal waters damage real estate or other personal property, common homeowners policies will not pay for the resulting losses. Therefore, anyone who wants protection against these risks must purchase optional flood protection.

However, not all water damage is considered flooding. Water damage that comes from wind-driven rain is not considered flooding. If rain enters your home through a hole in your roof or walls created by a fallen tree, the damage is considered windstorm damage and is covered under your homeowners policy.

Also, damage caused by frozen or broken pipes is covered under a typical homeowners insurance policy.

A homeowners insurance policy doesn't provide coverage for flood damage, but it does provide coverage for many types of water damage to your home. Just the opposite from flood damage, for insurance purposes, water damage is considered to occur when water damages your home before the water comes in contact with the ground. Some examples of water damage that would be covered include:

- a hailstorm smashes your window, permitting hail and rain free access into your home.

• a heavy rain soaks through the roof, allowing water to drip through your attic or ceiling.
• a broken water pipe spews water into your home.

But these events seldom cause the total losses possible during a flood. A handful of examples of flood damage include:

• a nearby river overflows its banks and washes into your home.
• a heavy rain seeps into your basement because the soil can't absorb the water quickly enough.
• a heavy rain or flash flood causes the hill behind your house to collapse into a mud slide that oozes into your home.

Even if flood damage is not covered by your homeowners insurance policy, losses from theft, fire or explosion resulting from water damage is covered. For example, if a nearby creek overflows and floods your home, and looters steal some of your furnishings after you evacuate, the theft would be covered by your homeowners insurance because it is a direct result of the water damage. However, the flood damage would be covered only if you have flood insurance.

It's important to note that flood insurance and homeowners insurance do not duplicate coverage for water damage. Instead, they complement each other.

In the December 1996 decision *Sallie Howard v. FEMA*, a federal court in Mississippi considered a dispute over denied flood insurance benefits. Howard purchased a Standard Flood Insurance Policy from a local insurance agency to insure her home in Canton, Mississippi. The policy included coverage up to $12,100 for the dwelling and $5,600 for contents. It was effective from June 7, 1994, through June 7, 1995.

On April 20, 1995, Bear Creek flooded near Howard's home. Water from the creek rose around the house and flowed into its interior. The next day, Howard's insurance agent filed a notice of loss informing NFIP that Howard had sustained a flood loss.

The claim was assigned to Charter Adjustment Company, and Jeff McGill was the adjuster assigned to inspect Howard's home. McGill investigated Howard's claim by inspecting her home. According to Howard, McGill—who had also investigated a claim by Howard from a flood in 1994—told her that she needed to get some estimates concerning the damage.

After completing his inspection of Howard's home due to the 1995 flood, McGill determined that at least some of the damage to Howard's home from the previous flood did not appear to have been repaired. Charter then requested documentation from Howard, in the form of "cancelled checks, material receipts, inspection reports, contractor agreements, or any other type of documentation," to verify that the flood damage from 1994 had indeed been repaired.

Howard argued that she did not have any proof that the repairs for the 1994 flood damage had been completed because "a lot of [her] papers had been damaged or destroyed" by the April 1995 flood.

In May 1995, a claims examiner for National Con-Serv Inc., a servicing agent for NFIP, sent a letter to Howard advising her that her flood policy required that a Proof of Loss be filed. (Although FEMA uses the services of various private corporations as fiscal servicing agents, the Federal Insurance Administration (FIA)—acting under the authority of FEMA—is ultimately responsible for handling all NFIP insurance policies.)

The letter stated, in relevant part:

> Your flood policy requires that a formal Proof of Loss be filed within sixty (60) days of the loss date. If this is not done, the terms and conditions of the policy would be violated and your claim could be denied. Your deadline for filing a Proof of Loss for the above captioned claim is 6/20/95. This letter is to inform you that you have until the above date to conclude your claim with the adjuster and file your Proof of Loss with us. If we have not received the Proof of Loss within the allotted time mentioned above, we will assume that you are not pursuing your claim and will close your file without further activity.

(An important point: The requested Proof of Loss is a different document than the Notice of Loss filed for Howard by her insurance agent.)

At some point prior to the final denial of her claim, Howard apparently sent an unsworn statement from Leroy Joyner to National Con-Serv which stated in part:

This will certify that we, me and my brother, Prentis Harris, did perform the work on her house located above, per our estimate dated 3/7/94. We furnished the materials and Sallie Howard paid us cash, as we completed this job. My brother, Prentis Harris is in Massassachusets [*sic*] with our sick father. This will acknowledge receipt of $5,000.00 cash for this job. The receipts have been misplaced for the purchase of materials, as no one was advised they should be kept.

On July 27, 1995, National Con-Serv sent a denial letter to Howard. That letter stated, in relevant part:

> We have received the report from the adjuster documenting your above captioned claim. The report advised us that the inspection of your property appeared to show that the repairs have not been completed from the prior loss. The adjuster has requested receipts and/or invoices to confirm that the repairs have been completed, but to date, none have been received. Your loss has exceeded the sixty (60) days for filing the Proof of Loss. Therefore, we are denying the claim and closing the file without payment for failure to pursue the claim. You have one (1) year from the date of this denial to file suit in the U.S. District Court for the district in which the insured property was located at the time of the loss.

After she received this letter, Howard hired a lawyer. The lawyer wrote a letter to National Con-Serv on her behalf, stating that Howard was disappointed with the denial and implying that she would appeal or take legal action.

In response, National Con-Serv sent a letter to Howard's lawyer. The correspondence was starting to focus on the details of the dispute. This letter read, in relevant part:

> We are in receipt of your letter of 1/10/96 concerning the denial of the above claim. We must advise you that after comparing the prior loss in 1994 file with the above, documents were requested to verify the repairs were made prior to the above loss. We were informed that the insured had no paid receipts, but a hand written letter was provided from Joyner stating that he and his brother had completed the repairs in 1994. Since the letter was written by hand and was not on a business letter head, numerous attempts were made to [contact] Joyner & Harris for verification of the letter. We reached Harris on 1/30/96, and he informed me that he had made no repairs to the damages from the flood, that he repaired only the roof. He also informed me that Joyner was not his brother and that he did not know him. Based on this information the only document received to support the above claim is not valid. Our denial must stand. However,

> if the insured can provide valid support (i.e., paid receipts, canceled checks (back & front)) we will be happy to review the file again.

During some of this correspondence, Howard was spending lengthy periods—as long as four to eight weeks—in the hospital. She acknowledged receipt of the letters but didn't understand their meaning. So, she passed them on to her insurance agent and lawyer.

Although she wasn't clear on the details, Howard did understand that the insurance company "was not intending to pay [her] claim." So, she instructed her lawyer to sue FEMA.

Considering the case, the federal court went back to the basic document—the Standard Flood Insurance Policy. Several provisions of the SFIP were relevant to the dispute. For one thing, the policy included a waiver provision which prohibited any amendment or waiver of any provisions of the policy "without the express written consent of the Federal Insurance Administrator."

However, the most important provision of the SFIP was the provision setting forth the requirements in case of a loss. This stated:

> Requirements in case of loss:
> Should a flood loss occur to your insured property, you must,
> 1. Notify us in writing as soon as practicable;
> 2. As soon as reasonably possible, separate the damaged and undamaged property, putting it in the best possible order so that we may examine it; and
> 3. Within 60 days after the loss send us a proof of loss, which is your statement as to the amount you are claiming under the policy signed and sworn to by you and furnishing us with the following information.
> a. The date and time of the loss;
> b. A brief explanation of how the loss happened;
> c. Your interest in the property damaged (for example, "owner") and the interests, if any, of others in the damaged property;
> d. The actual cash value of each damaged item of insured property after depreciation is deducted from the cost of replacement of the property...;
> e. Names of mortgagees or anyone else having a lien, charge or claim against the insured property;
> f. Details as to any other contracts of insurance covering the property, whether valid or not;

g. Details of any changes in ownership, use, occupancy, location or possession of the insured property since the policy was issued;
h. Details as to who occupied any insured building at the time of loss and for what purpose; and
i. The amount you claim is due under this policy to cover the loss, including statements concerning:
(i) The limits of coverage stated in the policy; and
(ii) The cost to repair or replace the damaged property (whatever costs less).

Another specific provision of the SFIP explained in greater detail the obligations of the insured person and FEMA with regard to the filing of a proof of loss. This provision stated:

> The insurance adjuster whom we hire to investigate your claim may furnish you with a Proof of Loss form, and she or he may help you to complete it. However, this is a courtesy only. And you must still send us a Proof of Loss within 60 days after the loss even if the adjuster does not furnish the form or help you complete it. In completing the proof of loss, you must use your own judgment concerning the amount of loss and the justification for that amount; the adjuster is not authorized to approve or disapprove claims or to tell you whether your claim will be approved by us.
>
> We may, at our option, waive the requirement for the completion and filing of a Proof of Loss in certain cases, in which event you will be required to sign and, at our option, swear to an adjuster's report of the loss which includes information about your loss and the damages needed by us in order to adjust your claim.

Finally, both the SFIP and the regulations contain provisions concerning the filing of a lawsuit. The SFIP contains the following provision:

> You may not sue us to recover money under this policy unless you have complied with all the requirements of the policy. If you do sue, you must start the suit within twelve (12) months from the date we mailed you notice that we have denied your claim, or part of your claim, and you must file the suit in the United States District Court for district [sic] in which the insured property was located at the time of the loss.

Similarly, the regulations contained a subsection entitled "Judicial Review" which provided that:

> Upon the disallowance by the Federal Insurance Administration or the servicing agent of any claim on grounds other than failure to file a

> Proof of Loss, or upon the refusal of the claimant to accept the amount allowed upon any such claim, after appraisal pursuant to policy provisions, the claimant within one year after the date of mailing by the Federal Insurance Administration or the servicing agent of the notice of disallowance or partial disallowance of the claim may...institute an action on such claim against the Federal Insurance Administrator in the U.S. District Court for the district in which the insured property or the major portion thereof shall have been situated, without regard to the amount in controversy.

Clearly, the regulations do not inspire a great deal of confidence with their convoluted language.

FEMA argued simply that Howard's failure to file a Proof of Loss required the Court to dismiss the lawsuit. Specifically, National Con-Serv, on behalf of FEMA, had requested proof from Howard that the damage caused by the 1994 flood had actually been repaired—so that FEMA would not pay benefits a second time in 1995 to repair damage which had occurred during a previous flood.

Howard's lawyer argued back that the requirement that Howard file a formal Proof of Loss was simply a pretext for denying her claim. After all, the claims adjuster who'd inspected her home after the recent flood observed that there had been damage.

The court focused instead on Howard's final claim—namely, that FEMA didn't require a Proof of Loss until it had decided to deny the claim on the suspicion that the repairs for damage from the 1994 flood had not been made. If true, this really could suggest pretext. Howard's lawyer claimed that, even after requiring that a Proof of Loss be submitted, FEMA didn't inform Howard of what information should be included in the proof of loss. It didn't even provide a proof of loss form for her to complete.

The only problem: Howard couldn't produce any evidence to support her claims.

The court tried to find some support for Howard's case. It referred to an earlier federal case in which another court had noticed FEMA's tendency to use "stunted technicalities" to avoid making NFIP payments. But, in the end, the court had little choice but to conclude that:

> ...no genuine issues of material fact have been properly presented by

> [Howard] and that summary judgment should therefore be granted to the [FEMA]. [Howard] essentially asserts that FEMA should be estopped from denying coverage based upon the SFIP provision requiring that a proof of loss be filed because of the actions of its employees in this matter. The Court finds that [Howard] has failed to submit any evidence to support her argument that FEMA should be estopped from requiring compliance with the terms of the SFIP policy.

The court sided with FEMA, finding that the agency correctly asserted that the proof of loss was required by the provisions in the SFIP. Furthermore, FEMA was not required to send a Proof of Loss form to Howard, nor was it required to instruct her on what the form should include—although Howard was given general instructions in two letters in May and June 1995.

Although the claims adjuster may have observed damage to Howard's home caused by the flood, Howard was still obligated under the provisions of the SFIP to submit a sworn statement of the amount of her loss. Furthermore, Howard did not assert that any agent of FEMA made any misrepresentations to her concerning benefits under the SFIP. She similarly did not offer any evidence that the Proof of Loss provision was waived by any FEMA representative.

Finally, although Howard claimed in one court filing that she never received a copy of the SFIP, she didn't submit any evidence to support this assertion and didn't even make this assertion in her affidavit. Faced with such "overwhelming evidence," the court found that Howard failed to create any genuine issue of material fact which would preclude summary judgment in favor of FEMA.

For these reasons, the court concluded that FEMA was entitled to summary judgment in its favor in the case.

Misuse and Abuse of NFIP

One problem with the way NFIP is administered: It's lopsided. More than 35 percent of the money paid out goes to a tiny fraction of the policy holders—2 percent get a whopping $2.5 billion. Said another way, in the 1990s—a decade of record flooding—Congress handed some $700 million to families who chose to live in swamps and on river banks.

In a series of angry news stories that appeared in newspapers during 1997 and 1998, various outlets referred...angrily...to one family that had made some 17 flood claims in less than seven years. In January 1998, the *NBC Nightly News* interviewed Harold and Lori Bray-Shere of Baton Rouge, Louisiana. The Bray-Sheres had collected $200,000—seven times more than they'd paid for the house.

Oliver Houck of Tulane University Law School summed up the problem:

> That it doesn't work doesn't bother them a bit. This is federal money pouring into Louisiana, and that's what politicians get elected to do. [People live near the water because] that's where cheap land is, and that's where developers are going.

At least some of the problem might be solved if NFIP more effectively encouraged homeowners to prevent flooding damage to their property. But it does a weak job of this. A simple preventative measure like a flood wall isn't covered by the policy.

Still, FEMA director James Lee Witt talked to the major media after Georges, calling the problem of houses that flood over and over again "a nightmare" for the federal flood insurance program. Witt said FEMA was aware that repetitive flood-loss properties were a drain on NFIP. His own agency's numbers showed that nearly 40 percent of the $6.8 billion in claims paid between 1978 and 1995 went to fewer than three percent of NFIP policyholders. But Witt defended FEMA as one of the busiest agencies in the federal government. It had spent $14 billion between 1993 and 1998 to deal with one disaster after another spread out among the 50 states. And that figure didn't include billions more spent by local and state governments and other federal agencies that respond to disasters.

Finally, Witt fell back to a familiar refrain: FEMA's problems stemmed largely from development decisions made at the local government level and solutions needed to come from local communities.

NFIP's Financial Problems

Witt's points wouldn't seem so urgent, except for one fact: As recently as 1998, NFIP owed the federal treasury $917 million—because premiums collected from policyholders were less than amounts paid in claims. In 1998, NFIP paid back $400,000 of that debt plus $96 million in interest, according to Federal Insurance Administrator Jo Ann Howard. She said that FEMA expected to be fully paid within a few years.

Policyholders of FEMA's NFIP can purchase regular flood insurance with coverage limits up to $250,000 of damage to the structure and up to $100,000 of damage to personal property, with a $500 deductible. However, to limit payouts and encourage policyholder care, only basement essentials such as a furnace and hot water heater are covered. As we've seen in the *Holtz* case from the previous chapter, a finished basement (sheet rock walls, ceiling, carpeting, etc.) and any other contents are not covered under the SFIP.

To prevent "day-before" purchases of flood insurance, the program requires a 30-day waiting period before the coverage takes effect. This 30-day period does not apply if you receive the coverage as part of a newly created home purchase/mortgage agreement. Still, this delay is one of NFIP's most effective cost controls.

There are other effective controls, though.

As with homeowners policies, policyholders must have insurance limits of no less than 80 percent of the replacement cost of the dwelling in order to qualify for full replacement cost coverage for the dwelling and contents.

For example: If you have a home that will cost $100,000 to replace, you must carry at least $80,000 of insurance to qualify for full replacement cost protection of the structure and your belongings. Otherwise, you will receive less than the full replacement cost value for your house and/or contents. This is often referred to as the coinsurance requirement.

As we've mentioned before, flood coverage carries the same coverage and price at all insurance companies since all policies are written by the NFIP. The premiums can range from a low of $85 up to an average $300 per year in higher risk areas. These rates seldom cover the true cost of the insurance; FEMA borrows the shortfall from the federal government.

But even high-risk homeowners may not respond to subsidized rates and flood insurance advertising. In April 1997, the Red River flooded several Plains States and caused a lot of damage. Hardest hit: South Dakota, with $225 million in losses caused by flooding.

South Dakotans had months to prepare for the flooding and federal emergency officials begged them to get insurance—but some resisted. Of 15,000 properties affected by the flood, only 900 were insured. In early 1997, residents of the Red River Valley in North Dakota and Minnesota were bombarded with flood insurance advertising. Because of heavy snowfall and waterlogged soil from the year before, flooding was a sure thing. Because of the 30-day waiting period, residents were urged to take advantage of flood insurance before the spring thaw and the inevitable flooding.

When March came and temperatures rose, massive amounts of runoff from melting snow had nowhere to go. Fargo, North Dakota, suffered some of the most serious flooding along with communities along the banks of the northward flowing Red River. Unfortunately, few residents had responded to NFIP's advertising blitz and fewer than 400 new policies were purchased during early 1997. A survey during the following summer indicated that 95 percent of the residents knew that flood insurance was available, but fewer than 20 percent of the residents actually purchased the coverage.

The flood, the worst in the region's recorded history, ultimately displaced upwards of 60,000 people and caused 10 deaths and an estimated $1.2 billion to $1.8 billion worth of property damage.

In April, hundreds of people were living in temporary Red Cross shelters. Others were returning home to pump stagnant water from their basements. Adding to the tragedy, only about 7 percent of homes in the six major towns most affected had flood insurance.

Flood Insurance Fraud

The June 1995 federal appeals court decision *Kevin Miller v. FEMA, et al.* considered allegations of flood insurance fraud that are fairly typical. In May 1985, Kevin Miller and Margaret Antoine—who lived together in eastern Missouri—bought a house and obtained an assignment of a lease. At the time of the purchase, the lower level of the house was flood damaged.

Miller, Antoine and their daughter moved into the house in the fall of 1985. They cleaned up the house and did some general cosmetic repairs. In November 1985, Miller and Antoine paid $210 for a one-year Standard Flood Insurance Policy from NFIP. The policy provided for coverage up to a limit of $30,000 on the building and $10,000 on the contents. On May 21, 1986, the house was flooded—though the damage was limited to the lower level of the house. Miller and Antoine filed a Proof of Loss claiming $7,283.87 in building damage and $4,174.15 in content damage. NFIP paid this claim in full.

On October 2, the house was flooded again. This time, Miller and Antoine filed a Proof of Loss claiming that the flood had caused $25,774.45 in building and content damage. According to Miller, the damage was larger because contents on the lower level were damaged—but the building was damaged on both the upper and lower levels.

William Hoover, an independent insurance adjuster, assisted Miller and Antoine in the preparation of their second Proof of Loss and the completion of a work sheet and building report required to be filed with the NFIP. In his report, Hoover wrote that the water level had reached eight feet above the foundation of Miller's house. As is common practice, Hoover included costs for the repair of both the first and second levels of the house—and replacement of the second level's subflooring.

On December 19, a Federal Insurance Claims Office manager for NFIP wrote to Miller and Antoine and acknowledged receipt of their Proof of Loss. However, Miller was promptly informed that, although the Proof of Loss had been timely filed, NFIP "reject[ed] any and all the statements thereon with regards to the amount of value and loss." Based on inconsistencies between the claims from the May and October floods, NFIP claims personnel suspected the second claim might be bogus.

On January 16, 1987, Kirby Gallagher—a fraud adjuster employed by NFIP—reinspected Miller's property. Gallagher concluded that the house had originally been built as an elevated building and that the first floor had later been enclosed to create permanent living space.

Under FEMA regulations "[e]nclosures, contents, machinery, building components, equipment and fixtures located at an elevation lower than the lowest elevated floor of an elevated building" are not insurable.

Gallagher also measured the interior and exterior water lines and determined that the water level had reached only seven-and-one-half feet and, therefore, he concluded that the October 2, 1986 flood did not damage the second level. He also found rotted subflooring, rusted steel support beams, and moldy exterior block walls from previous floods, indicating earlier unrestored damage. In all, Gallagher confirmed NFIP's decision to deny Miller's claim from the October 1986 flood. (Gallagher would later reinspect the property—twice—and confirm the findings of his first inspection.)

Miller filed a complaint against the director of FEMA, alleging that FEMA wrongfully denied his flood insurance claim from the October 1986 flood.

In response to Miller's suit, FEMA filed a counterclaim under the False Claims Act and common law fraud theories. FEMA contended that not only was Miller's claim arising from the October 1986 flood correctly denied, but that the October 1986 and May 1986 claims that Miller presented to FEMA were false claims.

The standard for proving a false claim is tough. The district court hearing the case on its first pass dismissed FEMA's fraud counts based on the Missouri statute of limitations—it had been too long (over nine years) since the alleged frauds had occurred.

However, the district court ruled that the federal statute of limitations had not run out on the false claims Miller made following the May 1986 flood. Following a three-day bench trial, the district court held that FEMA had not wrongfully denied Miller's claim from the October 1986 flood and that Miller's May 1986 flood claim violated the False Claims Act. This was very bad for Miller.

The court found that his house was, in fact, elevated. Since the losses occurred at an elevation lower than the lowest elevated floor of an elevated building, they were not covered under the standard NFIP policy.

The court also found that photographs and testimony admitted at trial showed that Miller claimed prior unrestored damage following both floods. It entered a $49,065.47 judgment against Miller. (The court cited federal law, which authorized triple damages—plus interest—and a civil penalty not less than $5,000.) Miller appealed.

The Court of Appeals ruled that the district court had erred in retroactively applying harsher penalty provisions of the False Claims Act that became effective after the government's claim ripened. The district court had concluded that the statute of limitations began to run on July 18, 1986—the date that NFIP paid Miller on his May 1986 flood claim.

The False Claim Act had been amended between that date and the lower court conclusion.

Before the amendments, the Act had provided for a penalty in an amount double the damages incurred by the government and a civil penalty of $2,000. The appeals court focused on this point. "[C]ongressional enactments and administrative rules will not be construed to have retroactive effect unless their language requires this result," it wrote. "Thus, it is necessary that we remand to district court so that it may impose a judgment in accord with the False Claims Act which was in effect on July 18, 1986."

Although the appeals court affirmed the district court's judgment against Miller, it sent the judgment back to be adjusted—downward. This was a small solace for Miller. The appeals court still rejected all of his arguments in defense of his claims.

Summary

People don't understand well enough that flooding is the catastrophic loss they're most likely to experience in their lives. When they do realize this, it's usually too late to do them any good.

In January 1997, a series of storms associated with the El Niño weather pattern in California dumped record amounts of rainfall throughout the state, leaving both homes and farms underwater.

Flood insurance purchases increased 16 percent between the January 1995 floods that hit several parts of the country and 1998, according to one FEMA spokesman.

"There's a renewed interest in flood insurance each time there's a big flood that catches their attention," he said. "Gradually, more and more people are coming to realize that their comprehensive homeowners policies don't cover floods."

In addition, FEMA launched a public education program in the fall of 1995 to acquaint businesses and individual property owners with the need and availability of flood insurance.

This may help. But the resistance is strong. Most people focus on more dramatic and direct disasters—earthquakes, fires and tornadoes. They only realize after muddy water has swept through their homes how powerful a destructive force it can be.

Insurance companies already know this. That's why they want consumers to buy the NFIP flood coverage.

CHAPTER THREE

El Niño and Other Weather Patterns

El Niño started showing up in cocktail party conversations in 1995 or 1996. It was the perfect topic—somewhat technical, somewhat colorful and inoffensive enough to be a safe topic of discussion with strangers.

Jay Leno and David Letterman used it as a standby punchline to shaky jokes. The popular press sprinkled it into headlines and sidebars. By the late 1990s, just about everyone had heard of El Niño—even if most people still weren't precisely sure what it meant. Or why it was such a big deal.

Weather experts describe El Niño as "a disruption of the ocean-atmosphere system in the tropical Pacific having important consequences for weather around the globe." Among these consequences: Increased rainfall and some flooding across the southwestern U.S. and south to Peru; high air pressure and west to east winds that push hurricanes away from the southeastern U.S.; drought in the West Pacific, sometimes associated with brush fires in Australia and New Zealand.

In normal, non-El Niño conditions, the trade winds blow from east to west across the tropical Pacific. These winds pile up warm surface water in the west Pacific, so that the sea surface is about two feet higher near Indonesia than near Ecuador.

The sea surface temperature is between 15 and 20 degrees warmer in the west, with cool temperatures off South America due to an upwelling of cold water from deeper levels. This cold water is nutrient-rich, supporting high levels of primary productivity, diverse marine ecosystems, and major fisheries. Rainfall tends to be found in rising air over the warmest water, so during normal times the east Pacific—including most of the western U.S.—is relatively dry.

In a world ruled by El Niño, an eastward displacement of the atmospheric heat source overlaying the warmest water results in large changes in the global atmospheric circulation, which in turn change weather patterns in regions far removed from the tropical Pacific. In other words, El Niño scrambles the normal weather patterns. As is so often the case, these phenomena are inherently neither good nor bad—but they can cause problems for the people in their paths.

During El Niño, the trade winds relax in the central and western Pacific leading to a depression of the so-called "thermocline" (the upswell of cool water from the deep) in the eastern Pacific. The result is a rise in sea surface temperature and a decline in primary productivity, which adversely affects commercial fisheries in the region.

El Niño was originally recognized by fisherman off the coast of South America as the appearance of unusually warm water in the Pacific ocean, occurring near the beginning of each year. El Niño means "The Little Boy" or "Christ child" in Spanish. This name was used for the tendency of the phenomenon to arrive around Christmas.

The Little Boy has appeared with growing frequency in the 1990s, which explains some of the extreme weather in the U.S. And there seems to be no end in sight. "With the newest figures, the long-term trend of increasing temperatures and precipitation in the United States continues," said Tom Karl, Director at The National Oceanic and Atmospheric Administration's (NOAA) National Climatic Data Center.

Recognizing El Niño

Observations of conditions in the tropical Pacific Ocean are essential for the prediction of short-term (a few months to one year) climate variations. To provide necessary data, the NOAA operates a network of buoys which measure temperature, currents and winds in the equatorial band.

NOAA has found that El Niño can be observed through measurements of the sea surface temperature.

In January 1991, the sea surface temperatures and the winds were near normal, with warm water in the western Pacific, and cool water—the so-called "cold tongue" resulting from the thermocline—in the eastern Pacific Ocean. The winds in the Western Pacific were very weak, and the winds in the eastern Pacific were blowing towards the west as they normally do.

In January 1998, NOAA found all of the signs that the Pacific was near the peak of a strong El Niño. Warm water spread from the western Pacific Ocean toward the east (in the direction of South America), the cold tongue had weakened, and the usually weak winds in the western Pacific were blowing strongly towards the east, pushing the warm water toward the Americas.

When an El Niño occurs, it makes itself known through its impact on U.S. weather. The National Weather Service—which is part of NOAA—reported that the winter of 1997-1998 was marked by a record breaking El Niño event and unusual extremes in parts of the country.

Overall, that winter was the second warmest and seventh wettest since 1895. Severe weather events during that season included flooding in the southeast, an ice storm in the northeast, flooding in California, and tornadoes in Florida.

The first two months of 1998 were the warmest and wettest in the 104-year record of temperatures and precipitation measurements for the contiguous 48 states. During those two months, the national average temperature was 37.5 degrees Fahrenheit compared with a normal national average of 32.1 degrees Fahrenheit. The previous record had been 37.0 degrees. For precipitation, 6.01 inches fell, compared with a normal of 4.05 inches. The previous record had been 5.7 inches.

"These are the patterns one would typically expect during a strong El Niño event," said Ants Leetma, director of NOAA's Climate Prediction Center. "This year, the strong El Niño on top of the continuing gradual increase of temperature and precipitation set the stage for many all-time state records."

Colorado State University's William Gray, a leading researcher who tracks and predicts hurricane activity, confirms that El Niño is responsible for—or at least associated with—increased tropical storm activity in the Pacific and decreased hurricane activity in the Gulf of Mexico and the Caribbean.

Following this theory, 1997—a strong El Niño year—saw very few hurricanes raging down Hurricane Alley.

La Niña and Other Variations

In May 1998, climatologists noted an abrupt cooling of the water in the eastern tropical Pacific Ocean, clearly signaling the end of the previous year's infamous El Niño and the beginning of the La Niña, the next swing of the planet's climatic pendulum. They predicted correctly that the Fall 1998 hurricane season would be much worse than the previous year's.

Hurricane Bonnie, which sent tens of thousands packing when it swept across the Carolina shores in late August, proved them right—as did Georges, which ravaged parts of the Caribbean and the Gulf Coast of the United States a few weeks later. Georges, in turn, was followed by Mitch—a category 5 hurricane which devastated central America.

Mitch killed thousands and left literally millions homeless.

La Niña is simply El Niño in reverse. Instead of the unusually warm water conditions that characterize El Niño, La Niña conditions exist when the water in the Equatorial Pacific is unusually cold. The "cold tongue" that exists in normal conditions stretches farther westward than usual.

La Niña means "The Little Girl." It's sometimes called El Viejo, anti-El Niño, or more prosaically "a cold event" or "a cold episode."
The 1998 La Niña episode began abruptly in May and was expected to strengthen during the rest of the year. If it followed previous cycles, it would linger into March, April or May of 1999. But some weather experts noted that the effects of an extreme La Niña are harder to predict than those of El Niño.

The effects of La Niña are, not unexpectedly, the exact opposite of El Niño's. In the U.S., winter weather temperatures are warmer than normal in the Southeast, and cooler than normal in the North. Unfortunately, La Niña years are associated with a higher incidence of hurricane activity in the southeastern U.S.

Both El Niño and La Niña influence the frequency and severity of global weather patterns in ways that are only partially understood. Especially in the 1990s, El Niño and La Niña have been blamed for weather phenomena. But even the experts are unsure of precisely which factors contribute to specific severe weather occurrence.

Jerry Levey, a trader at Natsource, a company that sells a kind of weather insurance to big companies, said that the insurance market had been betting that the winter of 1998/1999 would not be as severe as previously expected.

In fact, some weather watchers argue that the hype over El Niño and La Niña makes too much over a relatively small influence on catastrophic weather. Insurance companies and their risk experts have generally agreed with this skepticism. Through the late 1990s, most companies hadn't factored the Pacific weather patterns into their risk models with any particular focus.

But, as the experience of the 1990s confirmed the importance of indirect factors like El Niño—and as data processing capacity continued to grow at nearly geometric pace—some companies looked for ways to quantify the effects.

It was about time.

Why the Patterns Are Important

Even though El Niño's impact on catastrophic losses may be indirect, it is real. Like hurricanes, El Niño weather patterns do most of their damage with water. The problem that insurance companies and government agencies have with analyzing their impact is that the connection isn't very direct. An El Niño pattern can last for months and the patterns don't do much to help predict the storms that they generate or redirect. But they do have an impact.

One of the most extreme El Niño patterns in recent years began in late 1996 and continued for more than a year. California was particularly hard hit by this system.

As of January 1997, 43 of 58 California counties had been declared disaster areas. Sacramento was spared the worst of the flooding by a system of levees, although many nearby towns were not so fortunate. Numerous levee breaches and breaks occurred across the state. Some 16,000 residences were damaged or destroyed. State officials estimated at least $1.6 billion in damages to private and public property.

California wasn't the only state affected. The month of December 1996 and the first week of January 1997 brought tremendous amounts of rain and snow to parts of the states of Washington, Oregon, Idaho, Nevada and Montana. In particular, the period of December 26 through January 3 was especially severe—with over 20 inches of rain in some locations.

This, along with unusually warm temperatures, which produced tremendous snowmelt, resulted in record flooding in some areas. Emergency management officials in these states indicate that as many as a half a million people were forced to evacuate at one time or another during December and early January.

In Nevada, Reno alone estimated approximately $170 million in damages, with the state total possibly reaching $500 million. Damage to casinos and businesses in the Reno area was quite extensive.

The valleys surrounding the Sierra Nevada were especially hard hit, as the Truckee River reached its highest level on record. Lake Tahoe reached its highest level since 1917. The Army Corps of Engineers released a preliminary estimate ranking the flooding as a 50-year event (a 2 percent chance of occurrence in any given year) for the Sacramento River.

In Washington state, officials estimated that the storms and warm weather had caused $125 million in insured losses. Mudslides were a severe problem, especially in the Seattle area. State government agencies were worried—as they are inclined to be—about how much uninsured losses would add to the total. Uninsured risks often end up being absorbed by already overburdened state agencies that offer disaster aid.

In Oregon, areas along the Rogue River in the south and in the vicinity of the Tualatin River near Portland were among the most-affected areas of the state. However, damage totals for the state were lower than those in neighboring states.

In Idaho, about 400 miles of roads were closed, and over 10,000 people were isolated at one time by flooding and mudslides. Approximately one-third of the state's counties were declared disaster areas.

During the month of February 1998, a series of storms due in part to the effects of El Niño struck California. The estimates immediately afterward indicated over $550 million in damages for the state in that month. The state also reported 17 storm-related deaths for the winter, and 35 counties were declared federal disaster areas.

Clear Lake in northern California reached its highest level since 1909, flooding portions of Lakeport, about 90 miles north of San Francisco. In terms of precipitation, across California and the southwest, four weeks of nearly continuous storminess resulted in widespread flooding, mudslides, and agriculture disruptions.

Late in the month a shift in the weather pattern brought some of that storminess out of the southwest and into the northern plains. February precipitation records were set at nearly a dozen locations in the east and at least 19 stations in California. Santa Barbara received an incredible monthly total of 21.74 inches, breaking the old record of 17.33 set in 1962 and establishing a record for any month. Records for Santa Barbara date back to 1867.

To some extent, the focus on El Niño may be the result of a self-fulfilling prophecy. Because standard insurance coverages work relatively smoothly in the face of traditional risks, insurance companies often focus their analysis on exceptional risks—disasters.

This new focus gives them reason to look for exceptional causes—factors as indirect as the effect Pacific Ocean water temperatures have on the direction and magnitude of storms.

This is an important point that will occur again: As big insurance companies hand the easy risks off to reinsurance companies and the capital markets, they compete increasingly within a narrow band made up of riskier exposures. In this tight space, the difference between success and failure is narrow, intense and extreme.

The risk theorists who build the actuarial computer models have begun to look for all kinds of nontraditional and indirect causes of loss. These models ultimately determine our insurance premiums. That's why most of us have started hearing about El Niño in recent years.

Fishermen and sailors in the Pacific have known about the Little Boy for a hundred years—the actuaries in Hartford, Bermuda and Silicon Valley just started thinking about him in the 1990s. Insurance prices will depend on their predictions.

Summary

Ocean temperatures in the equatorial Pacific oscillate over the years, with El Niño characterized by unusually warm temperatures and La Niña by unusually cool temperatures. The intensity of the swings varies. But whichever way the pendulum swings, the effects are felt worldwide.

In the United States, temperatures during El Niño years are warmer than usual in the north central states and cooler than usual in the southeast and southwest; during a La Niña year, winter temperatures are warmer than usual in the southeast and cooler than usual in the northwest and northeast, according to NOAA.

Getting a handle on El Niño's full impact in the United States is complicated, though. FEMA's tallies cover only a fraction of the losses, and no central authority gathers data that include every loss.

The government agencies that have to deal with the losses and losers who fall through the cracks of the insurance industry will tend to focus more on the practical effects of flood exclusions and coverage that's too expensive for working-class homeowners to afford.

It's useful for FEMA and its state-level counterparts to know that El Niño sets in motion changes that result in rivers overflowing their banks. But officials are powerless when it comes to stopping the flood.

FEMA has to deal with the real implications of the rising water—the welfare families flooded out of their trailer park near the river when the levees give out. In the end, there are two different perspectives on disaster response wrapped around the same set of facts.

The risk guru wants to know about the river overflowing because that may help him figure out how to quantify El Niño's impact. The assistant director at FEMA is interested for a different reason—busy working with the Red Cross and local charities to get washed-out welfare families food and a place to sleep, he wants to know how many blankets he'll need that night.

These two perspectives will always be different. But, if they move too far apart, both become less effective. The actuaries can't afford to let their elegant formulas and NOAA buoys carry them too far away from the real damage that occurs.

The challenge in focusing on a fairly esoteric influence like El Niño is to understand why its important—and to keep the various parts of disaster response connected.

CHAPTER FOUR

Tornadoes

Tornadoes fascinate most weather watchers in a way that no other storm can. Credited by informed consensus as being nature's most violent event, tornadoes form when updrafts within a storm front lift rotating surface air currents into a vertical orientation.

Once the rotation is vertical, a tornado forms. A tornado acts something like a giant vacuum cleaner—a description also used for hurricanes. But tornadoes are much smaller, shorter-lived...and much, much more intense. Wind speeds within tornadoes can reach speeds approaching 280 miles per hour, though most twisters are considerably weaker.

Weak tornadoes usually have wind speeds in the neighborhood of 100 to 120 miles per hour (near the top of the scale for a hurricane) and last no longer than 10 minutes. According to NOAA, these weak tornadoes make up more than two-thirds of all reported twisters.

Stronger tornadoes have not only faster windspeed but also longer duration. This combination means they do considerably more damage than their more common, weaker counterparts. A strong twister can destroy a well-built home effortlessly. It can lift cars or trucks and hurl them hundreds of yards. And, twisters seem to have an almost animal sense for finding and upturning mobile home trailer parks.

Unlike hurricanes, tornado damage is usually confined to a very localized area. Tornadoes also may be accompanied by other significant weather events—including hail, wind gusts and flooding. Though tornadoes can occur virtually in all of the warmer parts of the world, the Southeast and Midwest experience the world's highest frequency of twisters.

In an average year, the U.S. will have about 800 reported tornadoes. But experts at NOAA and other weather tracking groups argue that the true numbers are actually much higher, since some twisters in sparsely populated areas are never reported.

Improved weather technology and Doppler radar (a tool that measures direction and speed of a moving object such as precipitation) have sharpened forecasting techniques to the point that fewer deaths occur each year due to tornadoes. Much as they do with hurricanes, weather scientists can track a tornado's path and make general warnings about direction and speed.

An important problem: It's impossible to predict the exact path of a twister. And predictions for tornadoes are more important because—unlike hurricanes—they offer so little warning.

The Damage Profile

The fact that tornadoes usually occur as brief, localized events means that losses from twister activity never reach the massive billion dollar levels caused by tropical storms that often span several hundred miles across. But, unlike a hurricane, a tornado spares little in its path—making up with intensity what it lacks in size.

On May 31, 1985, a single storm front spawned 41 tornadoes in one afternoon throughout parts of Ohio and Pennsylvania. The unusually potent front killed 75 people, injured 1,025 and caused $450 million in damage.

During the late evening of February 22 and early morning of February 23, 1998, the National Weather Service reported a series of tornadoes that ripped across central Florida. They were spawned by an unusual weather system that was blamed on the strong El Niño conditions of 1997-1998. At least one of the tornadoes reached the second-highest level of intensity on the widely-used Fujita scale—a fairly rare occurrence.

The hardest hit locations were Winter Garden, Altamonte Springs, Sanford, and Campbell—but the damage was surprisingly widespread. Overall, Governor Lawton Chiles declared 54 of Florida's 67 counties federal disaster areas.

Forty-two fatalities occurred, over 800 homes were destroyed and another 700 left uninhabitable, another 3,500 homes were damaged to some extent and 135,000 utility customers lost power at the height of the storms. Damages from the tornado outbreak exceeded $60 million—and

Florida's overall storm damage total for that year would ultimately reach nearly $500 million.

Noticeable among the damaged areas: Several mobile home trailer parks in the center part of the state.

It may seem like a tired joke that tornadoes and other wind storms seem to damage mobile homes and trailer parks...all the time. The reason that the things seem so often in the disaster news is that they're less structurally secure than traditional homes. A tornado or hurricane will often move through an area, doing minor damage to frame houses with foundations—and then do major damage to a park full of light and cheaply-assembled mobile homes.

It's not much of an exaggeration to say that a pewter stein is to an aluminum can what a traditional home is to a mobile home. Of course, it has to be this way. Mobile homes are designed to be inexpensive and...mobile. They're not going to hold up as well under 150 m.p.h. winds.

Tornadoes and hurricanes share some key attributes. For this reason, there's much that can be learned from response to hurricanes that can be applied to tornadoes.

The federal government takes its regulatory role in this matter seriously. The June 1995 federal appeals court decision *Florida Manufactured Housing Association, et al., v. Henry Cisneros* dealt in plain terms with the government's regulation of wind damage-prone mobile homes.

According to Congress, the 1974 Manufactured Housing Act was designed to "reduce the number of personal injuries and deaths and the amount of insurance costs and property damage resulting from manufactured home accidents and to improve the quality and durability of manufactured homes." (Manufactured home is the euphemism for mobile home that the makers of the housing prefer.)

In order to achieve these objectives, the Act authorizes the Secretary of the Department of Housing and Urban Development (HUD) to "establish by order appropriate Federal manufactured home construction and safety standards. Each such Federal manufactured home standard shall be reasonable and shall meet the highest standards of protection, taking into account existing State and local laws relating to manufactured home safety and construction."

This authority has a two-fold purpose. First, of course, it makes the homes safer for the people who live in them. Second, though, it creates safety thresholds that the insurance companies who cover mobile homes can count on to minimize losses.

Devastation caused by Hurricane Andrew in August of 1992 convinced HUD that the existing wind resistance standards for manufactured homes were inadequate. According to HUD, approximately 36 percent of all housing units destroyed by Hurricane Andrew were manufactured homes, a disproportionate share of the housing in the area.

Before HUD issued the new regulations, the agency's wind resistance standards for manufactured homes had divided the U.S. into two wind zones: a "standard" wind zone and a "hurricane-resistive" wind zone. Under those regulations, manufactured homes in the hurricane-resistive zone were required to withstand winds of approximately 80 miles per hour.

After Hurricane Andrew, HUD initiated field investigations as part of a general review of manufactured home standards. The investigations revealed various deficiencies in manufactured homes' resistance to wind storms, such as inadequate connections between roofs, walls and floors, and between exterior roof and wall coverings and supporting sheathing or framing. Those deficiencies led to other problems, including water damage, damage from increased internal pressures, and missile damage from flying debris.

In addition to HUD's investigations, the National Institute of Standards and Technology issued a "National Standards Report" comparing the wind protection provisions of selected codes and standards. In assessing the impact of Hurricane Andrew on manufactured housing, the National Standards Report found that: "Damage to manufactured homes ranged from loss of roofing to total destruction...."

On April 14, 1993, HUD published a Notice of Proposed Rulemaking, proposing that the manufactured home standards be amended to "increase the safety of manufactured homes in areas where wind-induced damage is a special hazard."

In order to have the new standards in place by the 1993 hurricane season, HUD used an abbreviated 30-day public comment period for the proposed rules. However, the deadline passed and HUD subsequently extended the comment period for another 30 days, because it decided that the new standards could not be implemented in time for the 1993 hurricane season.

HUD received comments from the public, manufacturers, and others with objections to the proposed standards, including criticism related to increased costs and predictions of deleterious effects on the industry and on low-income families.

The Manufactured Housing Act requires that HUD consult with an Advisory Council made up of scientists, public officials, and others "to the extent feasible" when amending manufactured home standards. However, in anticipation of having the rules in effect before the next hurricane season, HUD took the position that it was not "feasible" to meet with the Advisory Council; however, after the expedited schedule was relaxed, the agency convened the Advisory Council for a two-day session in July 1993.

The Advisory Council adopted a resolution that recommended further studies be conducted, and that the Advisory Council be reconvened to review public comments about HUD's analysis of these studies. However, HUD published the Final Rule in January 1994 without reconvening the Advisory Council. It explained that it had "considered the conclusions and recommendations of the Advisory Council" and did "not believe there is any significant advantage in, or that the public interest would be served by, reconvening the Advisory Council."

As a result, the Florida Manufactured Housing Association and several of its biggest members sued to block the proposed changes. The manufacturers argued that:

- HUD didn't adequately consult with its Advisory Council as required by law;
- HUD misinterpreted the meaning of "cost" as used in the statutory criteria; and
- the new wind standards were arbitrary and capricious.

Responding to the first charge, HUD insisted that it had complied with the law by convening the Advisory Council once and by carefully considering its comments. Although it disagreed with many of the Advisory Council's recommendations, the agency did make some modifications in its proposed standards based in part on the Council's recommendations. In view of the changes it made, HUD asserted that the manufacturers "have confused a requirement of consultation with one of 100 percent adoption."

On this matter, the federal court in south Florida concluded:

> Based upon its consultation with the Advisory Council, HUD did make some modifications to the proposed standards, with the result that they became less stringent. The Advisory Council wanted more modifications, more studies, and more consultation, but HUD is the decision-maker and the process must end sometime.

On the second charge, the Manufactured Housing Act set specific requirements for HUD to follow when establishing manufactured housing standards. One such criterion directed HUD to "consider the probable effect of such standard[s] on the cost of the manufactured home to the public." The manufacturers argued that this factor refers solely to the consumer purchase price of manufactured homes and that HUD misinterpreted the meaning of cost by giving it a much broader definition.

They referred to a statement that the meaning of cost is "not limited to [a manufactured home's] purchase price but includes the potential costs to the public if the home is involved in a disaster." Instead of simply considering consumer costs, they contend, HUD merged the consumer cost factor into a cost-benefit analysis and concluded that the benefits to society outweighed any price increases.

The manufacturers argued that when the price increases were subsumed into a more general weighing of societal costs and benefits, the true impact of price increases was minimized because they were offset by general benefits to the government and public at large. So, HUD's interpretation denied consumer price increases their proper consideration as an independent factor.

The court concluded that it didn't have to get into a philosophical discussion of the meaning of *cost* or *public*. The manufacturers acknowledged that HUD had considered the effect of the regulations on consumer purchase prices; in fact, they contested HUD's purchase price impact figures in a separate argument. So, HUD had met the requirement.

Finally, the manufacturers claimed that the new wind standards HUD proposed were arbitrary and capricious. Although this may seem like a ridiculously trivial dispute, it does show how the government regulates disaster risks—and how much the courts support this effort.

First, the manufacturers nitpicked about the cost and benefits of the new standards. HUD acknowledged that the new regulations would increase costs to consumers. It justified those increases on the grounds that the stricter standards would reduce losses from wind damage to manufactured housing occupants and the general public. It also figured that they would help to avoid the "inestimable costs of devastation to people's lives and emotional health and to the communities" caused by severe hurricanes and some tornadoes.

These "inestimable costs of devastation" did seem a little ambiguous—in terms of cost analysis. But HUD defended its conclusions. It explained that its statutory mandate required it to look at more than economic considerations in promulgating regulations. It also concluded that the new regulations were in the "optimal societal interest" because the "savings in storm damage repair, loss of personal property, and potential personal injury or loss of life, in addition to other expected benefits, exceeds the cost differential" for the new wind standards.

HUD quantified these costs and benefits in its Regulatory Impact Analysis ("RIA"). Using data from the damage caused by Hurricane Andrew, the RIA delineated three types of benefits that would result from the new standards:

- reductions in property damage borne by residents and insurers;
- reductions in federal disaster relief expenditures; and
- reductions in deaths and injuries.

Balanced against these benefits were increased costs of production caused by compliance with the new standards, although HUD determined that only a portion of the increased costs would be passed on to consumers in the form of higher prices. HUD concluded in the RIA that the new standards would produce an annual benefit of $83.8 million and an annual cost of $51.7 million, resulting in an annual net benefit of $32.1 million.

According to the manufacturers, HUD erred in its determination in RIA that the new wind standards would produce a net economic benefit. To the extent that HUD relied on projections indicating that the benefits of the new standards would outweigh the costs as the primary basis for issuing the new standards, the manufacturers asserted that the figures were flawed—making adoption of the new regulations arbitrary and capricious.

The manufacturers argued that the cost of producing manufactured houses complying with the new wind regulations would be double that of HUD's predictions. Moreover, they asserted that the RIA underestimated the amount of the cost increases that would be passed on to consumers as higher prices.

The court disagreed. It contended that HUD had given a logical explanation for the cost and benefit figures it relied on in promulgating the new wind standards, and that it provided in the Final Rule and the denial of the Application for Stay a reasoned response to the manufacturers' comments and criticisms.

Second, the manufacturers argued that the new wind regulations were arbitrary and capricious because they imposed on all manufactured homes, regardless of where they were located, standards based on stricter requirements. Thus, the wind regulations ignored the statutory criterion that the standards be reasonable "for the geographic region for which [they are] prescribed."

HUD explained that it had chosen a single exposure category so that dealers could stock inventories and would not be required to order each home based on the individual customer's location. This worked for the court, which concluded:

> Because HUD neither refused to consider the appropriate factors nor committed a clear error of judgment, the agency's decision to adopt [consistent] wind standards for all Wind Zone II and III areas was not arbitrary and capricious.

Third, the manufacturers argued that the new wind standards were arbitrary and capricious because they could not possibly achieve the "stated purpose" of the regulations: preventing manufactured housing damage from another Hurricane Andrew. According to the manufacturers, since Andrew's 145 miles per hour winds would cause damage even to manufactured homes built according to the revised standards, the cost increases associated with the new standards were not justified.

The court started to get a little sarcastic at this point:

> ...the manufacturers previously argued that the new standards are arbitrary and capricious because they go too far, and now they contend that the regulations are arbitrary and capricious because they do not go far enough.... [I]t is not at all clear that the "stated purpose" of the wind standards is to prevent damage from another Hurricane Andrew. Although Hurricane Andrew was the catalyst behind strengthening the standards, which even the manufacturers admit are too lax, the purpose of the changes according to the Final Rule is simply to increase safety "in areas where wind-induced damage is a particular hazard and risk."

This would include areas that have a lot of tornadoes.

In a last-ditch effort to fight the new rules, the manufacturers took a more political approach. They argued that, because hurricane risks cannot be eliminated completely, consumers must be given the option of sacrificing some hurricane protection in exchange for lower housing costs. According to the manufacturers, by including cost and geographic reasonableness criteria in the Manufactured Housing Act, Congress indicated that consumer choice should be accommodated.

Putting a fine point on their argument, the manufacturers insisted that HUD should be prevented from the kind of "governmental paternalism" that denied consumers the ability to choose to live more cheaply and less safely.

The court found this quasi-libertarian argument impersuasive because the wind standards promulgated under the Manufactured Housing Act were designed to protect not only the occupants of manufactured homes, but also other members of the public who could be affected by flying debris during high winds. Finally—and most fundamentally—said the court, the consumer's "right to choose" is not a criterion for decision-making under the Manufactured Housing Act.

Allowing consumers to knowingly assume the risk of unsafe housing may or may not be a good idea, but it is not one Congress included in the statutory scheme. If the manufacturers want the statutory criteria for promulgating manufactured home standards changed, they should direct their arguments to Congress.

So, the court rejected all of the manufacturers' arguments. HUD's new wind rules—and its prerogative to make such rules in the future—was left standing.

Measuring Tornado Intensity

Disputes over government rules seem trivial in comparison to challenges tornadoes represent. For starters, scientists have a hard time even measuring a twister. The best system available is an historical review, based on damage that has occurred.

And the difficulties go on. The size of a tornado is not necessarily the best indicator of its intensity. Large tornadoes are often weak while small tornadoes can be violent. Large tornadoes can also be strong and small tornadoes can be weak.

Since size is inconclusive and tornadoes are so fleeting, it is difficult to measure their internal wind speeds and intensity.

The Fujita Scale is used to rate the intensity of a tornado by examining the damage caused by the tornado after it has passed over a man-made structure. The Fujita Scale is based on damage, not the appearance of the funnel.

Although storm spotters and other weather observers make judgments about the intensity of a tornado when they are in the field, the Fujita Intensity estimate is made after the tornado has passed.

In the aftermath of a tornado, insurance coverage isn't the contentious issue that it can be in other disasters. Why? Because standard property policies don't exclude or even substantially limit coverage for wind damage. That eliminates the "Proof of Loss" disputes that so often arise in the wake of hurricanes or floods.

On a more cynical level, a critic might note that because of their geographic concentration, tornadoes tend to involve smaller total dollar amounts per incident, and this makes them less of an exposure to an insurance company's risk portfolio.

Whatever the reason, the importance is, of course, that the companies pay claims for tornado damage.

The Fujita Tornado Intensity Scale

F0 - F1 Weak Tornado
F2 - F3 Strong Tornado
F4 - F5 Violent Tornado

F0. Gale tornado (40-72 mph winds)
Light damage. Some damage to chimneys; break branches off trees; push over shallow-rooted trees; damage sign boards.

F1. Moderate tornado (73-112 mph winds)
Moderate damage. The lower limit is the beginning of hurricane wind speed; peel surface off roofs; mobile homes pushed off foundations or overturned; moving autos pushed off the roads.

F2. Significant tornado (113-157 mph winds)
Considerable damage. Roofs torn off frame houses; mobile homes demolished; boxcars pushed over; large trees snapped or uprooted; light-object missiles generated.

F3. Severe tornado (158-206 mph winds)
Severe damage. Roofs and some walls torn off well-constructed houses; trains overturned; most trees in forest uprooted; heavy cars lifted off the ground and thrown.

F4. Devastating tornado (207-260 mph winds)
Devastating damage. Well-constructed houses leveled; structures with weak foundations blown off some distance; cars thrown and large-object missiles generated.

F5. Incredible tornado (261-318 mph winds)
Incredible damage. Strong frame houses lifted off foundations and carried considerable distance to disintegrate; automobile sized missiles fly through the air in excess of 100 meters (109 yds); trees debarked; incredible phenomena will occur.

F6-F12. Upper ranges (319 mph to the speed of sound)
These are hypothetical limits. The maximum wind speeds of tornadoes are not expected to reach the F6 wind speeds.

Source: Journal of Atmospheric Science, August 1981, pp. 1517-1519

In late May 1997, a devastating tornado struck the Double Creek Estates subdivision in Jarrell, Texas (north of Austin). The tornado, an F4 packing winds of more than 200 m.p.h., cut a path a half-mile wide and two miles long through the Central Texas towns of Jarrell and Cedar Park.

It lifted homes from their foundations and asphalt from roads.

In the aftermath, residents returning to their homes in hard-hit Double Creek Estates said that only five homes were left intact out of more than 50 that once made up their neighborhood. Rescue workers called off their search for bodies when the death toll reached 27.

State emergency response officials said that any Texas town would have been sidelined by such an intense disaster; but Jarrell—an unincorporated town with no mayor, fire department or police force—was especially ill-equipped to deal with it.

The local Justice of the Peace stepped in as acting county coroner. Though he was getting help for nearby county agencies and Federal officials, he was still having trouble identifying victims. In fact, he was having trouble collecting victims remains. County officials were still collecting body parts hours before the stricken area was reopened to the public.

Randy Ackley of the Red Cross said his organization was recalibrating its aid package. The Red Cross usually focuses on relieving psychological traumas in the wake of a catastrophic tornado. In Jarrell, however, it was concentrating on meeting simple physical needs. "We're opening up a family services center...so we can begin to get them the basic necessities they need to get on with their lives," Ackley told a local newspaper. He explained that help would include everything from toothbrushes to temporary rent money.

At the time, authorities said state and federal disaster teams had finished a preliminary assessment of the damage within 24 hours of the twister, but it would be several days before they completed their estimates. In the meantime, Governor George W. Bush had declared Jarrell a disaster area and asked FEMA to set up its usual package of loans and recovery aid.

State Insurance Commissioner Elton Bomer said damage in the Jarrell area alone could reach $20 million. And he planned to pay close attention to how insurance companies with policies in the area paid claims. Of course, the profile of the Jarrell twister didn't offer much room for companies to dispute coverage. And, no matter how badly they are portrayed in movies and cheap fiction, insurance companies aren't politically foolish enough to save small dollars haggling with victims of an F4 tornado.

Sen. Kay Bailey Hutchison surveyed the area around Jarrell by helicopter and promised to aid the governor's office in its requests for federal disaster relief. Staffers for Hutchison, Bush and Bomer all agreed that—aside from the obvious political benefit—their bosses toured the area to send a message to the insurance industry that it couldn't quibble with Jarrell residents over their claims.

Summary

Tornadoes are covered by standard property insurance.

On the public policy level, it makes sense that insurance companies—and government agencies—should pay for tornado recovery without the hesitation or debate that sometimes follows other disasters. Why? Because tornadoes can and do occur throughout most of the U.S., so there's no issue of the government subsidizing people to live where nature suggests they don't. This eliminates the inequities created by millionaires living in waterfront Miami mansions and buying flood insurance subsidized by inland families living on $40,000 a year.

Also, tornado damage is furiously intense but short-lived. It's extremely rare for a single twister to stay on the ground for more than an hour. Combined with a tornado's small physical size, this means there's simply less total damage, no matter how devastating it may seem to the people who survive it.

For these reasons—and others we've considered—tornadoes may be the "purest" disasters that occur. They're common enough to model, but no one of them is broadly destructive enough to skew an insurance company's portfolio. In the 1980s and 1990s, tornadoes have been among the least complicated of disasters...at least for insurance companies. (Hypothetically, several dozen twisters touching down in the same location could stump actuaries. And this long-shot event could cause all kinds of financial problems.)

CHAPTER FIVE

Winter Weather

Every year, the National Weather Service provides a review of seasonal weather. The winter of 1995/1996 was a season of unusual extremes. Although December was not unusually active, January and February proved to be.

Those months included the following events: A January blizzard and ensuing flooding that disabled most of the Northeast; a severe cold wave in February that shut down most of the Midwest; February flooding in the Pacific Northwest; and unusual warmth and fires in the southern plains.

Another interesting development during that winter was the so-called "seesaw" pattern of temperature and precipitation over much of the United States. Extremely cold conditions were often followed by unusual warmth. The same applied to precipitation—the Pacific Northwest began the season on the dry side and then saw record rain. As is often the case in climatology, the averages of the season belied the extremes contained within.

Interesting or not, January and February of 1996 were deadly. Over 300 deaths could be attributed in some way to extreme weather during the winter of 1995/1996. Also, between $3 billion and $4 billion in insured property damage was inflicted by the combination of very heavy snowfall and severe flooding.

Moderate to heavy rains (one example: 3.03 inches in 24 hours at Williamsport, Pennsylvania) and rapid snowmelt triggered serious flooding along the Delaware, Susquehanna, upper Ohio, Potomac and James River basins, with crests as much as 20 feet above flood stage. The flooding killed 33 people, forced over 200,000 from their homes, and destroyed or damaged hundreds of roads and bridges.

Presidential disaster declarations included the states of Virginia, Ohio, Pennsylvania, Maryland, West Virginia and New York. Pennsylvania was especially hard hit. There were an estimated $1 billion in total damages and costs from the combined blizzard and flooding.

In April 1998, FEMA reported that it had committed more than $289 million to recovery from 1997/1998 winter disasters. That figure compared with $294 million in 1996/1997 and $280 million in 1995/1996. The winter of 1996/1997 saw severe flooding in the West and in the Ohio Valley, blizzards in the Dakotas and Minnesota and a tornado in Arkansas. The winter of 1996/1995's calamities included a 13-state blizzard and flooding in the Middle Atlantic States, Northeast and Pacific Northwest.

For the most part, the trend has been an upward one for more than a decade. FEMA's price tag for the winter of 1989/1990 was $170 million—and as low as $126 million in 1987/1988.

These numbers were only FEMA's expenditures. Insured losses were much larger for each of the years. And total losses—insured and uninsured—were larger still. Insurance industry insiders claim that, in the late 1990s, more than $2 billion in insured losses were claimed each winter.

Standard homeowners and auto insurance policies offer coverage for winter damage with few exceptions. Some of the most common covered winter losses include: collapsed roofs, frozen pipes and accidents that occur because of icy roads.

The United States has dealt with harsh winters since the eighteenth century. Why the sudden explosion of winter weather claims?

The generally increasing publicity of winter disasters seems to have spilled over from the usual hurricanes, earthquakes and floods.

One City's Response

Blizzards are particularly burdensome to local governments. In a reverse from most other natural disasters, winter storms do more damage to people, cars and infrastructure than they do homes and buildings. The main risk that snow poses to a house is damaging a weak roof before the Sun can melt it or the owner can remove it.

Much of the loss associated with heavy ice or snow is people not being able to move from one place to another—or accidents that happen when they do try to move.

The storms also cause problems for people—and local governments—because they hit municipal infrastructure hard. A blizzard or ice storm will usually cause telephone and power lines to break. They can cause water and sewage pipes to burst. (This is a big problem, because most standard homeowners insurance doesn't cover damages caused by failed sewer systems.) They can render bridges and overpasses unuseable. And the cost of response—specifically the man-hours and tools like road salt needed—can be high.

On October 23, 1997, a major early winter storm was brewing in the Rocky Mountains. On television and radio, weather reporters warned of the coming snow. Denver Mayor Wellington Webb called a press conference and stood before television cameras to declare that Denver was ready to meet any snow emergency.

On October 24, a blizzard with high winds and heavy snow swept across the Rocky Mountain states. The city of Denver was brought to its knees by one of the worst blizzards in its history. The blizzard covered eastern Colorado with up to four feet of snow and created snow drifts reaching 15 feet. The storm, in what is normally Colorado's driest month, closed virtually every highway across the eastern half of the state.

Denver International Airport was caught off-guard when nearly 22 inches of snow fell in less than 24 hours. The blizzard shut down DIA for a day-and-a-half and stranded more than 3,000 travelers in the airport's terminals. Hundreds more spent a Friday night and part of the following Saturday in their cars on the 10-mile-long airport access road, paralyzed by stuck and abandoned vehicles.

Then the blizzard swept into neighboring Nebraska—which received 23 inches of snow—and Kansas. The thick, wet snow threatened late-season corn crops in Nebraska and Iowa. It cut power lines and snapped tree limbs in Omaha, Des Moines and smaller outlying towns. And the southernmost edge of the storm dipped into Oklahoma and New Mexico.

At least 16 deaths in seven states—eight in Colorado, two in Nebraska, two in Illinois, and one each in Michigan, Iowa, Kansas and Oklahoma—were attributed to the weather. In Colorado alone, the snow caused more than $91.6 million in insured damages.

Within 24 hours, Denver found itself digging out under cloudless skies. In the meantime, eight inches of snow blanketed parts of Michigan, as the remnants of the storm blew northeastward into Canada.

Some weather experts blamed the blizzard on an old, familiar culprit. According to Klaus Wolter, research meteorologist at the University of Colorado's Climate Diagnostic Center in Boulder, the storm would have been quite a bit weaker without El Nino. "If you plot how much snow you get with each storm, what you find is the really high amounts of snow in a single snowstorm...tend to [occur] in El Nino years. It really loads the dice," Wolter told one newspaper.

In the aftermath of the blizzard, Denver officials took various steps to make amends for their shortcomings. They revised the city's emergency plans; they erected higher snow fences along the airport access road; and they bought more four-wheel-drive vehicles for police and fire departments. But only the next major blizzard would determine whether they'd done enough.

Almost exactly a year later, a major hail storm hit Denver. The storm pummeled buildings, vehicles and pedestrians with hailstones as large as 2 inches in diameter. A few anxious city employees thought the hail storm might be the next big opportunity. But it wasn't.

An official with State Farm Insurance estimated that the company would be paying out more than $12.5 million in claims for damage sustained by Denver-area homes and automobiles in the hailstorm. This was nothing compared to the Denver area's worst hail damage that occurred in June 1990, when property damage reached $657 million.

Of course, hail storms and ice storms can cause all kinds of havoc. An ice storm, especially, is a deceptive assault. As ice accumulates, it presses down on trees like a large hand. As the weight builds, treetops bend to the ground, massive branches break off and whole trunks snap in two. The ice also builds up on the ground quietly—often accumulating in some areas while leaving others relatively dry.

"Ice storms are the most dangerous winter storms because the stuff forms in patches," says one adjuster for a major regional auto insurer. "People will drive along half a mile of dry road and then hit a couple hundred yards of ice. They feel the car slide, they panic, then hit the brakes and—wham!—the wheels lock and smash into a telephone pole."

Once again, winter losses occur regularly enough that insurance companies pay claims with relatively few disputes.

Dealing with a Superstorm

Another major problem posed by big winter storms is that they tend to be very large in geographic reach. Especially when they pass through the East Coast, they can dump snow and ice on six...or ten...or a dozen states.

With all those various citizens stuck in their houses—if not airports or offices—six or ten or a dozen governors will be tempted to declare the stricken places disaster areas. This frees up the federal money. It also taxes FEMA to its limits.

In mid-March 1993, during a spell of unseasonably warm and pleasant weather, forecasters went out on a limb and predicted that warm and cold air masses would meet over the Gulf of Mexico and explode into a fast-moving storm of nearly unparalleled force.

And they were right.

Encompassing much of the eastern third of North America, the "superstorm" brought bitter cold, hurricane-force winds, deadly tidal surges and up to four feet of snow. It reached from Maine to Florida and left more than 270 people dead—three times the combined total of Hurricanes Hugo and Andrew—some of them in their own homes.

Insurance rating company A.M. Best would make a preliminary estimate on claims from the March blizzard of about $800 million. Within a few weeks, it would increase the estimate to $1.5 billion. Best's original estimate had been based on two previous late winter storms. The larger figure was based on surveys of insurers.

Although the blizzard lasted just three days, its impact on the country lasted the whole month. Various business and economic indicators for March 1997 dropped, as people concentrated on digging out from the storm. All but one category of retailing reported lower sales. The category that saw an increase: drugstores. They sold lots of flashlights, batteries and driveway salt.

In the meantime, FEMA and the biggest insurance companies were competing for adjusters and other specialists who could help sort through the various damages, start making estimates of losses and begin processing claims.

To use one example: Allstate flew and bused in adjusters from the West Coast and parts of the South that had been spared the worst of the superstorm. These people fanned out across the Northeast and Mid Atlantic coastal states, setting up temporary "on-storm" offices from which to handle claims. Adjusters were working from seven in the morning to past seven at night to process all the claims.

Another example: State Farm—the nations largest property insurer—has adjusters nationwide ready to travel to areas that need special attention. Members of this so-called NatCat team receive extra pay for the long hours and travel required for such assignments.

Why the rush? The intensity was the result of the short window of opportunity that follows a winter storm. Blizzard claims need to be made, documented and at least partially processed before the snow or ice melts. In the case of a late season storm, this can be two or three days. So the claims come in fast and furious. Literally.

Fortunately, for the adjusters, most seem to agree that winter storm claims are relatively simple to analyze, at least as compared to flood and earthquake claims. This is because cold weather damage is usually easy to identify and repair, rather than hidden and ignored.

FEMA often has more trouble than the big carriers in sorting out a sudden deluge of claims. It has to coordinate with various governors and other state officials inorder to do its job. And it has to administer loan programs and insurance claims—though it usually handles both of these functions through contractors and subcontractors.

"Basically, it's a bonanza for freelance adjusters and loan brokers," says one veteran FEMA adminstrator. "Like most government agencies, [FEMA] does worst when working under tight deadlines."

For this reason, there may be more questionable FEMA loans and grants made in the wake of a late season blizzard than after any other kind of natural disaster.

Summary

Winter storms may be the strangest of all natural disasters. If they aren't the most problematic for insurance companies, they certainly are for FEMA and local governments. While blizzards happen often enough, they don't do the kind of harm that floods, fires and hurricanes do. Still, they have a kind of lingering intensity that's particularly difficult for government administrators. And their effect on people and places is hard to measure.

Emergency response plans can help smooth out the aftermath of a blizzard. But there's an inevitable irony in the fact that the places hurt the most by snow are usually the ones that see it the least.

Cities like Buffalo and Minneapolis live with twelve-inch snow storms and six-foot drifts every winter. Therefore, a thirty-inch storm with ten foot drifts is only different by degree. Cities like Washington, D.C., Dallas and—surprisingly—Denver aren't as used to major accumulation. When they get serious snow, people panic and problems follow.

Government agencies, always willing to give assistance in the aftermath of a disaster, are also diligent about insisting that insurance companies stand by their assurances. Winter storm damage has become routine for insurance companies; consequently, most of the media attention that follows a blizzard focuses on the reactions of local governments.

CHAPTER SIX

Weather and Public Policy

Standard insurance policies provide coverage against most weather-related damage. But they don't cover everything. One notable exception: Floods. This issue is made more serious by the fact that some homeowners don't buy flood insurance because they mistakenly believe that Federal disaster aid will cover their losses. Unfortunately, Federal aid is often unavailable—and limited even when it is available.

For flood victims, insurance is much more reliable than government aid. The average FEMA Individual and Family Grant is less than $2,500. Most government disaster aid comes in the form of low-interest loans made by the Small Business Administration (even if the borrower is a person, not a small business). The average duration of an SBA disaster loan is 18.5 years and the average payment is $140 a month.

Most of the government programs are available only if the President—or the state's governor—declares a disaster. About one in 10 natural disasters are formally declared; that leaves nine of 10 ineligible for Federal disaster aid.

However, National Flood Insurance Program claims are paid even if the President doesn't make a disaster declaration. And federal law enacted in 1995 requires homeowners and businesses in flood zones to buy flood insurance as a condition for getting low-interest government loans to rebuild or repair damage. These policies were intended to force people living in flood areas to insure themselves properly. But they had some unintended consequences.

"The help people get is not without strings attached," California Insurance Commissioner Chuck Quackenbush said about government aid in early 1997—after a series of floods in the western states had caused several hundred million dollars in insured property damage. "They are becoming much more strict about that. Congress has said they want people taking care of themselves on the other end."

For those who don't have flood insurance, there is no guarantee of help. Not everybody who is uninsured is guaranteed the low-interest government loans that have become such a staple of natural disasters. Convicted felons and those who are financially strapped or default risk being denied. And in some cases, people who knowingly built or rebuilt in flood plains without obtaining insurance will not get loans.

But even these people will find help, both FEMA litigation specialist Ken Nauman and Quackenbush said. This was the fulcrum of the unintended consequence. Some cities give zero percent loans to avoid the blight that abandoned and damaged properties create. And the state will find some way to lend a hand, Quackenbush said.

"They'll move heaven and Earth to take care of consumers to make sure they get back on their feet," Quackenbush said.

The National Flood Insurance Program also offers coverage for small businesses with protection of up to $500,000 for building damage and $500,000 for contents coverage. (Under its emergency program, flood insurance for businesses is limited to $100,000 for the structure and $100,000 for the contents.)

For larger businesses, insurance companies offer flood protection along with earthquake insurance in a single policy called Difference-in-Conditions (DIC). The DIC contract fills gaps in property coverage created by the exclusions in the other property coverage forms and cause of loss forms.

DIC policies do not duplicate the coverage of other policy forms, but often extend existing coverage to cover the entire exposure. For example, DIC policies would extend flood insurance protection beyond the $500,000 NFIP business limit. It is important to note that DIC policies usually carry large deductibles.

Public Policy and Flood Insurance

Private insurance companies sell flood insurance, but these companies are not exposed to the profits or losses from writing flood insurance. They pass the premiums, less a small sales fee, along to the National Flood Insurance Program who administers the program and bears all of the risk.

Because flooding can affect wide areas in a single event, private insurance companies, even the largest, could face the risk of bankruptcy if a flood were to cause a sufficiently large number of claims. Consequently, private insurance companies do not take on the risk of flood insurance, with the exception of certain specialized commercial insurance programs.

For people interested in studying issues of public policy and economic theory, flood insurance poses some serious questions. FEMA claims that NFIP is a self-sufficient program that finances claims from premiums, borrowing any deficit from the U.S. Treasury. However, the NFIP ran deficits of approximately $550 million in fiscal 1996 and $40 million in 1997.

Reforms required by Congress in 1994 mandated that the NFIP reduce the level of taxpayer subsidies through premium increases and other measures. The deficits appear to be narrowing through more expensive and larger numbers of policies; at September 30, 1997, NFIP had written approximately $422 billion worth of coverage that generated $1.39 billion of premiums.

In a FEMA publication entitled "Myths and Facts about the NFIP," program administrators point out that a prior history of flooding does not exclude a property from participation in the flood insurance program. In other words, it doesn't matter how many times your house has been in a flood—you can still purchase flood insurance.

This hardly seems like a prudent policy.

Ruben Garcia lived in Miami, Florida. In 1984, he bought Villa 57—a townhouse located within the residential development known as L'Hermitage. When he purchased the residence, Garcia assumed the seller's then current flood insurance policy.

Later that year, Garcia filed a flood insurance claim with NFIP, which was paid. Upon expiration of that policy's term, Garcia continued the policy through Jose Diaz-Villalobos, an insurance agent from whom Garcia had purchased insurance in the past. At that time, the Federal Insurance Administration, which manages the National Flood Insurance Program, was the only entity providing flood insurance in the United States.

Sometime in 1989, Diaz-Villalobos became associated with the Tanenbaum-Harber agency. From that point, Diaz-Villalobos continued to service Garcia's insurance needs through Tanenbaum. Later that year, Garcia's policy was "rolled over" to Omaha Property and Casualty as a "Write Your Own" policy.

After the initial term, Garcia continued to renew his policy through Tanenbaum, in its capacity as an authorized agent of Omaha. So, Tanenbaum acted as a dual agent, representing both Garcia and Omaha, in the procurement of the flood insurance policy. This issue would become important later.

On August 24, 1992, Garcia's home suffered damages as a result of Hurricane Andrew.

Immediately after the hurricane, FEMA issued a memorandum to "Write-Your-Own" insurers of L'Hermitage properties directing the insurers to treat those properties as "elevated" buildings when adjusting flood insurance claims for them. Pursuant to the FEMA directive, Omaha denied the portion of Garcia's flood claim pertaining to damages sustained to building components and personal property located on the first floor, which are not covered for elevated buildings.

Omaha paid for damages to the higher floors of Garcia's three-level townhouse but denied payment with regard to most of the damages sustained on the first level.

Garcia sued the insurance company and the agent.

The case was a complex one. Half of Garcia's claims were thrown out by courts hearing the early procedural stages of the case. By the time it got to trial, four major points remained. These included:

- a claim for declaratory relief against Omaha, to determine coverage that should have been provided under the flood insurance policy,
- a claim against Omaha for the negligent actions of its agent,
- a claim against Omaha for breach of contract, and
- a claim against the Tanenbaum agency for negligent misrepresentations and omissions.

Omaha insisted that its handling of Garcia's claim was in keeping with a directive issued by FEMA after Hurricane Andrew. According to this directive, the homes at L'Hermitage—the development in which Garcia's townhouse was located—should have been treated as "elevated buildings."

Pursuant to these instructions, Omaha denied a substantial portion of Garcia's claim with respect to damage to the first level of his house. Tanenbaum, the agency, tried to blame the dispute entirely on Omaha.

It made two affirmative defenses against the claims involving it. First, it agreed with Garcia that the flood policy should provide coverage for the first floor. Second, it argued that Omaha and unnamed third parties were responsible for Garcia's loss.

On top of these defenses, Tanenbaum filed a crossclaim seeking indemnity from Omaha. This pitted the agency and the carrier—who should have been allies—against one another.

Garcia focused his sights on the insurance company. In a motion for summary judgment, he claimed that the policy as written provided full coverage for damages to the first level of his home. He sought a declaration of coverage and a judgment, as a matter of law, that Omaha had breached its contract of insurance.

Garcia also argued that he was entitled to judgment against Tanenbaum because the agency admitted all of the allegations in the complaint.

But Omaha wasn't about to fold. In a motion for summary judgment in its favor, the company argued that Garcia was not entitled to coverage based on the language of the policy, the applicable federal statutes, and local ordinances—which defined a minimum elevation for buildings located in the area of L'Hermitage.

The June 1995 federal district court ruling *Ruben Garcia v. Omaha Property and Casualty Insurance* sorted through all of the claims and counterclaims.

Both sides were pretty angry by the time the case made it to trial. Later, the court would refer—with what was surely unusual judicial irony—as enjoying "the benefit of oral argument from the parties." It also reviewed nearly a dozen other federal cases stemming from insurance disputes involving Hurricane Andrew and the development in which Garcia lived.

Like many of the people living in L'Hermitage, Garcia used the first level of his townhouse as living space...not for storage. As used by Garcia, this floor included a garage, carport, bedroom, bathroom and living room. However, the building plans for Garcia's townhouse showed the following designations for the various areas comprising the first floor: garage, carport, bathroom, laundry area, storage area and multipurpose area.

The policy's property description with respect to the building was "three or more floors with no basement, a single family residence." The property description with respect to contents is "household contents located on the first floor and above." The rating information shown on the declarations page included the following:

- construction date prior to 12/31/74;
- low elevation +16.0 feet;
- base elevation +12.0 feet;
- elevation difference +4 feet.

The declarations page also showed the notation "non-elevated building," below the building description. This was important because:

> The court's review of earlier declarations pages for Garcia's previous flood insurance policies, dating back to 1984 (the year when Garcia acquired the property), reveals that this notation does not appear in any of the declarations pages issued by the National Flood Insurance Program. The notation first appears in the Omaha declarations page for the policy term beginning May 19, 1989 and ending May 19, 1992.

At the heart of the controversy was FEMA's post-hurricane classification of Garcia's townhouse as an "elevated" building.

Garcia argued, based on the notation in the declarations page, that the building was "non-elevated," and that, under this classification, he was entitled to full payment on his claim.

The court didn't agree:

> Garcia's argument is flawed. Were the Court to consider the building as "non-elevated," Garcia would not be entitled to any payment whatsoever on his claim, since a non-elevated building...violates the community flood plain management regulations mandated by the National Flood Insurance Program.

Alternatively, Garcia asked the court to find an ambiguity in the insurance policy and to construe such ambiguity against Omaha. The ambiguity argument was two-pronged. First, Garcia argued that the exclusion provision for elevated buildings contained in the Standard Flood Insurance Policy was ambiguous.

In support of this argument, Garcia submitted the affidavit of Ronald B. Newman, Ph.D., an expert in the area of readability of the English language. The court did not find Newman's analysis persuasive: "Indeed, other courts, which have analyzed this exclusion provision, have found it to be unambiguous."

In the second prong of his ambiguity argument, Garcia argued that the "non-elevated" notation on the declarations page created an ambiguity vis-a-vis the rating information contained in that same page, and that such ambiguity had to be construed against Omaha.

However, a "Special Notice" appended to Omaha's Standard Flood Insurance Policy charged Garcia with the ongoing duty of insuring the accuracy of the information on the declarations page. The notice stated:

> The insurance coverage provided to you and the premium are based on the description of the property contained on your current policy. View the computer printed Policy Declaration page, which recites the information you have furnished to us, to make sure the information is correct. Your insurance protection can be jeopardized if you have made alterations or substantial improvements to your building which are not reflected on the policy and which are in violation of your community's floodplain management ordinances. This includes such modifications as changing an unfinished basement into a totally or partially finished basement or enclosing an area beneath the lowest floor of an elevated building.

Garcia, however, took no steps to correct this entry on the declarations page.

In addition, the original plans for Garcia's townhouse did not show any living areas on the first level. The declarations page dating back to Garcia's acquisition of the property showed the lowest elevation at +16 feet, an elevation higher than the first level.

Again, Garcia took no steps to correct the declarations page to reflect the fact that the lowest level in use at his residence was not at an elevation of

+16 feet. These things led the court to conclude:

> A determination that Omaha must provide full coverage for the flood damage to Garcia's first level would reward Garcia for failing to correct the inaccurate information reflected in the declarations page, in contravention of the policy terms. The Court declines to adopt such an approach.

So, based on these issues, the court ordered:
- Garcia's motion for summary judgment to be denied;
- Omaha's cross-motion for summary judgment to be granted; and
- Tanenbaum's cross-motion for summary judgment to be granted.

Summary

Many of us would like to live near the water, with the beautiful views and activities that accompany rivers, lakes and oceans. However, living near the water usually means higher risk of water damage as well as the potential for Hurricanes. Is it right that people who do not enjoy those same luxuries should be forced to subsidize those fortunate enough to purchase waterfront property? If the National Flood Insurance Program were self reliant, without constant help from the taxpayers, then by definition those subsidies would not exist and this would not be an issue.

But the presence of subsidized flood insurance that some property owners are forced to buy and taxpayers are forced to carry through bad times encourages overbuilding in flood prone areas. Should taxpayers in the high plains of Wyoming pay to subsidize the losses of residents in flood-prone New Orleans?

Few would argue that flood insurance should be abolished. If flood insurance became unavailable overnight, some property values would drop precipitously to reflect the new risk associated with at risk property.

Since private insurers are unlikely to supply large amounts of flood protection at any price due to the catastrophic nature of flooding, some government intervention may be warranted. Unfortunately, government has distorted the marketplace for real estate with the NFIP.

What could Congress do to correct the situation?
Congress could mandate substantially higher premiums to make the NFIP truly self-sufficient. Flood insurance should not be a mechanism by which

people are encouraged to build homes in harm's way. Flood insurance has been characterized as government's attempt to change the course of the river. That sort of activity is best left to the Army Corps of Engineers.

Until flood insurance takes on more realistic pricing and carries strict restrictions against multiple claims on the same property, we will continue to see taxpayer losses and building in flood plains that would never happen without such a Federal program. And everyone who is involved with disaster response knows that this is true.

At a National Press Club speech in November 1998, FEMA director James Witt announced his plan to move the agency away from making repeated bail-outs of the same properties.

He started his speech with an anecdote about his recent visit to a subdivision of 54 homes near Wichita, Kansas, that had been flooded when the Arkansas River had overflowed its banks. He had spoken with families who were slowly returning to their homes and going through the wreckage, sifting through the muck and stink left behind after the flood. It was a memorable image.

What Witt said next was equally memorable:

> The sad truth is, this scene should never have taken place much less been repeated.... We must change the way we think and plan and budget. It means that instead of responding to disasters. We must prevent them, instead of waiting to react.
>
> We have a responsibility as a government...to do all we can to save lives.... Building stronger, disaster resistant buildings will save lives—not rebuilding them where common sense says we shouldn't build will save more lives.

Witt was leading up to some major changes in the way NFIP is administered. He said that FEMA had identified 35,000 repetitive flood loss properties across the country. These were properties whose owners had made two or more flood loss claims in the previous ten years.

As a group, these claimants were costing NFIP over $200 million a year. These were the people that television news programs liked to profile—stubborn residents of riverfront developments and coastal enclaves. They insisted on returning and rebuilding, with government aid, in a way that seemed vaguely...criminal.

Witt had a proposal for fixing this abuse:

> We're preparing to implement a strategy that will cut annual losses by half in three years and save close to a billion dollars over the next ten years. We will propose that flood insurance not be available to homeowners who have filed two or more claims that total more than the value of their home and refuse to elevate their home or accept a buyout. People need to accept the responsibility and the consequences of their choice to live in high risk areas. We should charge people who live in high risk areas the fair market rates for insurance—instead of the lower, subsidized federal flood insurance rates.

And his new plan applied to more than just residences. FEMA was also proposing that public buildings be insured to 80 percent of their replacement value within two years. This would save federal taxpayers millions of dollars in rebuilding costs...and that essential public facilities would be back on line faster after a disaster.

Programs such as disaster aid from the Federal Emergency Management Agency serve a legitimate public policy objective: to give aid and comfort to people who have just suffered through a crisis. People do not purposely look to be disaster victims and they deserve a helping hand to restore some semblance of their pre-event lives.

Unlike flood insurance, FEMA disaster aid is relatively well considered in that it comes largely in the form of low interest loans. Grant aid is limited to $13,400 (adjusted annually for inflation), though the average grant is only $4,000, and is given only to those who truly need it.

The grants are considered last resorts and in most cases are available only if an applicant has been denied a disaster loan. FEMA funds 25 percent of the grant programs costs and 25 percent is covered by the state. The beauty of FEMA aid is that, for the most part, it encourages people to take care of themselves. The curse is that many people don't learn this until it's too late.

Since the average payback period of disaster loans is 18.5 years, property owners have every incentive to find insurance solutions to their catastrophe exposures rather than face lengthy loan repayment burdens.

Unfortunately, many property owners believe that Federal disaster aid will restore them to their pre-loss condition in one big grant. Perhaps the

American people need to receive an education about the true extent of their entitlement (or lack thereof) to Federal and state support in an emergency. With this knowledge, most people will make more responsible decisions about insurance protection.

PART TWO

Seismic Activity

In most parts of the country, earthquakes seem to be as remote as a Hollywood movie premiere—something uncommon that happens to other people in California. While serious earthquakes are not common anywhere, many parts of the United States are exposed to at least some risk of earth movement.

Scientists for the U.S. Geological Survey estimate that over one million earthquakes occur each year throughout the world as land masses known as tectonic plates shift, slide and float on the earth's molten core. Most of these earthquakes are detectable only with sensitive equipment and those that can be felt seldom do significant damage. But severe earthquakes can disrupt some of society's most basic services—roads, gas, water, power and telephone. Loss of these services and the enormous property damage cause incalculable productivity losses as people struggle to restore their surroundings to normal.

While earthquake prediction still remains a difficult enterprise, U.S. Geological Survey scientists still make 30-year predictions. In 1990, forecasters placed a two-thirds probability of a major earthquake in the San Francisco Bay area by the year 2020 and an 80 to 90 percent chance of a major quake in the Southern California region during the 1990-2020 period. It appears that the Northridge earthquake confirmed at least one of their forecasts.

The New Madrid Fault area in eastern Missouri will produce a serious earthquake with virtual certainty before the year 2040 and scientists place a 2.7 percent to 4 percent chance of a truly devastating quake (magnitude 8.3) during the same period.

Geologists use data on seismic activity and plate tectonic theory to estimate how much energy is stored in rock formations and when that energy will be released. Many smaller earthquakes can indicate that energy at plate boundaries, where two land masses strike and slip past each other, is being dissipated rather than stored. If energy is stored for extended periods of time, it can explode forth in one large event, causing serious damage. However, experts caution that many smaller earthquakes do not necessarily prevent a large event from occurring.

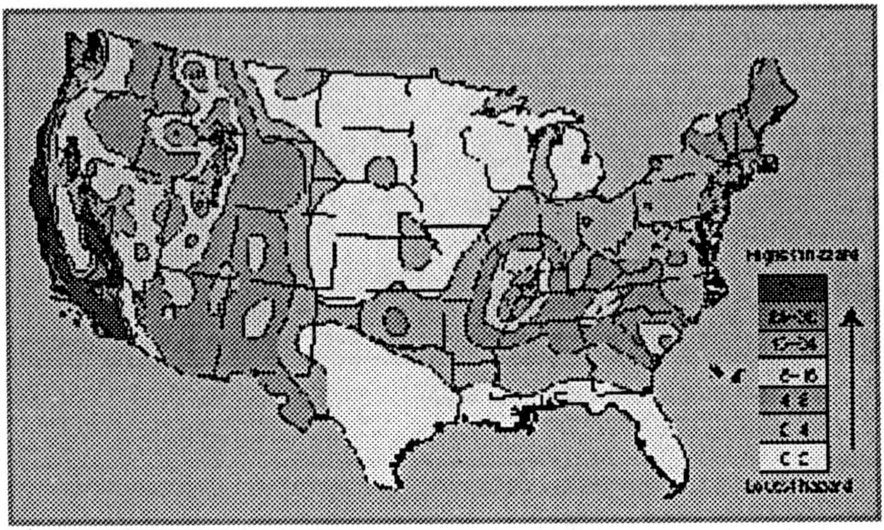

Seismic activity in the United States during the late 1990s

The seismic hazard map on this page illustrates the potential for the violent ground acceleration that causes property losses. Only a few areas of the U.S. have no exposure at all; the West Coast faces the most serious risk. Alaska and Hawaii include significant numbers of dormant and active volcanoes—seismic activity accompanies those geological formations.

CHAPTER SEVEN

Earthquakes

Financial losses from earthquakes concern Americans with good reason, the Northridge earthquake caused an estimated $20 billion in damage (12.5 in insured damage).

But losses of human life have been relatively less frequent in the U.S. and other industrialized nations than in less developed countries.

Most losses of life in an earthquake occur when structures collapse. Because construction and design standards of developed countries are superior to those of the third world, most buildings in the developed world remain largely intact during earthquakes.

For example: In 1990, an earthquake with a magnitude of 7.7 occurred in Iran killing over 40,000 people; a 1983 earthquake of the same magnitude in Japan (a more densely populated country) killed only 107.

Back in the U.S., people have more than just sturdy construction to protect them from earthquakes. They can also buy insurance designed especially for that purpose.

If you live on the West Coast or in any area near a major fault, you should strongly consider earthquake insurance. So says David DeSantis, executive director of the Natural Disaster Coalition in Washington, D.C. But most people don't need it. According to DeSantis, "Americans in large parts of the country are highly unlikely to ever experience a sizable tremor."

To find out about past and potential earthquake activity in your area, call your state's department of geology or visit the National Earthquake Information Center's Website (www.neic.cr.usgs.gov).

The Richter Magnitude Scale

Seismic waves are the vibrations from earthquakes that travel through the Earth; they are recorded on instruments called seismographs. Seismographs record a zig-zag trace that shows the varying amplitude of ground oscillations beneath the instrument. Sensitive seismographs, which greatly magnify these ground motions, can detect strong earthquakes from sources anywhere in the world.

The time, location and magnitude of an earthquake can be determined from the data recorded by seismograph stations.

The Richter Magnitude Scale was developed in 1935 by Charles F. Richter of the California Institute of Technology as a mathematical device to compare the size of earthquakes. The magnitude of an earthquake is determined from the logarithm of the amplitude of waves recorded by seismographs. Adjustments are included in the magnitude formula to compensate for the variation in the distance between the various seismographs and the epicenter of the earthquakes.

On the Richter Scale, magnitude is expressed in whole numbers and decimal fractions. For example, a magnitude of 5.3 might be computed for a moderate earthquake, and a strong earthquake might be rated as magnitude 6.3, or M6.3. Because of the logarithmic basis of the scale, each whole number increase in magnitude represents a tenfold increase in measured amplitude. As an estimate of energy, each whole number step in the magnitude scale corresponds to the release of about 31 times more energy than the amount associated with the preceding whole number value.

At first, the Richter Scale could be applied only to the records from instruments of identical manufacture. Now, instruments are carefully calibrated with respect to each other. Thus, magnitude can be computed from the record of any calibrated seismograph and compared globally.

Earthquakes with magnitude of about 2.0 or less are usually called microearthquakes; they are not commonly felt by people and are generally recorded only on local seismographs. Events with magnitudes of about 4.5 or greater—there are several thousand such shocks annually—are strong enough to be recorded by sensitive seismographs all over the world. Great earthquakes, such as the 1964 Good Friday earthquake in

Alaska, which did $2.28 billion (in 1994 dollars) damage, have magnitudes of 8.0 or higher. On the average, one earthquake of such size occurs somewhere in the world each year. Although the Richter Scale has no upper limit, the largest known shocks have had magnitudes in the 8.8 to 8.9 range.

The Richter Scale is not used to express damage. It's used to measure the intensity of an earthquake regardless of where it strikes and whom it affects. An earthquake in a densely populated area which results in many deaths and considerable damage, may have the same magnitude as a shock in a remote area that does nothing more than frighten the wildlife.

Similarly, large-magnitude earthquakes that occur beneath the oceans may not even be felt by humans.

What do the numbers on the Richter Scale tell us? Each unit of the Richter Scale is a tenfold increase in the relative size of an earthquake. A magnitude 6.0 is ten times the size of a magnitude 5.0, and one hundred times the size of a 4.0.

But energy release is a different matter. Each unit up the Richter Scale is around a 32 times greater release of energy. A magnitude 6.0 releases 32 times more energy than a magnitude 5.0, and about one thousand times more energy than a magnitude 4.0. The amount of energy released in a small earthquake is not enough to prevent a large one from occurring. A million magnitude 2.0 earthquakes would release the same amount of energy as one magnitude 6.0 quake. 32,768 magnitude 2.0 earthquakes would release the same amount of energy as one magnitude 5.0.

The Modified Mercalli Intensity Scale

According to the U.S. Geological Survey, the effect of an earthquake on the Earth's surface is called *intensity*. The intensity scale consists of a series of certain key responses such as people awakening, movement of furniture, damage to chimneys, and finally—total destruction.

Although numerous intensity scales have been developed over the last several hundred years to evaluate the effects of earthquakes, the one currently used in the United States is the Modified Mercalli Intensity Scale(MMIS).

The MMIS was developed in 1931 by the American seismologists Harry Wood and Frank Neumann. This scale, composed of 12 increasing levels of intensity that range from imperceptible shaking to catastrophic destruction, is designated by Roman numerals. It does not have a mathematical basis; instead it is an arbitrary ranking based on observed effects.

Mercalli Scale	Richter Scale	Description
I		Vibrations recorded by instruments
II	0-4.3	People at rest upstairs notice shaking
III		Shaking noticeable; hanging objects swing
IV		Dishes rattle; standing cars rock; trees shake
V	4.3-4.8	Liquid spills from glasses; sleepers awaken
VI		Windows break; pictures fall off walls
VII	4.8-6.2	Plaster and bricks fall; large bells ring
VIII		Chimneys fall; branches break
IX	6.2-7.3	Damage to foundations; general panic
X		Buildings destroyed; large landslides
XI	7.3-8.9	Railway tracks bend; roads break up
XII		Total destruction; "waves" seen on ground

Source: U.S. Geological Survey

The Mercalli scale is a semi-quantitative linear scale. The Richter scale is a quantitative logarithmic scale.

Severity	Mercalli Scale	Richter Scale
Mild	I-III	0-4.3
Moderate	IV-V	4.3-4.8
Intermediate	VI-VII	4.8-6.2
Severe	VIII-X	6.2-7.3
Catastrophic	XI-XII	7.3-8.9

Mitigation Efforts: Building Codes and Retrofits

Architects and engineers agree: We can construct buildings that resist earthquakes. But can we afford it? A 1985 National Institute of Standards and Technology (NIST) study of seismic-resistant features in new construction found that these designs added an average 1.6 percent increase to building costs. Fortunately, the three main national model building codes have taken some notice of seismic hazards.

However, these building codes are slow to change and do not affect existing structures. Therefore, it can take many years for the building stock to increase its overall resistance to quakes. But if loss mitigation does not begin now, our vulnerability will never decrease.

Retrofits are modifications that increase an existing building's ability to withstand earthquake activity. For organizations that want increased earthquake protection but cannot afford to rebuild their existing stock of buildings, retrofits may offer the only alternative. The most vulnerable buildings are unreinforced masonry (URM) since they face the highest probability of collapse during an earthquake. According to the Office of Technology Assessment, retrofits for URM buildings cost an average 23 percent as much as new construction. Faced with such high costs, some building owners may decide to rebuild. However, some organizations simply cannot afford to rebuild (23 percent is cheaper than 100 percent). The University of California at Los Angeles' plan to retrofit its campus was estimated to cost $500 million.

Retrofits are not exclusively for buildings. California has been an aggressive user of retrofits for structures such as bridges and overpasses. The initial results from the 1989 Loma Prieta and 1994 Northridge earthquakes indicate that the retrofits increase the survivability of structures.

Utilities such as power systems and water works often consider "hardening" their infrastructure to potential earthquake-related service interruption. The cost of failing to do so may be worse than the alternative. For example: In the 1995 Kobe (Japan) earthquake, an interrupted water supply prevented prompt fire extinguishment.

Paying for Earthquake Damage

Earthquake damage is not covered under the usual homeowners insurance policy—the coverage must be purchased as an optional endorsement, or as a separate policy from the California Earthquake Authority for residents of that state (See chapter 9 for a discussion of earthquakes and public policy).

Because seismic risk varies widely, prices and policies differ dramatically. In most areas, you can get an earthquake endorsement to your homeowners policy rather than a separate policy. Annual premiums can be inexpensive for people who live in low- or moderate-risk cities: For a

$100,000 house built in or after 1950 in Des Moines, for example, the yearly cost is just $15. Deductibles, on the other hand, are substantial: Most quake policies, offered by regular homeowners insurers, carry a deductible of 5 percent to 10 percent of the value of your house—meaning a $200,000 house can carry an deductible of between $10,000 and $20,000.

Major U.S. Earthquakes

Year	Location	Estimated Losses (Millions of 1994 Dollars)
1886	Charleston, SC	n/a
1906	San Francisco, CA	$6,000
1925	Santa Barbara, CA	60
1933	Long Beach, CA	540
1935	Helena, MT	40
1946	Aleutian Islands, AK	200
1949	Puget Sound, WA	220
1952	Kern County, CA	350
1952	Bakersfield, CA	60
1964	Anchorage, AK	2,280
1965	Puget Sound, WA	70
1971	San Fernando, CA	1,700
1975	Hawaii	n/a
1979	Imperial Valley, CA	60
1983	Coalinga, CA	50
1987	Whittier Narrows, CA	450
1989	Loma Prieta, CA	6,870
1992	Petrolia, CA	70
1993	Scotts Mills, OR	30
1994	Northridge, CA	20,000

Source: Office of Technology Assessment

Policyholders in earthquake territory, on the other hand, must pay more for less. You should find out your rights for filing claims before you sign on the dotted line for earthquake coverage. It's especially important to know how much time following a quake you have to file a claim. Although California's Northridge quake occurred in early 1994, claims are still being settled. This is because earthquake damage may not be apparent for some time. For example, cracks in a basement caused by the ground shifting may not be noticeable until a year later when water begins to seep into the cracks and worsens the problem. Also, as repair costs mount, many homeowners discover they've exceeded their deductibles and thus are suddenly eligible to file a claim.

Obviously, how insurance claims are adjusted in the wake of a disaster is a critical issue. But many people put too much faith in what adjusters say and do. Smart policyholders should be more skeptical. The October 1997 federal court decision *Krishan and Aruna Vashistha v. Allstate Insurance Co., et al.* shows why.

The Vashisthas owned four rental properties in Valencia, California, a suburb about an hour north of Los Angeles. These properties—which were insured with earthquake coverage by Allstate—were damaged to various degrees during the Northridge earthquake in January 1994, which measured 6.7 on the Richter scale.

In February 1994, Allstate insurance inspector Jack Martin responded to claims that the Vashisthas had filed with the company. Martin inspected the Vashisthas' personal residence for damage caused by the earthquake and produced a written estimate which stated that the damage to their residence was not greater than their 10 percent deductible and, therefore, not covered by their Allstate policies.

The Vashisthas accepted that assessment. During that same visit, though, they told Martin that they owned the rental properties—which were also insured by Allstate. They said that they believed the damage to the rental properties was less serious than the damage to their personal residence.

Based on these statements, Martin offered the opinion that the rental properties would also not qualify for coverage under the Allstate policies. Based on this conversation, the Vashisthas neither filed a claim with Allstate for the damage to the rental properties nor requested that an insurance inspector evaluate those properties.

As often happens in the wake of a disaster, the Vashisthas decided to wait until they could afford the necessary repairs on their home before beginning the work. In mid-1995, when they started talking to contractors, they were shocked to hear that the cost of the repairs would be well over $100,000—nearly eight times the amount of Martin's estimate and significantly greater than their 10 percent deductible.

Armed with the new information, the Vashisthas sought to obtain payment from Allstate for damage to both their personal residence and their rental properties. In August 1995, they made a claim to Allstate for damage to their rental properties. Allstate denied this claim on the ground that it was barred by the statutorily-mandated one-year limitations provision contained in the relevant policies.

In the meantime, several big insurance companies had settled charges from the California Department of Insurance that they had illegally denied claims based on Northridge quake damage. Stories about these settlements appeared in various southern California media outlets.

In June 1997, the Vashisthas filed a lawsuit against Allstate, alleging breach of contract, breach of the implied covenant of good faith and fair dealing, fraud and negligent misrepresentation.

The Allstate insurance policies at issue in the case did contain one-year statute of limitations provisions. The provisions read:
Suit against us. No suit or action may be brought against us unless there has been full compliance with all the policy terms. Any suit or action must be brought within one year after the loss.

Additionally, the policies contained provisions setting forth the proper notice procedures under the policy:
In the event of a loss to any property that this insurance may cover, you must do the following things: (a) Promptly give us or agent written notice.

The one-year limitations provision was a mandatory term required by California insurance regulations. The one-year period begins to run "when appreciable damage occurs and is or should be known to the insured, such that a reasonable insured would be aware that his notification duty under the policy has been triggered."

The court hearing the Vashisthas' case noted that "in the case of an earthquake, the limitations period begins to run on the date the earthquake occurs." In the immediate case, though, the Vashisthas did not make a claim for earthquake damage to their rental properties until August 9, 1995. This was more than a year after the limitations period began to run—namely, on January 17, 1994. And the lawsuit wasn't filed until June 4, 1997—more than three years after the quake.

So, the court ruled that too much time had passed. Unless they could prove that Allstate has done something to waive the limitations provisions in the policies, the Vashisthas would simply have to take their losses.

Of course, the Vashisthas tried to argue that Allstate had waived the limitations provisions. They didn't make any claims within the required limitations period because Martin had "advised them that they had no claim for damages respecting the rental properties." Because they had "reasonably relied on Martin's opinion," they argued that they should be allowed to make their proper claims.

The court reviewed the essential facts of the case, which it ruled were:

- the Vashisthas were the owners of the rental properties;
- they were aware of damage to the rental properties caused by the January 17, 1994 earthquake;
- Martin did not inspect, or view, the rental properties;
- the Vashisthas did not request that Allstate inspect the rental properties; and
- they didn't present a claim for damages to their rental properties.

These facts weren't good for the Vashisthas. In fact, the court ruled:

> Based on these allegations, specifically because Martin had neither seen nor inspected the rental properties, the Court finds as a matter of law, that [the Vashisthas'] reliance on Martin's statement was unreasonable.
>
> Therefore, Allstate is not estopped from asserting that [their] claim was untimely. The Vashisthas never provided Allstate with written notice of the loss to the rental properties as required by the policy provisions. Therefore, the limitations period applied.

The Vashisthas tried to plead ignorance as a reason for deserving special treatment. They claimed that, by giving oral notice to Martin on February 24, 1994, they acted within the limitations period and made a timely claim.

However, the court ruled that the limitations period applies from the time the policyholder reports the claim until the insurer indicates that it will not provide coverage. The Vashisthas argued that, after notifying Martin of the damage to the rental properties, he "advised them that they had no claim for damages respecting the rental properties. However, the court noted that—even if the ignorance argument were true—the Vashisthas' claim filed in August 1995 was time barred.

They tried another argument...really a variation on the first ignorance excuse. The second theory argued: Since Allstate effectively waived formal notice requirements and/or the statute of limitations respecting the claim on the personal residence, they should be deemed to have also waived those requirements on the claims made on behalf of the four rental properties.

The court didn't accept this variation, either. It ruled:

> This contention is incorrect. No claim for damages was ever filed by [the Vashisthas] with respect to the rental properties until August 1995. While this Court need not address the issue of waiver as to the personal residence, it would be impossible for Allstate to waive the notice requirements and/or the statute of limitations for the rental properties after the limitations period has already passed. Therefore, this argument fails.

The court found it undisputed that the Vashisthas' claim for damages on the rental properties was time-barred by the policies' one-year limitation provisions. It ruled that Allstate's non-payment of the belated claims was proper under the circumstances.

The court granted Allstate's request and dismissed the Vashisthas' claims.

As illustrated, in part, in the Allstate suit above, one of the biggest issues that impacts insurance claims in the wake of a natural disaster is timing. Some people take the approach of sorting through their troubles, setting things back on the road to recovery...and then dealing with the paperwork last. That can make things even more difficult. As unpleasant as the paperwork may be, it's important to attack early on.

The April 1997 federal district court decision *Gary and Donna Sullivan v. Allstate Insurance* considered some bad timing.

The epicenter of the January 1994 Northridge quake was just a short distance from the Sullivans' home. As soon as the shaking subsided, the Sullivans realized that their house and their personal property had suffered significant damage. Among other things, they noticed the plaster walls had chipped and cracked; their hardwood floors in their dining/living room had separated; and tiles had come unglued in their bathroom. In addition, there were cracks in the kitchen plaster and cuts in the kitchen linoleum; broken glass in their bedroom; cracks in their stairway; major cracks in their children's bedroom; and large and pervasive cracks in their retaining wall, exterior stucco and pool patio.

And the Northridge quake damaged more than just the house. A significant amount of personal property—including crystal, dishes, bottles of liquor and a television set—had been destroyed.

At the time of the quake, the Sullivans had an Allstate homeowners policy that provided earthquake coverage. The policy also included a provision that limited the insured's time within which to seek benefits to one year. As we've seen before, the policy stated that any lawsuits had to be filed within that one-year period.

Even though the Sullivans recognized that they had earthquake insurance and that they had sustained earthquake damage immediately after the Northridge quake, they did not promptly submit a claim to Allstate.

Instead, believing that the cost to repair their damages did not exceed their deductible, they waited more than a year to submit their claim. During that time, they took no action to determine the full extent of the damage or the cost of repairs. Donna Sullivan was expecting to inherit some money, so she and Gary decided to wait until they had the money in hand to begin their earthquake repairs.

But they waited too long. In February 1995, more than a year after the Northridge quake, their roof began to leak. Although the earthquake damage had not worsened over the year, the leaking water caused the existing cracks to enlarge and the existing plaster damage to get worse.

The Sullivans called a contractor to fix the leaks. He discovered the extent of their problems. In addition to needing a new roof, the Sullivans had sustained approximately $50,000 in earthquake damage to their home. So, on February 21, 1995, they submitted their first claim to Allstate for damage that had occurred during the earthquake.

After receiving the claim, Allstate inspected the property and took a recorded statement from Gary Sullivan. Based upon its investigation, Allstate concluded that the Sullivan's claim for earthquake benefits was barred by the one-year suit limitation provision set forth in the policy.

On March 27, 1995, Allstate sent the Sullivans a letter denying coverage for their earthquake loss.

The Sullivans—for reasons which remain unclear—then waited almost another full year after receipt of that letter before filing suit on March 25, 1996. Adding to the delay, they failed to notify Allstate formally about the suit for another three months.

In their lawsuit, the Sullivans charged Allstate with breach of contract, breach of the covenant of good faith and fair dealing, intentional infliction of emotional distress and negligent infliction of emotional distress.

The court saw the matter in fairly simple terms. The Sullivans' home had been damaged by the Northridge earthquake—and they had been aware that they'd suffered some damage at that time. Nevertheless, they failed to submit a claim to Allstate or institute suit for policy benefits within one year. Under these circumstances, their lawsuit was barred by the one-year contractual limitation period.

For purposes of coverage analysis, the California Insurance Code treats earthquake insurance as a variation of fire insurance. And it states clearly that all such policies shall contain a provision substantially similar to the following:

> No suit or action on this policy for the recovery of any claim shall be sustainable in any court of law or equity unless all the requirements of this policy shall have been complied with, and unless commenced within 12 months next after inception of the loss.

As if to emphasize the point further, the California Supreme Court had recently written: "[a] covenant shortening the period of limitations is a valid provision in an insurance contract and cannot be ignored with impunity."

The court defended the statute's purpose: to preclude the assertion of stale claims, require insureds to be diligent and prevent fraud. It went on to conclude:

> The one-year limitations period begins to run when the insured is aware of appreciable damage to his or her property. The standard for determining the date of loss is objective—when a reasonable person

> would be aware of damage which "deviat[es] from what a reasonable person would consider normal wear and tear." ...In the context of a loss caused by a single catastrophic event such as an earthquake, the date of loss can only be the date of that event. At that time, a reasonable person would be aware of the facts which might give rise to a claim....

The Sullivans argued that the limitations period did not begin to run until they'd realized they might have a covered loss (which they defined as a loss exceeding the policy's deductible). The court deemed this argument "untenable.... Indeed, all authority is to the contrary."

Besides, the Sullivans' argument was based upon a misreading of the policy. The notice clause in the policy stated: "In the event of a loss to any property that may be covered by this policy, you must...promptly give us or our agent written notice."

The plain language of this clause required the report of any loss "that may be covered" and not simply losses that actually are covered. The clear import is to require prompt reporting of all losses for which the insured might seek coverage so that the insurer may investigate the loss in a timely manner and avoid any prejudice caused by a lapse of time.

The Sullivans took one last pass: They argued that their earthquake damages should be considered progressive in nature, so that a so-called "delayed discovery rule" would apply. They claimed that Gary Sullivan "saw slight damage to his home become progressively worse." But the court concluded that their losses could not be characterized as a progressive loss "merely because they allowed their property to deteriorate rather than repair their damage."

The Sullivans had become aware of "appreciable damage" to their property on the day of the earthquake and the limitations period began to run on that date.

So, the court threw out the lawsuit:

> The limitations period began to run on January 17, 1994 when [the Sullivans] recognized they had suffered appreciable damage attributable to the earthquake. It expired one year later on January 17, 1995. As this lawsuit was not filed until March 25, 1996, it is barred. Therefore, Allstate's motion for summary judgment is granted.

Insurance companies are so guarded about catastrophe losses because they earn their profits by processing huge amounts of data on loss histories and pricing coverage precisely so that they can earn a fair return. The companies are usually positioned to absorb the occasional bad year—but disasters turn careful risk models inside out.

And there's another reason that insurance companies don't like disasters: People tend to slip minor losses not related to a disaster into their disaster claims. This is sometimes known as *claims build up*...and it makes a bad situation even worse.

The November 1996 federal court case *David Simon v. Allstate* illustrates how insurance companies react to this kind of claims fraud.

In 1984, Simon bought a house in Oakland, California. Allstate issued Simon a homeowners insurance policy, which was in effect between July 1986 and July 1993—and the policy included an earthquake endorsement. The endorsement was in effect when the Loma Prieta earthquake struck the San Francisco Bay Area on October 17, 1989.

When Simon purchased his house, the floors were noticeably out of level. Reports that he obtained from a structural engineer, a soil engineer and a pest-control service reflected that the house had settled demonstrably in the past. In addition, the foundation had been capped, the house had been jacked-up to correct previous settlement—and the jack was still in the basement. The walls and ceilings had been patched to repair cracking. A regular build-up of moisture in the basement was the result of poor drainage. The house was a fixer-upper.

After the 1989 Loma Prieta earthquake, Simon immediately noticed cracking in the interior walls of his home and cracking in his foundation. Within a day or two of the earthquake, he realized the house had settled near the front entrance. He didn't notify Allstate—his insurer at the time—of any of the damage caused by the Loma Prieta earthquake. And he didn't make a claim at that time.

Republic Insurance Company issued Simon a homeowners insurance policy beginning in June 1993. The Republic policy, although designated an "all-risk policy," specifically excluded losses caused by earthquakes as well as traditional flood losses.

In about June 1994, Simon hired David Thompson, a friend with a general contractor's license, to remodel his upstairs bathroom. Neither Simon nor Thompson obtained a building permit. During the bathroom remodel, Simon decided to relevel his floors. Thompson, who had looked at the house shortly after Simon had purchased it, testified that by 1994 the house was considerably more out of level than it had been in 1984—when he first bought it.

While working in the basement, Thompson found the near-surface soil was saturated with water. He determined the pipes were cracked in places and the cement mortar holding the pipe sections was no longer intact. This allowed water to seep out at the cracks and/or joints when the backfill was removed.

Simon reported a claim to Allstate—in October 1994—for the damage he discovered since the time of the Loma Prieta earthquake and for the costs of releveling his home and performing the foundation work. He contended that during the time the Allstate policy was in effect, the Loma Prieta earthquake of 1989 damaged the underground sewer lines, causing them to rupture and leak. He also reported a claim for the releveling and foundation work to Republic—his new insurance company—that same October. In this claim, he argued that the failure of the sewer line was caused by wear and tear and other events covered by the Republic policy in effect at that time.

Republic denied coverage in a letter to Simon dated November 9, 1994. Allstate sent him a letter dated January 27, 1995, which said the company would investigate but which amounted to a denial of coverage. Simon sued both companies.

At trial, Simon's expert witness testified that he believed the settling of Simon's home was caused by the Loma Prieta earthquake, which ruptured the sewer pipes and resulted in soil saturation. However, Simon offered no proof of when the pipe cracked and conceded that he had not been aware of problems with his sewage system prior to the foundation work.

Allstate, by contrast, produced credible testimony from Larry Russell, an expert in sanitation engineering, and Allan Kropp, a soil engineer, that the soil conditions would not have resulted from a cracked sewer line. Both

Russell and Kropp attributed the conditions at Simon's house to long-term settlement due to the poor drainage conditions.

Republic presented the testimony of Joel Baldwin, an expert in engineering geology and geohydrology, who testified that the soil under Simon's home was saturated as a result of natural and perennial ground water. Baldwin opined that the saturated soil conditions were not caused by seepage from cracked sewer pipes.

The court hearing the case started its analysis by laying out how the law applied:

> Under California law, the policyholder has the burden of proving a claim within the insuring grant of his policy. If he meets this burden, the burden shifts to the insurer to prove an exclusion applies. However, if the evidence fails to show that a covered peril is more likely than a noncovered one, judgment must be entered for the insurer.

Except for the cracking, for which no claim was filed at the time, Simon had failed to prove his home suffered any physical damage caused by the Loma Prieta earthquake. The evidence demonstrated that the cause of the losses to Simon's home was subsurface water conditions and poor drainage on the lot.

Another point of California law: The time of a loss under a first-party insurance policy, at least for progressive damage caused by gradual events, is when the damage becomes "manifest"; that is, when the policyholder learns or should have learned through reasonable inspection that the damage occurred.

Simon's testimony, and that of his expert witness, was that no settlement damage was discovered or discoverable by reasonable inspection until September or October of 1994. Allstate's coverage terminated July 7, 1993, well before manifestation of Simon's alleged loss. So, the court ruled that the Allstate policy provided no insurance coverage for Simon.

Republic was still on the hook, though. It argued that the losses to Simon's house were subsurface water conditions and poor drainage on the lot. These losses were specifically excluded by Republic's policy. The court agreed with this argument—and ruled that Republic didn't owe Simon a settlement, either. Two big insurance carriers went away from the trial reasonably content but out some substantial legal fees. The consumer who lost would have to do the fix-up out of grocery money.

The New Madrid Fault

During a three-month period in late 1811 and early 1812, a series of earthquakes struck the area near New Madrid, Missouri, consuming land and changing the course of the Mississippi River. Though measurement techniques had not yet been developed, geologists estimate that the main shocks, the three largest earthquakes, were estimated to be greater than magnitude 8.0.

These quakes originate from a fault zone commonly known as the New Madrid Fault, but more technically a geological structure known as the Reelfoot Rift.

Geological experts believe that the North American tectonic plate has a "scar" where the plate once made a failed attempt to break apart. That failed attempt has left a region vulnerable to seismic activity.

The New Madrid fault system, or the New Madrid seismic zone (NMSZ), cannot be seen on the surface. The fault system extends 150 miles southward from Cairo, Illinois through New Madrid and Caruthersville, Missouri, down through Blytheville, Arkansas to Marked Tree, Arkansas. It dips into Kentucky near Fulton and into Tennessee near Reelfoot Lake, and extends southeast to Dyersburg, Tennessee. It crosses five state lines, and crosses the Mississippi River in at least three places.

The entire fault system is believed to have ruptured in the series of earthquakes in 1811 and 1812. Aftershocks included two events around magnitude 8.0, five around magnitude 7.7, ten around magnitude 5.3, and eighty-nine estimated at magnitude 4.3. Aftershocks were felt in the region for more than a year. This was the largest release of seismic energy in the continental United States. The only other larger event was the so-called "Good Friday"Earthquake, in Alaska in 1964.

Of greatest concern in the near future, then, are the 6.0 to 6.5 events. Damaging earthquakes in this magnitude range are possible within the lifetimes of our children. Two have occurred since 1811/1812, one in 1843, and another in 1895.

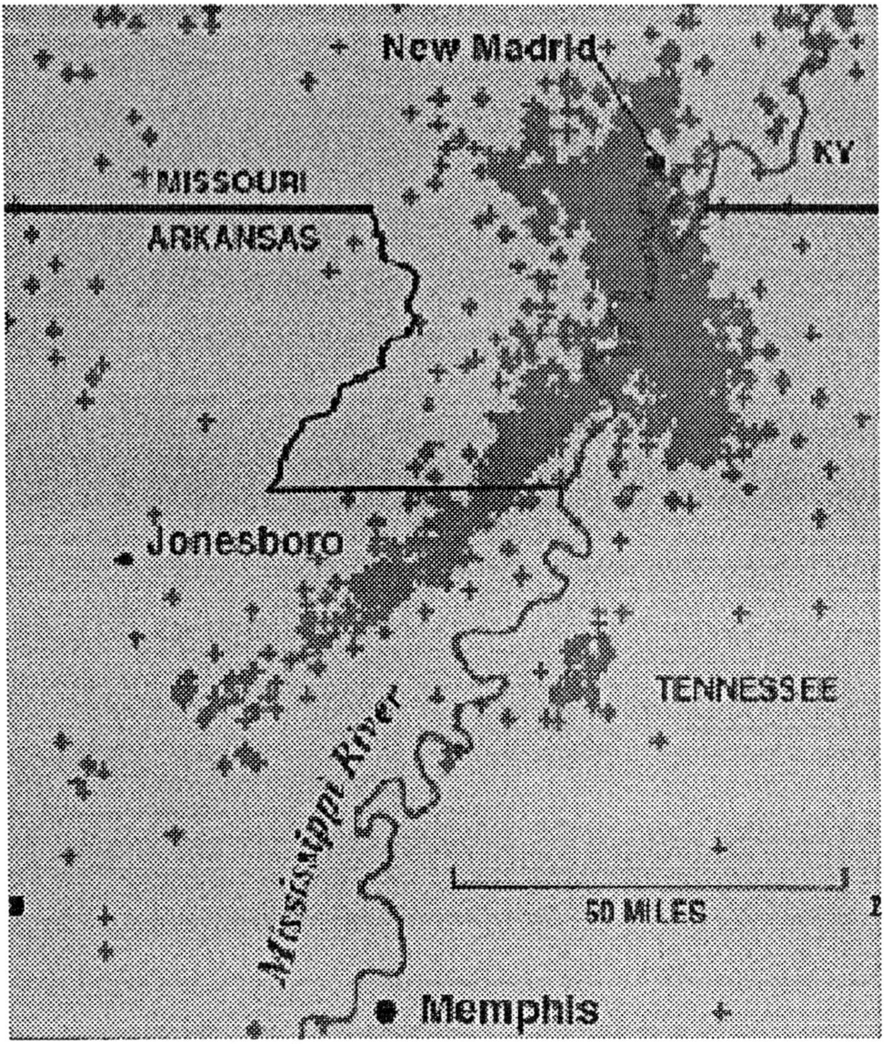

The New Madrid Seismic Zone, as defined by noted activity

Today, forecasters believe that a repeat of the 1811/1812 New Madrid experience would cause over $100 billion in losses. Most people in the lower Midwest know about the risk of earthquake in the region, but relatively few carry an earthquake endorsement. Recent insurance company efforts to limit their exposure to a New Madrid catastrophe have forced deductibles in the region from as low as two percent up to the 10 percent level while other companies are limiting the number of new policies that they write.

However, the possibility of a great earthquake happening soon in the New Madrid seismic zone is small. Scientists believe that catastrophic events like those of the 1811/1812 happen in the New Madrid region every 550-1,200 years. This means there is roughly a 0.3 to 1.0 percent probability of an event greater than magnitude 8.0 within the next 15 years, and a 2.7 to 4.0 percent probability within 50 years. Even though the probabilities are small, there is no reason to be complacent, for there have been other damaging earthquakes in the region since 1811 and 1812.

A damaging earthquake along the New Madrid Fault, magnitude 6.0 or greater, happens every 70 to 90 years and has a probability of 40 percent to 63 percent within the next 15 years, and 86 percent to 97 percent within the next 50 years. An earthquake of this size would cause damage to older structures, especially those of masonry construction. For this reason, there could be serious damage to many schools in the region.

The New Madrid fault system is quite active averaging more than 200 earthquakes per year. Of these, eight to ten are large enough to be felt. There are approximately forty-six earthquakes in the magnitude 2.0 range, and seven in the magnitude 3.0 range per year.

A major earthquake, magnitude 7.0 or greater, happens in the U.S. every 254 to 500 years—and has a probability of five percent to nine percent within the next 15 years. An earthquake of this size in the NMSZ would be felt throughout much of the central and eastern United States. Damage could amount to tens of billions of dollars.

Magnitude	Expected Timeframe
4.0	14 months
5.0	10 to 12 years
6.0	70 to 90 years
7.0	254 to 500 years
8.0	550 to 1,200 years

Insuring Midwest Earthquakes

Reflecting some lack of preparation for a potential New Madrid quake, there is no midwestern earthquake insurance facility similar to the

California Earthquake Authority.

About a quarter of the homes in California have earthquake insurance, with that percentage higher in areas considered most prone to quakes. Earthquake insurance premiums totaled nearly $550 million in 1993, according to A.M. Best Co. figures cited in an Insurance Information Institute report. This was more than 13 times the business done in any other state.

Missouri has the second highest premiums from earthquake insurance with $40 million, followed closely by Washington at $39 million. Because of the New Madrid Fault in the Midwest, many homeowners in several states are relatively religious purchasers of quake protection. Earthquake insurance premiums are highest in California and considerably lower elsewhere in the U.S.

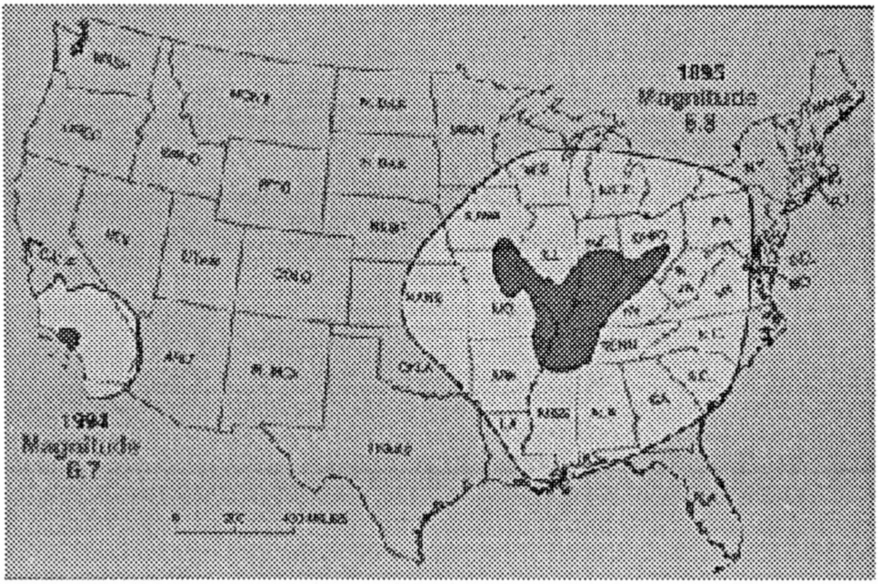

The relative impact zones of similar intensity earthquakes

However, between 1996 and 1998, many property casualty insurers have dramatically increased deductibles on earthquake endorsement coverage for homeowners and businesses in and around the Mississippi Valley.

Deductibles that averaged in the 1.5 percent to 2 percent range for carriers writing insurance in the region have climbed to between 10 percent and 15 percent. Some insurers require a 25 percent deductible for earthquake endorsement coverage. In this environment, rate hikes are sure to follow.

What's changed in the past few years? Keep in mind, the loss ratio for quake coverage in the region is zero, carriers traditionally provided the coverage for a few dollars more, and to our knowledge insurers have never had to pay a quake claim in the NMSZ.

But scientists estimate the probability of a magnitude 6.0 to 7.0 earthquake occurring in the zone within the next 50 years is higher than 90 percent. Such a quake could hit the Mississippi Valley at any time, according to the U.S. Geological Survey

Unlike rates or loss costs for risks like California quakes or Florida windstorms, where a plethora of historical data is available, the historical record is not sufficient to predict quake risk in the NMSZ, critics of the models say. While the models may be the best tool available to underwriters, they're new and subject to extreme variations, these same critics argue.

What does this all mean for regulators who recognize that loss costs haven't changed in 20 years or so and who are charged with monitoring solvency in the wake of a major quake?

As Coit Holbrooke, Tennessee's director of property casualty filings, said in a recent interview: "We want to maintain the availability of earthquake coverage, but at the same time, the rates should be affordable."

However, homeowners insurers cannot simply push through high increases or abruptly pull out of the market. As one agent in Memphis tells us, "Consumers understand moderate increases over time and we can accurately and effectively communicate those increases."

But moving from a 1.5 percent deductible to a 15 percent deductible on a $200,000 home equates to an increased financial exposure of $27,000 for the insured. "Most people can't afford that," nor understand what's changed over the course of a year to warrant the increase, the agent says.

CHAPTER EIGHT

Landslides

The term *landslide* includes a wide range of ground movement, such as rock falls, deep failure of slopes, and shallow debris flows. Although gravity acting on an over-steepened slope is the primary reason for a landslide, there are other contributing factors:

- erosion by rivers, glaciers, or ocean waves create oversteepened slopes;
- rock and soil slopes are weakened through saturation by snowmelt or heavy rains;
- earthquakes create stresses that make weak slopes fail;
- volcanic eruptions produce loose ash deposits, heavy rain, and debris flows;
- vibrations from machinery, traffic, blasting, and even thunder may trigger failure of weak slopes; and
- excess weight from accumulation of rain or snow, stockpiling of rock or ore, from waste piles, or from man-made structures may stress weak slopes to failure and other structures.

Slope material that becomes saturated with water may develop a debris flow or mud flow. The resulting slurry of rock and mud may pick up trees, houses, and cars, thus blocking bridges and tributaries—causing flooding along its path. U.S. Geological Survey (USGS) scientists are working to reduce long-term losses and casualties from landslide hazards through better understanding of the causes and mechanisms of ground failure both nationally and worldwide.

Landslides, including debris flows, are a national problem. They occur in significant numbers in all 50 states and are widespread in the U.S. island territories. Landslides disrupt communities and lifelines, transportation corridors, fuel and energy conduits, and communication linkages. It is estimated that landslide-related fatalities average from 25 to 50 per year, and that direct and indirect economic costs to the nation range up to $2 billion per year. The Pacific Coast, the Rocky Mountains, and the Appalachian Mountains are particularly susceptible to the effects of landsliding.

The Landslides Hazards Group conducts research, gathers information, responds to emergencies and disasters, and produces scientific reports and other products for a broad-based user community. The group provides the results of investigations to private consultants in geology and geotechnical engineering, and to government planners and decision makers.

The National Landslide Information Center (NLIC) is responsible for distributing information about landslides to the lay public, researchers, planners, and local, state and federal agencies. The NLIC provides a toll-free number (1-800-654-4966) and a webpage, where anyone can make inquiries about landslides.

Where do landslides occur?

Landslides occur in every state and U.S. territory. The Appalachian Mountains, the Rocky Mountains and the Pacific Coastal Ranges and some parts of Alaska and Hawaii have severe landslide problems. Any area composed of very weak or fractured materials resting on a steep slope can and will likely experience landslides.

Although the physical cause of many landslides cannot be removed, geologic investigations, good engineering practices, and effective enforcement of land-use management regulations can.

Insurance companies are so guarded about catastrophe losses because they earn their profits by processing huge amounts of data on loss histories and pricing coverage precisely so that they can earn steady profits. The companies are usually positioned to absorb the occasional bad year—but disasters turn careful risk models inside out. No matter how carefully the insurance companies analyze natural disasters, they seem to resist planning.

Landslides are not covered by standard property insurance policies. Separate coverage is available under earthquake insurance—but these policies have low limits and conditions that make it a problematic form of insurance. Furthermore, a landslide claim is a difficult one to make.

The April 1995 federal court decision *Inez Humphrey, v. NFIP, FEMA et al.* raised some major points about why FEMA's methods of running the flood insurance plan are frequently called into question.

Humphrey lived in Pontiac, Michigan, but owned a piece of real estate located in Lonaconing, Maryland. The Maryland property abutted Jackson Run, a tributary of George's Creek. The home on the property, which Humphrey lived part of the year, was insured against damages caused by flooding pursuant to the NFIP. The policy limit was $25,300.

During the later 1980s and early 1990s, Jackson Run has experienced consistent erosion along the riverbank. During a wind and rain storm in October 1991, George's Creek overflowed—worsening the existing erosion problem and damaging Humphrey's house.

NFIP hired Joseph Garlena, an independent adjuster, to evaluate Humphrey's loss. Garlena noted that, due to its poor maintenance and age, the home was in imminent danger of erosion. Humphrey indicated to Garlena that she had no objection to the destruction of the house under FEMA's so-called Upton-Jones provisions, as long as she was adequately compensated her for her loss.

The Upton-Jones provisions pose one of the major problems in this story—and they raise some questions about the NFIP.

In 1988, Congress passed the Upton-Jones Amendment to FEMA. The amendment extended the coverage of existing Standard Flood Insurance Plan (SFIP) to include coverage to insured structures in "imminent danger of collapse due to flood-related erosion." To be eligible for coverage under this amendment, the structure must be either condemned or certified by an appropriate state official to be in imminent danger of collapse due to flood-related erosion.

FEMA is required to promulgate regulations and guidelines to implement provisions of the Upton-Jones Amendment and the same coverage restrictions applicable to the existing SFIP's apply to claims made under the Amendment.

The amendment also provides specific methods of property valuation for determining the amount to which a claimant is entitled. Specifically,

> [f]or purposes of paying flood insurance pursuant to this subsection, the value of a structure shall be whichever of the following is lowest...(A) The fair market value of a comparable structure that is not subject to imminent collapse of subsidence. (B) The price paid for the structure and any improvement to the structure, as adjusted

> for inflation in accordance with an index determined by the Director to be appropriate. (C) The value of the structure under the flood insurance contract issued pursuant to this title.

If this sounds unduly complicated, you're starting to get good at recognizing problems in government disaster policy.

FEMA's instructions to pay for demolition of damaged properties may make sense from a public policy perspective. It's not a good idea to have dilapidated buildings waiting around to collapse when a storm or earthquake happens. But these instructions cause a lot of trouble when the time comes to apply them to real situations.

On March 2, 1992, Lonaconing Township condemned Humphrey's Maryland house and, subsequently, the NFIP secured an appraisal. Allan Stevenson, an independent broker, performed three appraisals. Using the "market value" appraisal, he valued the structure at $11,500. Using the replacement cost appraisal, he valued the structure at $13,551, the original value being $45,169 less 70 percent depreciation for age, obsolescence, and the structure's generally poor condition. Stevenson also used a valuation based on information provided by the insurance consulting firm Marshall Swift; this valued the structure, using a 60 percent depreciation rate, at $27,138.52.

On February 14, 1994, the NFIP issued a Final Determination for demolition benefits. Based on the structure's $11,500 market value, the NFIP authorized total payment of $12,150 to Humphrey. The NFIP forwarded two Proofs of Loss reflecting the amount authorized for payment for loss of the building and its contents. Humphrey did not return the Proofs.

Humphrey's attorney contacted the NFIP by letter dated March 9, 1994 to contest the NFIP's valuation. The NFIP responded that, under the Upton-Jones Amendment to the National Flood Insurance Act, the correct value of the structure was the lower of fair market value or the replacement cost less depreciation.

Humphrey retained a new attorney who contacted NFIP and asserted Humphrey's belief that the policy provided coverage up to replacement value. NFIP responded this line of argument by stating that the Standard Flood Insurance Policy, a copy of which it had provided to Humphrey, allowed replacement cost coverage only for a principal residence.

On October 12, 1994, Humphrey filed a lawsuit alleging that the Maryland house had a fair market value of $25,000; that, under the insurance contract, she was entitled to payment of replacement costs; that the fair market value exceeded the policy limit of $25,300; and, that the NFIP negligently misrepresented the coverage provided.

NFIP countered that Humphrey's complaint should be dismissed. It cited various reasons for this:

- Humphrey's failure to file a sworn and certified Proof of Loss mandates dismissal;
- under the SFIP and the Upton-Jones Amendment, Humphrey is not entitled to recover replacement costs;
- the NFIP is not estopped to deny coverage;
- National Con-Serv is not a proper defendant; and
- Humphrey is not entitled to a jury trial.

Having considered the parties' respective memoranda and attached exhibits, the court deemed a hearing unnecessary. Even giving Humphrey every benefit of doubt or uncertainty, her case was in trouble.

The court cited the section of the SFIP which dealt with timely communciation between a policyholder making a claim and the NFIP:

> Within 60 days after the loss, send us a proof of loss, which is your statement as to the amount you are claiming under the policy signed and sworn to by you and furnishing us with the following information. a. The date and time of the loss; b. A brief explanation of how the loss happened; c. Your interest in the property damaged and the interests, if any, of others in the damaged property; d. The actual cash value of each damaged item of insured property after depreciation is deducted from the cost of replacement of the property (unless the policy's "REPLACEMENT COST PROVISIONS" apply, in which case the replacement cost without allowance for depreciation should be furnished) and the amount of damages sustained; e. Names of mortgagees or anyone else having a lien, charge or claim against the insured property; f. Details as to any other contract of insurance covering the property, whether valid or not; g. Details of any changes in ownership, use, occupancy, location or possession of the insured property since the policy was issued; h. Details as to who occupied any insured building at the time of loss and for what amount; i. The amount you claim is due under this policy to cover the loss....

Rather than grind through the fine points of valuing the condemned property, FEMA focused its argument on Humphrey's failure to file a sworn and certified Proof of Loss. This, the agency argued, excused its obligation to pay an otherwise valid claim.

In other words, since Humphrey never returned proof nor certified her loss she was not entitled to recovery. Humphrey didn't deny that she'd never returned a sworn and certified Proof of Loss.

Instead, she argued that FEMA didn't conduct appraisals in accordance with the regulations. She focused on FEMA's mistakes in considering comparable properties and using the wrong date of valuation for her property. She further maintained that, because FEMA didn't demand precise compliance with the SFIP, it shouldn't deny her claim on technicalities and points of strict compliance.

The court didn't buy her arguments. It referred back to the language of the Upton-Jones Amendment. Specifically, it noted:

> The record...indicates that [FEMA] considered comparables in valuating [Humphrey]'s property. Moreover, the relevant regulations provide that certification by the appropriate authority that the structure is in imminent danger of collapse is a prerequisite for Upton-Jones benefits.... the Township condemned the structure.

The court also rejected Humphrey's theory that FEMA couldn't use her failure to file a sworn and certified Proof of Loss. In order to make this argument work, Humphrey would have to show "affirmative misconduct going beyond mere negligence."

She didn't. FEMA had provided her with a copy of the SFIP when she purchased the flood insurance. It was not required to "demand" separately that she comply with the contract. The regulations themselves provide the necessary incentive and consequences for noncompliance.

The court concluded that FEMA had conducted its part of the processing and valuation of Humphrey's claim as required by law. Humphrey was the one who had not followed the rules. Her case was dismissed—and she was encouraged to accept FEMA's lower offer.

CHAPTER NINE

Earth Movement and Public Policy

Following the Northridge Earthquake in January 1994, companies writing insurance in California began to discuss the implications of a second earthquake of equal or greater Richter Magnitude to the 6.4 event that had just occurred. It did not take long for insurers to decide that they could no longer bear the risk of additional quakes that could cause anything like the $12.5 billion in insured damage caused by the Northridge tremor.

Prior to formation of the California Earthquake Authority, insurers that wished to write homeowners insurance policies were required under California Insurance Regulations to offer their policyholders an optional earthquake endorsement that extended their coverage to earthquakes for an additional cost.

While this insurance was expensive and often carried percentage deductibles that amounted to tens of thousands of dollars, insurance companies still did not want to bear the potential risk of an "eggs in one basket" loss in the Los Angeles or San Francisco area. This led many insurers to restrict writing new insurance or stop writing new policies altogether.

After intense lobbying activities and 18 months political wrangling, the California Earthquake Authority (CEA) was born in late 1996. The CEA provides protection on homes through a privately funded but state run system in which private insurance companies offer earthquake insurance but do not bear any direct earthquake exposure. Instead, insurers retain an administrative/sales fee and pass the remaining premium onto the CEA.

CEA resources include the premium revenue from policyholders and up to $10.5 billion from assessments on insurers, reinsurance coverage, and lines of credit to be repaid from future premiums. The actual allocation of losses is a detailed finance topic; but the intent is to spread risk across many different parties (insurance and reinsurance companies as well as policyholders) and across time (through borrowing). While the CEA claims that it should have sufficient resources to withstand any earthquake that has ever occurred in California, critics argue that it will not be enough if a severe quake strikes the heart of Los Angeles or San Francisco.

Following the $12.5 billion 1994 Northridge earthquake, 90 percent of insurance providers in the state either stopped selling any kind of homeowners insurance or significantly scaled back their underwriting.

Why? Because state law makes insurers offer earthquake coverage with every homeowner's policy. To limit future earthquake exposure, insurers were forced to limit their non-earthquake homeowners business as well. But the advent of the CEA eased the insurance availability crisis.

In October 1996, the same month that the CEA made it through the legislature, both Allstate and Farmers Group said they would begin writing homeowners policies again. In November, State Farm followed suit. As a result, the CEA achieved one of its goals, which was to make traditional homeowners insurance available again. However, it could be argued that delinking homeowners insurance and earthquake insurance offerings could have achieved the same result more easily.

CEA Policy Coverage and Rates

CEA policies do not offer extensive amounts of coverage. First and foremost, CEA homeowners policies carry a deductible that amounts to 15 percent of the home's value. Therefore, earthquake coverage on a $300,000 dwelling carries a whopping $45,000 deductible.

Unlike traditional homeowners coverage, CEA policies offer only bare bones coverage for contents/personal property inside the home ($5,000) and temporary living expenses ($1,500). Furthermore, CEA policies do not cover other structures on the property such as walkways, fences, detached garages or pools—only the house itself is covered.

Policies that extend the CEA's basic contract, usually known as "wrap-around contracts," may eventually be widely available. One company that filed for approval to offer such coverage, United Services Automobile Association (USAA), sells to officers and family of the Armed Forces—but the firm is spreading beyond its base. And even its additional coverage is limited to increased limits on personal property and additional living expenses.

Most companies are not offering wraparound coverage, for three basic reasons. First, the companies say they are too busy training agents in the basic CEA guidelines. Second, companies note that 90 percent of insurers pulled out of the homeowners market after the 1994 Northridge quake precisely because of their increased exposure to liability. If they had to be coaxed back into the market with CEA's frugal policy limits, they are not likely to want to increase their liability by providing additional coverage. Third, offering wraparound coverage requires going through the state department of insurance for processing—a complicated and time-consuming process.

This bureaucratic hurdle, combined with the financial risks involved in offering supplemental coverage, has made some insurers less than enthusiastic about providing wraparound coverage now or in the near future. As long as your house doesn't have any pre-existing earthquake damage, you will be able to get coverage from the CEA. There's no guarantee that you will get coverage from non-CEA companies, since many of them have more stringent criteria for homes that they will cover.

Areas are graded on a 1-5 scale for likelihood of quakes, and these zones may be reflected in insurance rates offered to homeowners in those areas. Wood homes get better rates than brick ones because they withstand quake stresses better than brittle brick structures.

In early 1998, California's earthquake insurance market got its biggest jolt since the state had created a government-run agency to sell policies 15 months before. A new private competitor, Pacific Select Insurance Co., offered a broad range of products that offer meatier coverage than the skeletal policies sold by the California Earthquake Authority. (CEA had become the de facto earthquake carrier for the biggest homeowners insurers in the state.)

The thousands of California homeowners infuriated with a CEA pricing system that tripled and quadrupled annual premiums won't find much rate relief from Walnut Creek-based Pacific Select. In many parts of the Bay Area, Pacific Select's prices actually may be slightly higher than the CEA's rates. But Pacific Select customers will almost always get more for their money than CEA policyholders.

"A lot of people want to know that if their home is completely destroyed by an earthquake, it will be rebuilt so it looks like the same as it did before. Our policies can assure them of that," said Richard Campagna, Pacific Select's chief executive officer. "I'm sure people would rather see our premiums half what they are, but we think we are providing a good value," Campagna said.

Pacific Select's start-up at least provides consumers with their first meaningful alternative to the CEA, said Philip Roberto, research director for the Prop. 103 Enforcement Project, a consumer group that has consistently blasted the CEA.

Pacific Select gives it customers greater peace of mind largely by offering a lower deductible than the CEA. The most popular of Pacific Select's five earthquake insurance products has a 10 percent deductible compared with 15 percent at the CEA.

Other advantages to Pacific Select's premium policy include: coverage for detached structures, a feature unavailable from the CEA; more coverage for earthquake damage to a home's contents (up to 50 percent of a policy's face value compared to a $5,000 maximum at the CEA); and a maximum of $25,000 to cover post-quake living expenses compared with $1,500 at the CEA.

This top-of-the-line coverage isn't cheap. Pacific Select's rates for frame-construction homes in the highest-risk neighborhoods run between $5.52 and $6.18 per $1,000 in coverage compared with a range of $3.90 to $5.00 per $1,000 in coverage at the CEA. Pacific Select's lowest prices on the high-end policy run between $2.03 to $2.27 per $1,000 in coverage compared with a range of 80 cents to $1.10 per $1,000 at the CEA.

With the help of computer models, Pacific Select hopes to limit its losses to a maximum of $2.5 million by buying coverage from reinsurers around the world.

A few other homeowners' insurers have sold earthquake policies outside the CEA, but most of the alternatives also have provided bare-bones coverage at a steep price. All of California's biggest homeowners' carriers—State Farm, Farmers, Allstate and the California State Automobile Association—have been diverting their earthquake business to the CEA.

As of March 12, the CEA had 931,000 policies in effect with an average premium of $456. Pacific Select's average premium so far is running closer to $900, Campagna said.

CEA spokesman Mark Leonard said the entity's biggest fear about Pacific Select is that it will "cherry-pick" the market—that is, sell policies primarily in low-risk neighborhoods and leave the most earthquake-prone communities for the CEA, which must take all comers.

Since the CEA was formed in late 1996, there have been no serious tests of its efficacy. However, effectively zero claims have led to premium reductions and a large pool of funds from which to draw in the event of an earthquake.

Premiums are based on location (by zip code), and range from 80 cents per $1,000 of coverage in low-risk areas up to $4.50 per $1,000 of coverage in high-risk areas—sometimes within a single county. A home costing $100,000 could be facing annual premiums for quake coverage—on top of ordinary homeowners' protection—ranging from $80 to $450. Prices can go as high as $5.70 per $1,000 for older homes and $11.85 per thousand for mobile homes, depending on where they are located.

Much of the criticism of the rates—apart from purely political considerations—stems from the method used in arriving at them. Traditionally, insurance companies have used historical data in establishing their premiums. If an earthquake struck a town in the past, actuaries assumed another one would hit there sometime in the foreseeable future. The premiums for that town would be set higher than surrounding, quake-free zones in the expectation that the risk of loss would be greater.

For the CEA, however, California Insurance Commissioner Chuck Quackenbush turned to a new method of determining the risk of future earthquakes based on computer modeling. Ironically, the insurance department had earlier opposed the same technique when State Farm applied for a rate increase for its commercial earthquake business.

But now, faced with the need to establish prices for the new state-run agency, the department asked EQE International, a structural engineering firm based in San Francisco, to create a seismic model of the whole state. The model would take into account all of the risk factors that could result in damage to individual properties in the event of a quake.

EQE specializes in analyzing buildings and recommending steps to reduce the risk of damage during earthquakes, hurricanes and other natural disasters. In the 1994 Northridge earthquake, it won plaudits when a brewery, which was located near the epicenter of the trembler and had been retrofitted according to EQE's recommendations, suffered only minor damage and was able to go back into full production in less than a week.

The brewery's owners estimated their losses would have been $500 million if they had not followed EQE's suggestions. For the CEA rates, EQE used data from geologists' reports of soil types, claims data from previous earthquakes and structural analysis of various types of buildings. That allowed the company to develop a risk profile that showed how likely a home was to suffer damage in an earthquake. Seismic data were analyzed to determine how likely each of California's hundreds of fault lines was to rupture.

The results were initially divided by ZIP codes, which would have created an unwieldy 2,000-plus rating zones. Instead, regions with similar risk characteristics were combined into a more manageable 19 zones, or bands. Finally, cost factors were assigned to each of the rating bands, taking into account the amount of money the CEA needed to generate to be able to function as well as overhead and administrative costs.

One surprising result of the computer modeling was a lower-than-expected degree of risk for cities and regions that had suffered earthquakes in the past. The engineering studies found that a seismic fault that had "blown off" recently is likely to be more stable than faults that have been relatively quiet.

No one knows whether or not the new rates correctly reflect the actual risk of an earthquake. That will only be determined after they've been tested by real-world events, i.e., devastating earthquakes. EQE and other risk management firms are continuing to refine their data in hopes of making the numbers more exact. Meanwhile, everyone is hoping that the test won't come any time soon. In the event the CEA is forced to borrow to fund claims payments, future CEA policyholder premiums may carry a surcharge to cover the repayment of any borrowings.

CEA critics argue that initial coverage premiums were too high and that insurers have underreported their ability to bear earthquake risk. Moreover, they point out that most insurance companies still made a healthy profit during 1994. But insurers argue that they must stay healthy to provide continuing protection even after a catastrophic event.

Without solid balance sheets and an adequate flow of premiums, many insurance companies could not absorb the losses from a Northridge earthquake and a Hurricane Andrew in the same year. Such a year will happen eventually—it is only a matter of when.

A well-established funding mechanism is needed to see insurance companies through such a "double whammy." Therefore, the establishment of the CEA may have deepened the pockets of the industry in a less disruptive way than if insurers had to scramble for funds after several expensive catastrophes have already struck.

PART THREE

Catastrophic Fires

Unlike hurricanes, earthquakes and floods, structural fires usually strike a very specific location, such as a single home, factory or warehouse. This kind of fire can devastate those directly affected by its aftermath, but it seldom affects more than a handful of people—and insurance companies can easily absorb the usual structural fire's financial impact.

In these ways, structural fires are like tornadoes.

But there remains a certain group of fires, sometimes known as wildfires, that spreads beyond man's control and can cause billions of dollars in insured losses. These are catastrophic fires.

From 1985 to 1998, wildfires destroyed more than 10,000 homes and other insured properties in the United States.

It is a strange phenomena of nature that most wildfires strike areas that face other catastrophic exposures such as hurricanes and earthquakes. Southern California and Florida experience numerous wildfires due to their hot, dry climate, which produces fuel for the fires in the form of dried out underbrush. Experts say that both human and nonhuman events cause wildfires, including arson, careless campers, lit cigarettes, lightning, and malfunctioning electrical equipment. Once a wildfire has started, wind speed and direction may determine the extent of the damage more than man's ability to contain it. The extreme heat of a wildfire not only destroys everything in its path but also prevents firefighters from approaching the flames at close range. A well-timed rain can—and often does—help the cause.

Fires—and wildfires in particular—don't pose the $10 billion-plus megacatastrophe threat presented by hurricanes and earthquakes, but the threat of large losses still exists. The Oakland fires of 1991, for example, totaled nearly $1.7 billion, and some areas of Southern California present billions of dollars of exposure under worse conditions.

Certainly we cannot prevent wildfires. But we can curtail development in areas that face high risk of wildfire.

Private land use rights need to be protected, but they should also carry with them well-defined responsibilities. People who build in high-risk areas should expect to experience wildfire losses and pay more for insurance protection.

The insurance market has not yet responded to the wildfire threat with the same vigor that it has recoiled from earthquakes, floods and hurricanes, but both rates and underwriting restrictions are increasing. It would be prudent for the insurance industry to focus homeowner and government attention on the wisdom of adequate wildfire prevention measures while maintaining adequate availability of financial protection against fire losses of any kind.

"Any time you allow development in high-hazard areas for fires or floods, you are setting yourself up for major losses...or even loss of life," said Scott Bollens, a professor of political science at the University of California, Irvine. "It's not just about environmental concerns. It has to do with public safety and major economic loss."

CHAPTER TEN

Wildfires

In October 1996, wildfires fueled by strong winds burned from the hills near Los Angeles towards the Malibu shore. The fires sent thousands fleeing from a two-mile wide wall of flames that cast an eerie red glow over the nearby Pacific Ocean. Blown by the wind, flaming embers soared several miles ahead of the 9,000-acre fire, which burned vegetation and destroyed at least one home. A massive plume of brown smoke rose several thousand feet and floated ominously over the area.

"We're advising people to pack up their things," said city spokeswoman Sara Maurice at the time of the fire. "Malibu has a natural, built-in fire break. Unfortunately, it's the Pacific Ocean."

The firestorm was one of five wind-whipped wildfires that October that charred about 13,000 acres across southern California, destroying or damaging at least 28 homes. Thousands of children at area schools were evacuated. Flames came to within 200 feet of A.E. Wright Middle School in nearby Calabasas. In Malibu alone, October 1996 fires caused more than $1.4 million in damage, fire officials said. More than $100 million in property at the edge of the fire faced total loss, but for the efforts of firefighters.

Meanwhile, in Carlsbad, about 40 miles northeast of San Diego, wind-driven flames destroyed more than 30 houses as authorities scrambled to evacuate residents from the path of a 2,400-acre fire. "We're writing off the houses that are already on fire and getting to the ones we can save," said Fire Battalion Chief Sonny Hilliard at the time. "We're overwhelmed. Most of the area has already been evacuated."

President Clinton issued a disaster declaration for Los Angeles County and also for San Diego and Orange counties, where the firestorms had chased thousands from their homes. The President's declaration authorized federal funding for fire victims from a variety of federal assistance programs.

"Today, federal firefighters have joined with state and local forces to form a human fire wall from Malibu to the Mexican border," said Clinton, who also dispatched James Lee Witt, director of the Federal Emergency Management Agency, to survey the damage.

Witt toured the scorched hills of Malibu, praising brush clearance efforts that saved hundreds of homes and promising federal resources to help prevent mudslides that could come with winter storms. "I know it's going to get serious if you get a lot of rain and we want to do everything we can," Witt said.

Mark Lorimer, interim Malibu city manager, said he hoped Witt's visit would help expedite $2.9 million in disaster relief still unpaid from the 1993 Malibu fires and the 1994 and 1995 floods.

The millions in damage caused by the 1996 wildfires throughout southern California did not compare to the devastation of the 1991 Oakland/ Berkeley Tunnel wildfire in northern California that totaled over $1.7 billion in insured property losses. For those who witnessed the aftermath, the Oakland fire looked as close to Armageddon as anything they had ever seen.

State Farm catastrophe consultant Dan Carrigan was on site immediately after the 1991 event. "The Oakland Hills fire was the most overwhelming catastrophe site I have ever experienced—the fires were so intense, the homes and property were burned beyond recognition," Carrigan said. "The inferno appeared to burn everything to an absolutely pristine state of cleanliness, like a self-cleaning oven."

A Familiar Habit: Building in Harm's Way

Despite the predictable pattern of wildfire, homeowners continue to build in areas exposed to uncontrollable fire hazards. Compounding the problem is the coverage provided by insurance companies. Unlike other catastrophic risks, the risk of fire is covered under the standard homeowners contract. While insurance companies may charge more for homes located in fire zones, insurers know that they can recover their losses through increases in homeowners premiums across all policies.

Wildfires usually occur in the western states but, under the right conditions, wildfires can affect virtually any part of the United States. In California, where the wildfire risk is greatest, the population has grown particularly rapidly in forest regions. From 1970 to 1996, the population of 11 California counties grew by more than 150 percent, and nine of those counties are in forest areas. Meanwhile, the population of the entire state rose by just 60 percent.

Fires can occur virtually anywhere, and wildfires present the chance that large areas can be consumed by wildfire. Contrary to popular belief, wildfires are not confined to the western part of the United States. "Although the most destructive wildfires have historically been concentrated in the West, we now recognize that the fire hazard from wildland/urban interface is a national problem," says John J. Kollar, vice president of ISO's Actuarial Services & Research Department. "In 1996, wildfires occurred in every state. More than 113,000 conflagrations burned a total of 6.4 million acres that year."

In an article written for *Wildfire* magazine, forestry expert Neil Sampson explains:

> Fire was a very common phenomenon in the North American environment. One estimate of the wildfire frequency in the pre-settlement period, based on estimates of the extent of different ecosystems and their fire return intervals as developed by modern fire scientists, indicates that 4 to 11 percent of our land may have burned on an annual average. Obviously, fire was a very different factor in different ecosystems. For example, in Florida the fire return interval in the Everglade system was estimated as 5 to 10 years, while in the Mangrove system, fire occurred only every 500 to 1,000 years.

Today, people have too much at stake to allow wildfires to burn freely.

Market forces have a powerful effect on property development in high-risk areas and loss mitigation efforts. But markets' focus on short-term results can overwhelm the wisdom of sound responses to the threat of wildfires. This kind of situation calls for strong public policy to encourage responsible development with adequate protection against risk. While regulation is often not the answer, building codes, adequate fire access roads, landscaping ordinances, hazard fuel-reduction programs and zoning can shape residential and commercial development in a constructive way that can save both property and lives from the next *real* barn-burner.

To save lives, widespread readiness has become imperative in recent years, as communities have found themselves threatened by racing flames that hours or even minutes before seemed to pose no threat. Pre-planned routes for evacuations, water drops, and airlifts have kept casualties to a minimum. But even with the best planning, emergencies occur.

As for property, wildfires destroy thousands of buildings and cost hundreds of millions of dollars each year, but most people already know this. Their actions (or inaction) reflect an "It won't happen to me" attitude.

Should government take steps to protect people from themselves? Most fire experts firmly believe they should and they act on that belief. The Federal Wildland Fire Policy calls wildfires a major problem that will escalate as the nation moves into the Twenty-First Century. What is government doing about it?

Most fire prevention efforts take place at the grass-roots level in the form of municipal ordinances and building codes. In southern California, brush regulations—which require homeowners in high risk areas to keep grass, brush and other vegetation trimmed to three inches high around their homes—have been vigorously enforced since the 1993 wildfires, according to Los Angeles County Fire Department Captain Steve Valenzuela. In fact, homeowners resisting the regulations have been cited and, on occasion, prosecuted.

There have been some important preventive changes since 1993, but some experts believe the changes were not enough. In Orange County, California, the Board of Supervisors and some municipal officials refused to designate very high fire hazard zones that require special safety measures. The officials and residents of such beautiful but high-risk canyons and hillsides complained that the high-risk designation would increase insurance rates and depress property values.

They may have kept premiums down in the short term but history has proved those residents' thinking to be shortsighted. A 1993 fire in the exclusive Lemon Heights area of Orange County damaged or destroyed 26 expensive homes as flames jumped from house to house, pushed by winds gusting to 71 miles per hour. Residents used garden hoses, swimming pools and anything they could find to wet their rooftops in a frantic bid to save their homes.

The Lemon Heights area includes many $1 million-plus mansions with large swimming pools and tennis courts surrounded by stately old trees. Some residents packed belongings and fled. Others stayed behind to battle the flames. At one house, two people scooped water from a swimming pool, handing containers up to each other on the roof, where they dashed to soak wooden shingles touched by wind-borne embers. Other residents hurled dirt by the shovelful at a wall of fire along a street. When it was all over, fires that included the Lemon Heights blaze had charred about 37,000 acres scattered across Southern California.

Following the Lemon Heights fires, the Orange County Board of Supervisors enacted fire prevention measures and regulations, but the damage already had been done.

It took the Los Angeles County Board of Supervisors two years to pass an ordinance requiring automatic interior fire sprinklers in new or remodeled homes in high-risk areas. The 1995 regulations also require any home improvement that costs 50 percent or more of the home's value to include replacement of wooden roofs with flame-retardant materials. Fire officials believe wooden roofs are a major reason that many homes are destroyed in wildfires. However, the powerful wood shake and shingle lobbyists in the various state capitols often thwart ordinances and other regulatory measures that would encourage or require homeowners to replace wooden roofs on their homes.

Since 1991, Malibu ordinances have required the roofs of all new homes to be built with fire-retardant materials, although no regulations have been adopted for homes built before that time. A proposed law being considered by the Malibu City Council would require homeowners with pools to register with City Hall. The homeowners would post signs on their properties so that firefighters would know where to find extra sources of water in case of a fire.

A month after the devastating 1996 Malibu fires, the Los Angeles County Board of Supervisors agreed to form a task force that looked for ways to prevent the mudslides that often follow the fire season in mountain and canyon areas. The Post-Fire Watershed Recovery Task Force was charged with helping control heavy erosion on the charred hillsides of the Santa Monica Mountains.

Consisting of members from federal, state and local agencies, the task force was formed (ironically) right after a rainstorm dropped as much as

6.5 inches on the area, causing further erosion on the scorched hillsides. The storm also loosened boulders that future rains could send tumbling onto Malibu Canyon Road, one of the few north-south links in the area. A similar pattern of fires and subsequent mudslides occurred in 1993, after a deadly wildfire swept across Santa Monica Mountains canyon lands only to be followed by heavy rains that caused destructive slides. But it took the 1996 Malibu fire experience to effect change.

California municipalities face the largest wildfire threat, but federal officials play an important macro-level role. The National Forest Service (part of the U.S. Department of Agriculture) and the United States Fire Administration (part of FEMA) both contribute to fire prevention efforts, research, and public awareness. But budget cuts and priorities that include urban fire losses, firefighter training and other natural disasters have relegated wildfire issues to a secondary position at the federal level.

A 1998 Blue Ribbon Panel explained the problems in a review of the United States Fire Administration, but the panel did not focus on wildfire issues. Consequently, local officials must take the lead in shaping public policy for their own particular areas. According to Neil Sampson of the Forest Policy Center:

> From the federal viewpoint, the urban/wildland situation is a political nightmare. Federal policy or law cannot be seen to be imposing restrictions on private landowners. That is a well-established fact in American political life. Any regulation of private land use is left to state and local governments and they, as we have all seen, must be very careful with this as well. Americans value private property rights about as much as any aspect of our personal freedom, and recent court rulings have established guidelines that set out the need for financial compensation when any significant economic value is removed from private property as the result of public regulation.

Sampson's point is well taken: regulation is best done locally and in moderation. Financial support from the federal government for wildfire prevention efforts and research initiatives is vitally important.

But the key to structural survival in a wildfire is fuel management by communities. Although site specific, this includes choosing native, drought-resistant vegetation while phasing out nonnative species, using fire safe building materials, selecting appropriate structure placement and providing adequate access roads and water supplies.

Those communities that don't could get burned.

Overview of Fire Risk

For much of this century, fire-suppression policies have sought to extinguish wildfires as quickly as possible. Rather than focusing on prevention, these policies have encouraged the accumulation of brush and other vegetation that feed future fires.

Neil Sampson writes, "If you look at the wildfire statistics for the Twentieth Century, you see a nice U-shaped curve. We had lots of wildfires in the early years of the Century. Logging practices left a lot more fuels untreated, arson was common and suppression capability was nearly nonexistent. Most of that changed."

As fire suppression policies gathered support, wildfire activity diminished throughout the mid-Twentieth Century. Unfortunately, wildfire activity has once again assumed an upward trend. The fires that ravaged southern California's suburbs in 1996 provided a blazing finale to the nation's worst wildfire season since 1952. Wildfires burned 6.4 million acres in 1996, the most since 1952 when 6.7 million acres burned, according to the National Interagency Fire Center. "These new fires have flames hundreds of feet high, where in the past they may have gone 20 feet high," said Leon F. Neuenschwander, a fire ecologist at the University of Idaho. "They are jumping canyons. The only way to fight them is to change the weather."

The 10 Most Costly Fires in U.S. History

Date	Event	Estimated Loss (Mill. of 1995 $)
April 1906	San Francisco Earthquake/Fire	$5,915
October 1871	Great Chicago Fire	2,129
October 1991	Oakland-Berkeley Tunnel Area Fires	1,678
November 1872	Great Boston Fire	951
October 1989	Polyolefin Plant/Pasadena, TX	923
February 1904	Baltimore Conflagration	545
April/May 1992	Los Angeles Riots	616
October 1993	Laguna Wildfires/Orange County, CA	557
December 1995	Massachusetts Textile Mills	500
February 1942	USS Lafayette	496

Source: National Fire Protection Association; Property/Casualty Insurance Fact Book

Of course, wildfires are not the only fires that cause significant property losses. Most significant fire losses have occurred in urban areas from causes that are not related to hot, dry conditions. In fact, of the ten most costly U.S. fires, only three are considered to be wildfires.

Wildfires typically do not have high death tolls. Fire deaths often originate when people cannot escape the blaze. For this reason, chemical and mine workers also have suffered from explosive fires throughout history.

The 10 Worst Multiple Death Fires in U.S. History

Date	Event	Deaths
April 1865	Lower Mississippi River/S.S. Sultana	1,547
October 1871	Great Chicago Fire	1,152
June 1904	New York, S.S. General Slocum	1,030
December 1903	Chicago, Iroquois Theater	602
October 1918	Cloquet, Minnesota Area	559
November 1942	Boston, Cocoanut Grove Night Club	492
April 1947	Texas City Chemical Plant	468
September 1894	Hinckley, MN Area	418
December 1907	Monongha, WV Mine Explosion	361
June 1900	Hoboken North German Lloyd Pier	326

Source: National Fire Protection Association; Property/Casualty Insurance Fact Book

Wildfires are quite predictable but their damage doesn't stop with burned property; another problem is the fire-flood cycle. Destructive floods have followed most of the bigger wild fires. When vegetation is charred in places like Malibu, gulches and palisades become carbonized waterways. Damage caused by floods and mudslides has cost Los Angeles County about $100 million in lawsuit settlements alone. Taxpayer advocates have long complained about the huge bill for protecting and cleaning up areas known to be home to celebrities and high-rollers.

Erosion in areas affected by wildfire not only strips away valuable topsoil, but also contributes to significant pollution downhill/downstream as silt fills streams, rivers and lakes. Silt traps, new plantings and man made dikes can stop some of the runoff from a sloped area scorched by wildfire. But exposed landmasses can become waterlogged resulting in landslides. Landslides may pose more of a financial threat than wildfire, since the standard homeowners insurance policy does not cover losses that result from landslides.

Nature and Its Contribution to Wildfires

Wildfires find most of their origins in nature. Hot, dry weather combined with an abundance of low-level vegetation makes excellent kindling for a large fire. But wildfires are a natural occurrence serving a natural purpose: to clear the waste on the forest/prairie floor. "Fires are part of the normal cycle of the ecosystem," said Malibu City Attorney Christi Hogin. "Everybody out here says it's not a matter of if the fires will come, but when."

It is not nature's fault; rather it is man's intervention in a natural and inevitable process that makes wildfires financially crippling. U.S. Fire Administration experts all the way down to local planners understand the risks of building in the path of nature's fury. Homes built in fire prone areas really do not stand much of a chance if conditions favor wildfires.

Most wildfires begin with weather conditions. In the fall, southern California experiences a weather phenomenon known as the Santa Ana Winds. Dry, desert winds push toward the coast, picking up speed as they squeeze through southern California's canyons and mountain passes. These warm, dry winds plague Southern Californians in the fall, draining moisture from the air and fanning the flames of wildfires. It's no coincidence that brush fire season peaks during these yearly wind events. Santa Ana winds dry out the shrubbery and fine grasses that fuel wildfires. Fire officials estimate that fires pushed by Santa Ana winds spread five to six times faster than other brush fires.

Strange as it seems, hot Santa Ana winds start out as cold air hundreds of miles away from Los Angeles. Those winds are the result of several meteorological events and are part of a complex weather system that extends throughout the Western states.

Three characteristics of Santa Ana winds:

1. Hot: The sinking movement of the high-pressure system wind causes it to warm; air temperatures increase 5.5 degrees for every 1,000 feet it descends. Moving across the hot deserts of Nevada and eastern California adds to the warming effect.
2. Fast: Wind gains speed as it squeezes through the narrow moun-

tain passes and canyons of the San Gabriel and San Bernardino Mountains.

3. Dry: The sinking air motion can cause humidity levels to drop to single digit levels.

The following weather conditions contribute to the Santa Ana effect:

1. **Low Pressure: A low-pressure area with counterclockwise winds develops off or along the California coast.**
2. **Jet Stream: Powerful Santa Ana winds need a strong jet stream over southern California. The jet stream is what guides storms, and its position and strength vary.**
3. **High-Pressure: The cold, dense air from an Alaskan storm helps create a high-pressure system centering roughly over the northern Utah- Nevada border. For strong Santa Ana Winds, the high-pressure system must exist for a greater vertical depth over California, extending from about 18,000 feet above sea level to the ground.**
4. **Cold Front: Cool air from a cold front moves from the Gulf of Alaska into the Great Basin states.**
5. **Air Circulation: Air circulating clockwise in the high-pressure system moves west toward southern California, becoming the northeasterly winds called Santa Anas.**

Sources: James Murakami, Meteorologist at UCLA Atmospheric Science Department; National Weather Service.

Nature also contributes that which fuels the fire: vegetation. Wildfire professionals in California have coined a new term to denote the wildfire threat at the Urban-Wildland Interface or Intermix. "I Zone," for "Interface Zone," denotes an area that includes wild land vegetation, exotic/ornamental vegetation and structures. In fire parlance, all vegetation, native and exotic/ornamental, is termed "fuel." But ornamental (nonnative) vegetation appears to contribute most to the problem. If burning structures were the results of the fast-moving flaming front, ornamental vegetation was the wick.

Most hillside residents live in chaparral-covered canyons because they enjoy the ambiance. But instead of landscaping with deep-rooted native California vegetation, they tend to use shallow-rooted, exotic species to landscape their property. The dry conditions of these canyons deprive the ornamental vegetation of moisture and, lacking a deep root structure, the vegetation becomes very dry, making these plants excellent fuel for a wildfire.

One example of ornamental vegetation is the Eucalyptus tree. Experts say eucalyptuses—containing highly flammable oils, with easily felled old branches—are dangerous in cities and should be cut down in some cases. A nonnative to southern California, the Eucalyptus tree arrived from Australia more than a century ago.

In most wildfires, structures that survive display smaller amounts of nearby ornamental vegetation. One structure, with a wood roof and wood siding, survived the 1993 Malibu fire, according to fire department officials, due primarily to an aggressive vegetation management program by the property owner as well as owners of adjacent property.

CHAPTER ELEVEN

Fire Insurance and Prevention

Fire insurance is one of the oldest coverages offered by insurers. Since most fires do not consume many houses at a time or even a single house in its entirety, fire insurance is readily available and usually at reasonable cost as part of the homeowners insurance policy. Earthquakes are excluded from all standard homeowners policies and some insurance contracts exclude hurricane coverage, but all homeowners insurance policies cover fire losses.

The Homeowners 3 policy (special form) is the most common homeowners insurance contract. The HO-3—as well as most other contracts—covers the dwelling itself as well as personal property against "hostile" fire losses. A "hostile" fire is defined as a flame outside its normal confines. Lit cigarettes and hot water heater pilot lights are considered friendly fires, but become hostile fires once they spread to other areas.

Smoke damage to your home's interior and contents from a sudden and accidental fire is covered and so is water damage resulting from fire fighting activity. Although homeowners insurance does not cover earthquake and flood losses, fire losses caused by earthquakes or floods (such as an explosion and fire from a ruptured gas line or shorted electrical appliance) are covered.

In short, nearly all fire losses are covered by insurance, except intentional losses (arson) and losses on property that has been left vacant for over 30 days.

Such broad coverage with very few exclusions provides homeowners with little in the way of incentive to avoid fire-prone areas. Insurance premiums for at-risk properties reflect some of the increased exposure but homeowners generally have no trouble finding willing insurers. The result has been plenty of development in hazardous territory.

But times may be changing. Having been burned in California (pun intended), some insurance companies have cut back on their writings in areas exposed to wildfires. As California insurance companies start withdrawing fire insurance from high-risk areas, homeowners across the West will have to come to grips with the essential role of fire, ecologists say. "The solution is recognizing the inevitability of fire," said David L. Bunnell, a fuel specialist for the U.S. Forest Service. "It is like building in a 35-year flood plain."

"Population shifts to wildfire-prone areas—and the development patterns in those areas—have put many homes and other insured structures at risk," says John J. Kollar, vice president of ISO's Actuarial Services & Research Department. "As a result, insurers today face the potential both for catastrophic wildfires with unequaled losses and an increasing stream of losses from smaller but more numerous fires."

Faced with these risks, insurance company underwriters and actuaries continue to seek additional tools to evaluate the extent of the wildfire risk. The challenges confronting insurers that underwrite properties exposed to the wildfire hazard include:

- developing and implementing appropriate underwriting criteria;
- understanding and managing the aggregate amount of wildfire risk in an entire book of business, sometimes known as probable maximum loss (PML);
- managing the geographic concentration of risks;
- educating insureds about what they can do to make their properties safer; and
- working with government and other groups to mitigate potential wildfire losses.

Fortunately, both the government and private associations have undertaken to protect both public and private property from the wildfire risk. The National Fire Protection Association has identified three critical factors in assessing risk and replacement value in areas exposed to wildfire risk. Those primary factors are:

- Fuel—This factor considers whether an area is covered in grass, trees or dense brush, giving an indication of how intensely that area will burn.
- Slope—This factor identifies whether a risk is located on a steep grade. Slope can affect how quickly a wildfire may spread and can be a significant factor in reconstruction costs.

- Access—This factor identifies whether a risk is located on a dead-end, winding or narrow road that fire trucks may have trouble negotiating.

Through premium surcharges and underwriting restrictions, insurance protection against fire loss should encourage builders to construct fire safe structures away from fire-prone areas. But, like flood insurance, homeowners policies may actually motivate development of at-risk properties. Given that insurers are unlikely to exclude fire as a covered peril, government and insurance companies should measure fire risk and take steps to reduce it.

Tools for Measuring Wildfire Risk

Predicting property losses from wildfire is a major challenge. The process of deciding which areas are more or less likely to experience fires has always been difficult at best. In early 1998, the Insurance Services Office (ISO) tried to move fire prediction forward by offering a satellite imagery risk assessment tool to gauge wildfire risks. The FireLine system uses satellite imagery to pinpoint heavy concentrations of highly flammable brush near homes and businesses. It produces maps of much greater detail than traditional aerial maps and provides data previously not available.

Insurers also can use FireLine to develop overall wildfire hazard ratings for all of the risks in their books of business to gain a better understanding of their overall amount of wildfire risk and whether that risk is geographically concentrated. "Now we're able to offer insurers a service that will enable them to make better business decisions and assess wildfire hazards even more accurately," says Patrick McLaughlin, ISO's senior vice president of risk decision services. "In addition to providing greater accuracy, FireLine offers insurers greater consistency in applying their own underwriting guidelines."

In addition to systems like FireLine, fire underwriters can use information about a location's accessibility and the quality of its municipal fire department. Underwriters use an index, often known as the Fire Protection Class (FPC) or Public Protection Class (PPC), that combines a property's proximity to fire hydrants and fire stations, measures of fire department effectiveness and the number of firefighters available per unit of area to determine premium. The FPC and PPC are calculated by ISO as part of its Public Protection Classification Service. Fire Chiefs closely monitor their department's FPC and PPC to avoid costly premium increases for citizens—and their own embarrassment.

In 1998, ISO added the Community Outreach Program as a new component of its PPC service. Under the new program, ISO reached out to communities and fire districts to identify changes in fire protection features that will enhance the accuracy and reliability of its PPC database. The group's goal was to contact every participating community over 30 months for information on any significant changes.

ISO's PPC database contains detailed information on the fire suppression capability of approximately 43,000 fire districts and municipalities countrywide. Under the Community Outreach Program, municipalities will receive a public protection information update form and a detailed street map showing the boundaries of the fire protection area and fire station locations. The form and map, once returned to ISO, will be compared with information in the PPC database. If significant differences are found in fire protection features, ISO will schedule a field survey after consulting the appropriate community officials. With these updates, insurance premiums will reflect a more accurate measure of fire risk.

In addition to ISO's private sector efforts, government agency initiatives have pursued identification of at-risk areas. Vegetation maps of the Santa Monica Mountains produced from a NASA airborne sensor taken before and after the 1996 Calabasas/Malibu brush fire are helping scientists improve predictions of fire hazards in the area and may one day reduce the risk of catastrophic fires. Maps of chaparral vegetation are created with advanced measurements from NASA's Airborne Visible and InfraRed Imaging Spectrometer (AVIRIS) which was developed and is managed by the Jet Propulsion Laboratory (JPL) in Pasadena, California.

According to Dr. Dar Roberts of the University of California, Santa Barbara:

> With AVIRIS, we've been working on techniques to use the spectral information measured by the instrument to map different vegetation communities in the Santa Monica Mountains.... This information should improve our ability to assess fire risk and predict fire behavior, and perhaps could provide more effective information for planners and agencies concerned with fire prevention. We can also predict moisture content in the foliage which helps us understand how different areas will burn.

The AVIRIS instrument flies aboard a NASA aircraft traveling at an altitude of 12 miles above sea level. Scientists use AVIRIS to conduct research across a range of scientific disciplines, including ecology, geology, snow and ice, coastal and inland waters, and wildfires.

"We are measuring in detail how light is absorbed or reflected by various materials on the Earth's surface," said Robert Green, the AVIRIS experiment scientist at JPL. "In the case of the Santa Monica Mountains, we are measuring the presence of molecules such as chlorophyll, leaf water and cellulose. By measuring these molecules we can map different vegetation types, vegetation moisture and the overall amount of vegetation, all of which play a role in predicting wild fire hazards."

According to NASA and JPL, scientists and fire agencies will use AVIRIS vegetation maps and measurements they have taken on the ground to forecast how and where a fire would burn in the area.

"An accurate fire model could be very useful in allowing us to strategize by staying one or two steps ahead of an actual fire as it burns, allowing more efficient deployment of resources during an emergency," said Herb Spitzer, assistant fire chief at the Forestry Division of the Los Angeles County Fire Department. "The AVIRIS information can tell us what kinds of fuel are present and that could help us plan safe and effective 'prescribed' burns. If we could burn the vegetation more frequently and in small patches, then it would reduce the risk of catastrophic fires."

Despite these technological advances, most insurers still rely heavily on historical actuarial data to calculate premiums and determine underwriting criteria. Insurers actively support fire prevention technology, but they can only do so much. Consequently, government must take an active role in fire prevention and suppression to keep the public's fire losses and premiums as low as possible.

Wildfire Fighting Technology and Prevention Efforts

In May 1998, a series of wildfires swept across North-Central Florida as high winds combined with extremely dry conditions to burn over 37,000 acres of forested land. Officials believe that the dry pine and palmetto forests were set on fire by lightning strikes. Some 30,000 residents of Flagler County were evacuated and Interstate 95 was closed from Jacksonville to Cocoa Beach because of fires and smoke.

U.S. Forest Service firefighters, FEMA bulldozers and fire engines airlifted from California were brought to Florida to combat the blaze. Over 2,100 people from all over the U.S. battled the blaze, including personnel from the Florida National Guard. Helicopters dumped water on the flames to stop the wildfire's advance. But fire officials conceded that a good rain was the only hope for an end to the blaze—and they got it in early July.

The most primitive of wildfire suppression technologies—the firebreak—proved ineffective against the wind-driven flames. Workers used bulldozers and shovels attempting to break the fire's continuity, but to no avail. The fire lasted over six weeks and burned over 140 homes. The sheer size of the fire and its firebreak-jumping ability rendered useless most of today's fire suppression technology.

Firefighters have employed airborne tankers in most wildfire battles in the 1990s. These air tankers can transport dozens of loads of water to remote locations during the course of a single day. In one high profile move, Los Angeles County leased two airplanes known as Super Scoopers equipped to pick up large quantities of water from reservoirs or the sea and to drop it on the flames. The County leased the planes for two years before deciding to commit to a long-term agreement in early 1998. Some county officials were concerned that the planes would not perform well in high winds and in steep canyons because of a lack of maneuverability but supporters dismissed those criticisms.

To reduce property losses, some real estate developers are paying heed to the lessons of the past. Most homes built post-1980 tend to have double-paned windows, tighter, energy-efficient construction—and noncombustible roofing. Most important, ornamental, exotic landscaping is not as prevalent in post-1980 developments. These factors have diminished fire losses in some cases.

Public preparations to combat the next blaze also qualify as fire suppression. In Laguna Beach, California where a disastrous fire struck in 1993, consuming 16,864 acres of land and damaging 441 homes, officials nervously watched in 1997 as flames flared in nearby Lemon Heights.

They voiced tempered confidence in steps taken after the last big fire. During the summer of 1996, the Laguna Beach County Water Department completed a three million gallon reservoir. In addition to the reservoir, more fire hydrants were installed near open space areas and new water lines now connected different reservoirs to each other allowing them to feed one another. Officials also enlisted hundreds of goats to gnaw away dry brush and the city expanded the firebreak around the city limits.

In addition, the City Council declared the entire city a severe fire hazard zone, which required the use of fire-resistant materials in new construction and banned use of wood roofing. City building codes also were tightened. For example, wood siding can be used on the outside of homes, but only with dry wall boards underneath.

Laguna Beach also invested about $100,000 to outfit fire engines with fire-retardant foam that firefighters can spray on the blaze directly or on homes if a fire is threatening.

In 1993, wildfires in the Malibu hills destroyed over 300 homes—including the $4 million estate of actor Sean Penn—and blackened nearly 18,500 acres in Malibu and neighboring Topanga Canyon. It was the ninth catastrophic blaze to roar through Hollywood's favorite beachfront since the 1950s.

But regulations implemented in 1991 prevented the blaze from becoming even more costly. "It's a great credit to Malibu residents [that] their brush-reduction program has allowed for a significant reduction of homes lost," Governor Pete Wilson said during a visit. Later, he declared three counties disaster areas to secure federal and state aid.

Solving the Wildfire Problem

Ironically, solving the problem may mean allowing wildfires to happen—in a controlled way. For over half a century, American firefighters have largely eliminated the kind of small, naturally occurring fires that have cleaned forest floors since antiquity.

"In the 1960s the order was, 'Every fire contained by 10 a.m. the following day,'" Les Rosenkrance, the Bureau of Land Management fire center's director, said of the total suppression policy. Consequently, a massive buildup of fuel—dead branches, leaves and small trees—cover many forest floors. Some ecologists believe the nation has a limited window of opportunity to use controlled burns to defuse these forest "time bombs." By burning into the wind, or at humid times of the year, forest managers can replicate the small, low-level fires that kept Western forests healthy in the past. "In Arizona, the Ponderosa pine forests used to burn every two to four years," said Melanie Miller, a fire ecologist here for the Bureau of Land Management. "Now you have forests that haven't burned in 80 years."

After a cautious start, some forest officials in the West are embracing a policy of managed burns. The price of keeping fire out of a forest for decades is a single, catastrophic blaze that races from tree crown to tree crown, destroying thousands of mature trees.

Since 1990, the U.S. Forest Service has doubled the average amount of forest burned under controlled conditions. And over the next decade, the Forest Service plans to increase this amount sixfold, to 3.5 million acres a year in the year 2005. Even at this rate, the Forest Service estimates that most areas will burn every 25 years, which may not be often enough.

The 1998 wildfires in north-central Florida may have been exacerbated by fire suppression that works too well. Dry conditions may have only accelerated or called attention to the natural pruning of wildfires that should have occurred years ago. Unfortunately, urban areas may not have the luxury of controlled burns since most at-risk areas already have been heavily populated.

Regions such as southern California will have to pursue different strategies for controlling the wildfire risk. Using goats to consume dry bush/fuel is one answer, but just a start. Aggressive regulations such as restrictions on vegetation and wooden roofing may do little more than halt the increase of property value at-risk, but these ordinances are steps in the right direction.

Insurance companies need to address the shortcomings in their own premium structures. Most builders and property buyers will take notice if premium levels reflect the nature of the risk. While the market for fire insurance is getting tighter and more pricey, perhaps only an extreme experience similar to the Florida windstorm insurance market will get developers' attention.

Forest fire expert Neil Sampson attributes most of the wildfire prevention deficiencies to a lack of political will. In an article for the magazine

Wildfire, Sampson wrote, "[Wildfire risk] is an increasingly complex situation in virtually every part of the Nation; one for which good solutions simply have not, in many places, been put in place. But even as this problem gets more difficult and expensive, we are not implementing the solutions we know."

Sampson may be right; but we can expect prevention efforts to fall short until private market forces—insurance costs and property values—fully reflect the wildfire risk.

PART FOUR

Man-Made Disasters

When thinking about disasters and catastrophic losses, it's easy to focus only on hurricanes, earthquakes, fires and floods. These are the disasters that impact most people in most situations. However, some people have their lives upended by disasters created by other people...rather than by Mother Nature.

Some of these man-made disasters are not intended to harm. The best example of this unintentional assault is the much-trumpeted Year 2000 computer software problem. Insurance companies and risk experts are convinced that this software bug—the accidental result of a programming shorthand from the 1960s—could do serious harm to people when computers around the globe flip their internal clocks to 01/01/00. As a result, people and companies are working hard to mitigate the damage.

And the whole episode serves as a useful study in how to avert a catastrophic loss—with sufficient forewarning.

Other man-made disasters are intentional. These events...think of Timothy McVeigh killing scores of people in Oklahoma City...occur to most people as moral parables. For the purposes of our exercise, though, they remain morally neutral. We'll consider how government agencies, insurance companies and individual people respond to terrorism's growing risk profile.

Intentional or not, man-made disasters have the same impact on people's decision-making processes and the broader capital markets that natural disasters do. The main distinction is the anger that's inevitable when you realize that someone...somewhere...put these catastrophes in motion. But, as we've said before, that anger is beyond our investigation.

CHAPTER TWELVE

The Year 2000 Problem

The Year 2000 problem—also known as *Y2K* or the *Millennium Bug*—is a computer software glitch that could interrupt many of the computers used for personal and business applications on January 1, 2000.

The operating systems and software applications used on most machines refer to all specific dates in the following formats: MM/DD/YY or DD/MM/YY. In these formats, the DD refers to the day, the MM refers to the month, and the YY refers to the year. For example: May 7, 1996, could appear as 05/07/96. The month and date work fine in the system; but the year is problematic.

In the 1960s, when government and military programmers were first developing the operating systems and software applications that preceded the ones most people use today, they didn't hesitate to shorten the year in their dates to its last two digits. They simply designed their programs and machines to assume the first two digits—19—when doing any kind of chronological calculation.

Computer memory was astronomically expensive in those days and all the "19"s that they saved made a big difference. The smart programmers realized the shortcut would cause problems in the year 2000. The machines would assume "00" and "01" meant 1900 and 1901. But the year 2000 seemed a lifetime away...and there was a Cold War to win.

Well, here we are.

In the early 1990s, with January 2000 fast approaching, a number of businesses and government agencies began to realize they were going to have big problems if they didn't do something to fix their computers. Loan amortization schedules would get confused. Magazine subscriptions would have errors. Projections and models of various sorts would turn inside out.

There were other problems that made Y2K even worse. These included:

- The leap year problem. To make matters worse, 2000 is a leap year—with an extra day in February—and 1900 was not. So, even the date numbers are wrong after the 59th day of 2000.
- The null set problem. Some programs are designed to read "99" as shorthand for the logical concept of nothing (as opposed to the number 0). This is what logicians call "no data" or "null set."
- The re-initialization of system date in some Global Positioning System ("GPS") transceivers have a date error in them that will reset August 22, 1999 to January 6, 1980.

That last item made some pessimists worried that airplanes in the sky and ships at sea would be lost as of 08/22/99. However, many GPS manufacturers have assured customers that newer versions of their products will continue to function beyond this date.

"Companies with U.S. exposures are more likely to take a greater interest in Y2K problems, because they'll likely face the largest liabilities," said Jacques Blondeau, chairman of the French insurance company SCOR S.A. "U.S. lawyers are already at the starting blocks," he laughed—ruefully.

SCOR reduced its exposure to Year 2000 liabilities by non-renewing insurance contracts with heavy professional liability exposures, especially those programs covering computer manufacturers.

The Lawyers Are Already Moving

If the Y2K losses and liabilities are as severe as some people think, lawsuits—and the resulting insurance claims—are sure to follow. Many insurance companies think of this risk just as they thought of environmental liability claims in the 1980s—namely, as an uncontrollable risk that doesn't have any sensible connection to an underlying economic factor. Faced with an avalanche of unpredictable claims, insurance companies are likely to conclude that they have no choice but to deny coverage and litigate Y2K claims aggressively. This could mean major problems and higher premiums for everyone.

In the mid-1990s, insurance companies that did a lot of business in commercial liability already were beginning to demand that policyholders attest that they were "Y2K compliant." This meant, basically, that they had reviewed their computer systems and made any changes necessary to minimize the impact of the two-digit date.

The significance of this compliance is that it allows insurance companies to reduce major liability exposures when—and if—angry customers, shareholders or other business contacts sue companies for losses caused by Y2K problems.

So, the old irony emerges. Unless a company is willing to become Y2K compliant, commercial liability insurers are likely to exclude coverage for the damages.

Still, some financial analysts insist that in every major business sector there is at least some Y2K litigation potential. Medical-device manufacturers, for example, face possible claims from devices with embedded software and devices that work in conjunction with external systems that are not Y2K compliant. Warehousing companies and distributors that use software for inventory management could reject or dispose of stock that the computer erroneously believes to be a century old, which could lead to third-party claims for damages. And rail-switch manufacturers could be subject to claims should scheduling-related accidents result from their mechanisms switching trains to the wrong track.

And shareholder lawsuits—already a scourge of the computer industry in the 1990s—pose an even larger threat. As a result, a company's directors and officers face the prospect of claims by shareholders concerning their handling of the process of identifying Y2K exposures and remediating them.

The likelihood of big shareholder claims increased following a 1997 ruling from the Delaware Chancery Court which held that:

> ...a director's obligation includes a duty to attempt in good faith to assure that a corporate information and reporting system, which the board concludes is adequate, exists, and that failure to do so under some circumstances may, in theory at least, render a director liable for losses caused by noncompliance with applicable legal standards.

A director has the responsibility to protect the company from losses to tangible assets and business operations—as well as from third-party liability claims and losses. To give directors some freedom to make good decisions, the courts have created a safe-harbor in the form of the so-called "business judgment rule." In simple terms, this rule states that a board of directors can be held liable for broad issues of action or inaction—but not for details of specific choices.

In this context, most companies have protected themselves by taking management or board-level action to mitigate the Y2K problem. But the specific choices a board makes to handle Y2K risks would likely fall within the business-judgment rule.

Still, Y2K losses could first manifest themselves in the directors and officers liability market, said Brian O'Hara, chairman and CEO of X.L. Insurance Co. Ltd., a leading directors and officers liability carrier based in Hamilton, Bermuda. He predicted a blast of litigation against corporate executives as a result of Y2K losses. "We see opportunity in Y2K risks because we aren't exposed," O'Hara said.

While Y2K exposures are often regarded as a liability problem, there is also a significant property exposure if a failure to fix a system results in property damage to the items the system controls, said Herve Cachin, chairman and general manager of Societe Anonyme Francaise de Reassurances (SAFR), a French unit of Partner Re—another liability carrier based in Bermuda.

SAFR asked its reinsurance clients to review their books of business to ensure that policyholders had plans to deal with the Year 2000 problem. "If they do so, we tell them that we are ready to cover the residual risk.... If we are not sure that they have done this, we will put in an exclusion," Cachin said. This exclusion would eliminate Y2K coverage.

On the public policy front, in 1998, the Securities and Exchange Commission issued a legal bulletin declaring that companies must disclose Y2K problems if either the cost of addressing the issue—or the cost of a failure to address the issue—is likely to have a material financial impact on the company. Brian Lane, director of the SEC's division of corporate finance, told the Senate Banking Committee that "companies that fail to take this requirement seriously and do not provide adequate disclosure in the Commission filings run the risk of Commission enforcement action."

Y2K Insurance...and Reinsurance

Insurance companies are increasingly concerned about Year 2000 liability and property losses, and their reinsurers are similarly sizing up the problem. Given the lack of market-wide response to insuring Y2K exposures, during the 1990s individual insurers and reinsurers were left alone to assess their appetite for risk, premium, and market share in determining whether to adopt Y2K exclusions.

For liability policies, one exclusion would totally exclude computer-system related losses "due to the inability to correctly recognize, process, distinguish, interpret or accept the year 2000 and beyond." For property policies, there is a proposed total exclusion for losses "due to the inability to correctly recognize, process, distinguish, interpret or accept one or more dates or times. An example is the inability of computer software to recognize the year 2000."

(Property insurers may simultaneously offer limited, $25,000 coverage for Y2K problems, similar to what they have offered for environmental coverage.)

In addition to these total exclusions, partial exclusions are in circulation: for liability policies, there is (i) an exclusion of all Y2K exposures except for specified locations and (ii) an exclusion of all products and completed-operations Y2K losses (which would preserve premises-operations coverage for Y2K losses under standard liability policies).

In view of the possible introduction of Y2K exclusions and the likelihood of coverage disputes for the losses under standard insurance policies, some insurers have responded by introducing special Y2K insurance policies to these exposures separately. Many of the new policies cover directors and officers liability, business interruption costs, and extra expenses related to operations.

The reinsurance industry is keenly aware of the Y2K risk but generally is counting on ceding companies to manage the exposure.

For those insurers that can't demonstrate that they are responsibly underwriting the exposure, reinsurers may walk away from the risk, some reinsurance executives say.

Even though many questions remain over how the Y2K problem will play out and what policies could be triggered, reinsurers are preparing for losses to be significant. For the most part, there is uncertainty about what Y2K will bring. However, Dirk Lohmann, chief executive officer of

Zurich Insurance Co.'s reinsurance operations, says: "the general consensus is that even for those doing all they can to mitigate the exposure, there will be losses."

Even for those insurance companies that end up not having to pay claims, litigation expenses will likely be large.

Some insurers and reinsurers are taking the position that the Y2K bug is not a covered event, though they may cover other losses that result from Y2K-related malfunctions. But this may not work from a business perspective. Reinsurers can't put a blanket exclusion on all Y2K exposures, said James Bryce, with International Property Catastrophe Reinsurance Ltd. in Bermuda: "It's easy to say `exclude everything,' but then you would sit back and you wouldn't have any business."

Consultants and Coverage Triggers

Most Y2K policies require a detailed risk analysis and engineering assessment whose purpose is to identify loss exposures and their possible magnitude. These audits, which are paid for by the applicant, can cost upwards of $50,000. Some of the insurance policies require the insured to pay for semi-annual or even quarterly risk assessments, and some higher-risk insureds no doubt will be asked to do the same even if the particular insurer does not generally require it.

The complexity of these exclusions—and new policies—has been a bonanza for insurance coverage consultants. (These people seem to crowd around the volatile crisis points of disaster insurance.)

If the 1980s crisis over environmental impairment liability (having mostly to do with asbestos insulation) is any indication, insurance companies will probably try to avoid Y2K coverage by contending that, if any one is responsible for paying out under the standard liability insurance policy language, it is some other insurance company.

This type of finger-pointing between or among insurers will largely be resolved by the determination of the "trigger" of coverage, that is, what event must occur during the policy period for a policy to be activated, which determines which carriers are responsible for the claim.

"Trigger" disputes for other new, mass and expensive liabilities, such as medical-implants, environmental, asbestos and pharmaceutical claims, have taken years—sometimes a decade or more—to resolve.

The trigger positions for Y2K liability claims would appear to lie at either end of a chronological continuum:

- the moment of actual physical injury or the manifestation of physical injury; or
- the moment of the installation of the causative software or the sale of the product incorporating the software, which in most instances will be some years earlier.

In considering the trigger of coverage for Y2K liability claims based on some physical injury or damage, it is useful to group the resulting claims into two categories:

- incidental-injury claims, that is, injury or damage to third parties that has occurred as a result of and collateral to a Y2K failure; and
- intrinsic-failure claims such as a product's inability to perform its intended function because of a Y2K glitch in the governing software.

The courts may be inclined to find that coverage for incidental injury claims is provided by the policy in effect when the physical injury actually occurs; that is, the policy in place in 2000 or beyond. For intrinsic failure claims, the courts are more likely to reach back and trigger the policies in effect when the software was installed or the product utilizing the software was sold.

For both incidental injury and intrinsic failure claims, a compelling case can be made for triggering these earlier policies as courts have done in other contexts.

One example: In cases involving asbestos-in-buildings claims, the courts have found that policies in effect when asbestos-containing building materials were installed in the 1940s, 1950s and 1960s provide coverage for asbestos-related claims made in the 1970s and 1980s. These policies—known as occurrence policies—have become relatively rare in the 1990s. Currently, most liability coverage is offered on a claims-made basis, meaning only claims made during a stated period of time will be considered for coverage.

Where a defective component has been incorporated into a larger system, which in turn fails, courts routinely find that a policy is triggered when the component is installed; there is no reason to differentiate what one court described as a "ticking time bomb" from a leak-prone plumbing system.

This is an extremely bad situation for companies whose businesses will be affected by the software bug.

Government Agencies Are Part of the Problem

When it comes to disasters caused by Y2K bugs, government agencies may not be able to step in and insulate people from loss. They may be up to their bureaucratic necks in the problem themselves.

The General Accounting Office (GAO), the investigative arm of the U.S. Congress, put the situation in unusually breathless terms:

> At 12:01 on New Year's morning of the year 2000, many computer systems worldwide could malfunction or produce incorrect information simply because the date has changed. Unless corrected, the impact of these failures could be widespread and costly.

According to the GAO, "system and application programs that use dates to perform calculations, comparisons, or sorting may generate incorrect results when working with years after 1999." Among its examples for the federal government:

- IRS tax systems could be unable to process returns, which could jeopardize the collection of revenue and the entire tax processing system.
- Payments to veterans with service-connected disabilities could be severely delayed because the Veterans Affairs' compensation and pension system either halts or produces checks that are so erroneous the system must be shut down and the checks processed manually.
- Federal systems used to track student education loans could produce erroneous information on loan status, such as indicating that an unpaid loan had been satisfied.

Reports by the Office of Management and Budget (OMB), which monitors federal computer conversion efforts, noted that—as of November 1997—only 27 percent of mission critical systems were already Year 2000 compliant, and 54 percent are under repair (the remaining are being retired or replaced). However, this did not appear to be aggressive enough to ensure that all such systems would be ready in time.

For example, at the Social Security Administration, which has been addressing the problem for several years and is in the lead among government agencies, some 80 percent of mission critical systems were compliant as of November 1997. At Health and Human Services, 33 percent of systems were compliant.

So, FEMA might have as much trouble bailing itself out of Y2K trouble as everyone else.

CHAPTER THIRTEEN

Arson, Theft and Insurance Fraud

Without any doubt, arson is one of the most common—and most devastating—disasters made by people. It is a major issue because intentional losses like fraud are not covered by standard insurance policies. Your house is not covered if you burn it down yourself (ironically though, a bank that issued you a mortgage will get paid). It may be if someone else burns it down.

Arson is defined legally as "the act of deliberately setting fire to a building, car or other property for fraudulent or malicious purposes." It is a crime in all states; and certain kinds of arson—notably, church arson—are classified as federal crimes.

In late 1997, Richard Geist Jr. and Douglas Moyer, both in their early twenties, were charged with going on a drunken arson spree and causing at least $276,946 in damage in less than two hours the early morning of November 6, 1996.

On their nocturnal rampage, they'd set fire to two buildings, two cars and scarecrows outside the Lower Macungie Elementary School. A house being built in the Hopewell Farms development on Lone Lane in Upper Macungie Township was severely damaged, along with three connected condominiums under construction at the Fairways at Brookside in Lower Macungie. A fourth condominium was destroyed.

Geist entered guilty and no contest pleas to numerous charges, including arson, risking a catastrophe, conspiracy, institutional vandalism and burglary. Moyer pleaded no contest to the same charges.

Defense lawyer James Katz said Moyer was sorry about what happened and realizes it was a "silly thing" to do. "'Silly' is probably a little bit too weak," Lehigh County, Pennsylvania, Judge Thomas A. Wallitsch responded.

Assistant District Attorney James Anthony asked for long maximum sentences for Moyer and Geist so they have a chance to work and pay restitution to individual victims and insurance companies. "I want these individuals...to realize they have significant responsibility to pay back the victims," Anthony said.

Other than that morning when they got drunk and decided to do "some potentially dangerous" things, the prosecutor said, both men led law-abiding lives. "They are lucky they didn't cause any serious bodily injury," Anthony said. A long period of supervision, he added, would ensure that if the men step out of line with the law, they will go to a state prison. "I want them to realize there is a price to pay for their stupidity," he concluded.

The sentencings were delayed briefly when the prosecutor and defense lawyers renegotiated the terms of the plea bargains so the men could serve their sentences in Lehigh County Prison instead of a state correctional institution.

Defense lawyers feared that if the men were sent to a state prison, their chances of release would be slim because of the state Board of Probation and Parole's apparent reluctance to parole defendants. Wallitsch told the men he didn't think they belonged in a state prison now, but warned them they will be headed there if they violate conditions of their parole over the next 10 years.

Judge Wallitsch ordered Geist and Moyer to make regular payments on restitution during the 10 years they will be under court supervision. Failing to make payments could result in a parole violation and their incarceration in a state prison.

Moyer, who'd been free on bail but spent several days in jail after his arrest, was sentenced to nine months to six years in Lehigh County Prison, plus an additional four years' probation. Geist, who was considered the ringleader of a small group of young losers, was sentenced to one to six years in the county jail and four years' probation. He also was ordered to pay a $1,000 fine.

Both men would have to do community service.

"It's a sobering fact: in the last year, 500,000 arson fires were set. They killed more than 500 Americans and destroyed more than $3 billion of property," says FEMA director James Witt. "Arson is the leading cause of death for pre-schoolers, accounting for 85 of every 100 deaths. What is disturbing is that one out of every four fires is intentionally set."

Insurance companies have an interest in preventing arson-because the fires cause needless loss of life and property and also push up the cost of insurance for homeowners, vehicle owners and owners of commercial buildings. But insurance companies have an even more immediate interest in detecting arson-because, in many cases, they don't have to pay arson claims.

An important tool arson investigators use for sharing information is the Property Insurance Loss Register (PILR), administered by the American Insurance Services Group, Inc. Nearly 900 insurers representing more than 90 percent of all the fire insurance premiums written in the United States now file their claims with PILR. Of the nearly 70,000 reports PILR receives each month, about 14 percent are flagged as suspect, thereby increasing dramatically the chance that an arsonist will be caught.

The information in the system, which helps identify suspicious fire patterns, is available to insurers investigating claims and, on occasion, to law enforcement agencies. Most fire fighters and police officers have basic training in arson detection.

To further this effort, a series of recent state laws allow a free exchange of information between insurers and law enforcement agencies in suspicious cases (these laws eliminate the threat of civil suits for libel or violation of privacy).

These moves are having an effect. According to the National Fire Protection Association, in 1997 the number of structure fires that were suspicious or deliberately set dropped to the lowest level in the previous 10 years. The NFPA estimated that there were 78,500 structure fires of an incendiary or suspicious nature in 1997, down 8.2 percent from 1996. (In 1988, there had been 99,500 such fires.) The cost of these fires declined by 6.8 percent from 1996 to $1.3 billion.

Still, arson remains the second leading cause of residential fire deaths and accounts for approximately 25 percent of all fires in the United States. The crimes are hard to solve-only about 16 percent of cases end in arrests, according to the FBI.

Fires that were deliberately set or suspected of being deliberately set accounted for 13.8 percent of all fires in structures and vehicles in 1997 and for 18.2 percent of property loss in structure and vehicles.

Studies point to vandalism as the leading cause of arson. An Insurance Research Council study suggests only 14 percent of arson suspects are motivated by a desire to defraud an insurance company but other studies suggest the arson-for-profit rate is higher. And arsonists are surprisingly young. People under 18 years of age account for more than half of all arson arrests. Analysts note young people commit arson out of a desire to vandalize property and for the thrill of seeing a building burn. These factors make fire claims more complex when arson is the cause of insured fire losses.

Arson rates are highest in large cities. In 1996, cities with over 1 million inhabitants had an arson rate of 90 per 100,000 people. In cities of all sizes, the rate was 51. Suburban counties registered an arson rate of 33 offenses per 100,000 people, and rural counties had a rate of 19 per 100,000 people.

Insurers have other basic methods of controlling arson. They can ask prospective insureds to fill out an investigative questionnaire, known as an anti-arson two-tier application, that may alert agents and underwriters to prior fire losses, tax liens against properties, fire-code violations and other indicators of danger ahead. It also can signal to the insured that the company is aware of these problems; that knowledge, in turn, may deter an arsonist. Another strategy is to ensure that the policyholder signs the application, thus giving the insurer grounds to deny a claim if false statements are made.

Anti-arson efforts represent one of the earliest organized activities of the insurance industry in America. The National Board of Fire Underwriters, one of the oldest business organizations in the country, was formed in 1866, partly in response to the problem of arson. In 1926 the Association of Casualty and Surety Companies was founded. One of its major divisions was a fraud bureau.

Theft

Under most personal insurance policies, theft losses are covered. However, commercial policies written for businesses offer more limited coverage. And FEMA offers a stripped-down crime insurance policy for businesses in rough neighborhoods, which creates some complex disputes.

The July 1996 federal court decision *Joel Sherman v. Federal Emergency Management Agency* dealt with a dispute over a FEMA commercial crime insurance policy.

Sherman owned and operated Sherman's Liquors, a small grocery/liquor store located in Baltimore. In June 1994, he had obtained robbery insurance from FEMA under the National Insurance Development Program.

This program, designed to help insure businesses operating in economically distressed areas, was created by Congress as part of the National Housing Act of 1970. It is administered—like the flood insurance program—by FEMA. However, when you consider how the coverage works, questions invariably arise about why FEMA is in this line of business.

On his application Sherman indicated that he owned a retail liquor store—but failed to advise FEMA that he also operated a check cashing business, apparently because he considered this operation a "sideline." (He was consistent in this practice, describing his business as a liquor store in his tax filings.)

But the sideline changed the nature of Sherman's operation. He kept large amounts of cash on the premises in order to conduct his check cashing business.

A month after Sherman bought the insurance, two armed bandits robbed him at the store. They got away with $9,285, most of it in cash. On the following day, the bandits returned and stole another $5,150— again with the bulk of the loss in cash.

Sherman filed a claim and requested payment from FEMA in accordance with the terms of his commercial crime insurance policy.
In late July 1994, an independent adjuster retained by FEMA indicated that "it was likely" that Sherman was robbed of the amount he claimed. This adjuster recommended that FEMA pay Sherman's claim. However, FEMA refused to pay because Sherman had failed to document his losses adequately. The agency argued that the sloppy record-keeping at

Sherman's "mom and pop" operation made it difficult, if not impossible, to verify the amount of the loss.

Sherman tried to satisfy FEMA's demand for documentation. He produced more substantial documents, including bank statements and the like. FEMA retained an accounting firm to conduct a review. Ultimately, on the recommendation of that firm, FEMA issued a final decision declining Sherman's claim.

Sherman sued, seeking to recover approximately $15,000 from FEMA. The agency countered with a multi-part request that the court throw out Sherman's suit.

The court started out by defining the issues it would consider. "Although FEMA has expressed skepticism over the timing of the robberies, there is no suggestion that Sherman has perpetrated a fraud."

The program under which Sherman obtained his crime insurance spoke pretty directly to the claims. It required that "the insured shall keep records of all the insured property in such a manner that [FEMA] can accurately determine therefrom the amount of the loss, and if the insured maintains cash funds for the purpose of check cashing, a complete record of each check negotiated shall be kept by the insured...."

FEMA argued that Sherman did not comply with these record-keeping provisions, so it could not verify the amount of loss that he had suffered. In support of its argument that Sherman's record-keeping was inadequate, FEMA pointed to an admission by Sherman that "I do not keep in a ledger the amount of money I bring in each day to the store. However, be assured that I am aware of exactly how much cash I do bring to the store each day."

Even though he couldn't use his own records to provide an accurate account of his losses, Sherman wanted FEMA to accept his good faith effort at recollection as to how much cash and property the robbers had stolen.

Making matters worse, Sherman's own expert witness was unable to verify the amount of the claim after reviewing Sherman's records. Under questioning, the expert stated "I was never able to determine the amount of available cash on hand at the time these robberies occurred."

So, the court concluded: "The uncontroverted evidence reveals that Sherman failed to meet his contractual obligation to maintain records of all insured property in such manner that [FEMA] can accurately determine therefrom the amount of the loss."

In a previous crime program coverage dispute, an earlier federal court had held that, although the insured's bank statements provided some record of its check cashing activity, those statements were "insufficient because they provide no indication as to the actual amount of money and checks on the premises at any given time."

The court hearing the Sherman case ruled that the same reasoning applied. Specifically, it wrote:

> Although it is likely that the culprits stole a substantial amount of cash from Sherman's store during the two robberies, his failure to maintain adequate records makes it impossible to determine exactly how much money (or property) was stolen. The indisputable purpose of FEMA's record-keeping requirements is to make available verifiable proof that a specific loss in fact occurred. When verifiable proof is not available because the insured failed to comply with the record-keeping requirements, FEMA need not pay such claims.

Sherman relied heavily on the fact that the independent adjuster initially hired by FEMA to investigate the loss determined that "it was likely" that Sherman had been robbed and recommended payment. Sherman argued that the investigator's statements proved that he had complied with the record-keeping requirements. The court didn't agree: "This argument is flawed. The independent adjuster does not represent FEMA and his statements cannot bind FEMA."

In fact, the burden of proof on making a claim against FEMA was more heavy than Sherman realized. Federal courts have held consistently that, in order to "maintain an action against a federal agency on an insurance policy, there must be strict compliance with the terms of the government issued insurance policy."

This is an important point for anyone thinking about suing FEMA. The conditions applicable to Sherman's insurance policy required that "the insured shall keep records of all the insured property in such a manner that [FEMA] can accurately determine therefrom the amount of the loss, and if the insured maintains cash funds for the purpose of check cashing, a complete record of each check negotiated shall be kept by the insured...."

From this starting point, the federal court concluded that Sherman had failed to present facts sufficient to show he had complied with the record-keeping requirements of the policy. It wrote:

> It is not enough to show, as has Sherman, merely that a loss was suffered. Neither FEMA nor a fact finder at trial is required (or allowed) to engage in guesswork to determine the exact amount of the loss, or to assume that some minimum or "conservative" estimate of the loss is compensable. More than that is required.

So, the court ruled that FEMA didn't have to pay Sherman's claim. The moral of the story: He should have kept better books.

Bogus Insurance Claims and Other Scams

According to the National Insurance Crime Bureau, approximately 10 percent of all insurance claims are fraudulent—though some experts believe the figure is much higher.

People who are looking for fast money after a disaster don't have much shame. Unscrupulous solicitors may ask for donations for bogus support charities. If you do not recognize that the organization is affiliated locally, make your contributions to the Red Cross or other locally known charity.

"There are groups of people who go from one disaster area to another trying to defraud unwary victims," said Gailee Cardwell of the Florida Department of Emergency Management. "They know there's quick money to be made."

Another common form of fraud occurs after floods and other disasters. Homeowners not affected by the disaster try to obtain financial grants or inflate their damage estimates. "People see an opportunity to make some easy money from the government, so they take it," said Mary Hudak of the Federal Emergency Management Agency. "It takes away from real victims."

FEMA has a system in place to identify the very small percentage of applicants taking advantage of the system by obtaining disaster assistance which they are not qualified to receive. It performs on-site inspections immediately after the disaster to confirm the damage to each house. The initial inspection is done in a couple of hours and is meant to get financial assistance to victims as soon as possible.

The agency audits a random sample of 5 percent to 10 percent of the aims a couple of months after the disaster. Some audits ask for receipts and other paperwork through the mail, but others include another on-site inspection. "It's in everybody's interest to make sure that the money is appropriately received and appropriately spent," Hudak said.

"Managing a multi-million dollar disaster program always means walking a fine line between speedy service to those who need it and ensuring that taxpayer dollars are not misused," Federal Coordinating Officer José A. Bravo of FEMA's San Juan, Puerto Rico, office said in the days following Hurricane Georges.

According to Bravo, a number of methods are used to detect fraud. An automated system cross-checks information with other agencies and insurance companies to weed out duplicate applications. Field inspections are conducted to verify losses and damages for every person who applies. Potential cases of fraud or misuse are referred to the U.S. Justice Department for prosecution.

Other types of applicant fraud include:

- people who claim residences that are not their primary residence;
- applicants who leave out a spouse's information when registering;
- self-inflicted damages;
- spouses claiming different addresses; and
- people that fail to disclose insurance coverage.

"Federal disaster aid is paid with taxpayers' money," said Paul J. Lillis, assistant inspector general for the Investigations Division of FEMA's Office of the Inspector General. "While we do not want to deter anyone from applying for federal assistance, we will enforce the law to protect honest citizens and keep disaster funds out of the hands of those who would commit criminal acts."

Still, the most common type of abuse that plagues disaster relief systems is less flamboyant than fake charities or fabricated losses. Most of the harm is done by claims padding—the less noticeable inflation of real claims.

The problem is serious. One example: California's insurance industry takes in about $63 billion each year in premiums. About a third of that figure is used to pay for fraud committed by various parties—including consumers, contractors, auto-body shop owners and others.

To gather evidence on claims that appear fraudulent many insurers have set up their own Special Investigation Units (SIUs). Almost every major insurance company has formed an SIU or a unit with a similar function to investigate such claims, and most were using these units to investigate vehicular and homeowner arson. One chief executive officer stated that there was a savings of about 6-to-1—meaning that for every dollar spent, six dollars are saved in payments for fraudulent claims.

Under most state laws, it is a felony to submit knowingly a bogus or inflated repair bill for a property loss insurance claim. But the person submitting the insurance claim isn't always in on the fraud. In fact, the most common frauds after a disaster are often perpetrated by contractors. "After every significant natural catastrophe, there are some individuals and businesses who flock to the area to prey on homeowners," said Henry (Butch) Viccellio, president of USAA Property and Casualty Insurance Group. "There are a number of red flags that homeowners should notice."

Among the red flags, homeowners should not do business with contractors who:

- arrive at your home without being called;
- have no local office or telephone number;
- lack proper references or equipment to do work;
- estimate costs that are below-market;
- demand cash or up-front fees before starting repair work; or
- cannot show licenses, proof of insurance or bonding.

There may be no way to prevent a bad, determined contractor from ripping off insurance companies—and consumers. But a few common sense tactics can make it harder for the crooks. In the wake of a disaster, consumers should:

- contact their insurance companies;
- obtain at least three quotes before authorizing repair work—and get all estimates in writing;
- never deal with unlicensed contractors;
- never pay large (that is, more than 20 percent) down payments;

- set priorities for repairs that need to be done immediately to preserve a homes condition.

Some repairs, like fence rebuilding or removal of downed tree limbs that do not threaten homes, can be reserved for a later date.

In many states, it's a felony for an unlicensed contractor to make repairs in a disaster area. According to C. Lance Barnett, who heads the California Contractors State License Board, there's good reason for this. One of the most common tactics is for the scam artists to demand large, upfront deposits from customers, and then to disappear without performing any work.

"Whenever there's a disaster, these people come out like locusts," Barnett says. "Unscrupulous contractors often inflict more damage than what follows a natural disaster. We're just trying to stop a natural disaster from becoming a man-made one."

The June 1996 federal court decision *Plywood Property Associates, et al., v. NFIP, et al.*, dealt with a situation that was either a considerable bureaucratic error...or an ingenious fraud. In either case, it shows how FEMA proceeds when it thinks someone is making a false claim.

Saul and Morris Friedman owned Plywood Property Associates, which they operated out of offices and a warehouse building in Bergen County, New Jersey.

On December 11, 1992, a severe storm occurred in many areas of the northeastern United States. Due to the intensity of the storm, a limited state of emergency was declared in all of the counties of New Jersey by Governor James Florio.

Plywood's warehouse was apparently damaged as a result of floods produced by the storm. The Friedmans quickly made a claim on their SFIP, in force on the date of the storm. On or about December 11, Plywood retained Merit Adjusters, Inc. as a public adjuster to review its claim. Merit and Plywood entered into an unusual contingency fee agreement, whereby Merit was to receive 12.5 percent of any amount received pursuant to the Proof of Loss submitted under the SFIP.

Merit insisted that, as an adjuster, it merely acted as a conduit between

Plywood and FEMA for the submission of the claim. However, many of Merit's actions would credibly suggest that Merit's principals were more intimately involved in several aspects of the preparation and submission of Plywood's claim.

Merit's principals met with FEMA's public adjuster and inspected the property in January 1993. As a rule, they also represented Plywood in discussions with FEMA.

Plywood submitted two separate Proofs of Loss—through Merit—to FEMA. The first document was submitted February 9, 1993. The second, answering specific questions raised by FEMA, was submitted April 8. In each document, Plywood notified FEMA of its intention to recover under the SFIP for damages allegedly sustained during the storm.

In the second Proof of Loss, Plywood indicated that it had sustained damages to company property in an amount of $484,000. Therefore, it sought to recover the full policy limit of $250,000. In a letter dated May 24, 1993, FEMA informed Plywood that its claim was being denied.

Almost a year later, on May 19, 1994, Plywood filed a lawsuit against FEMA and the Pennsylvania Lumbermans Mutual Insurance Company to assert its right to insurance coverage under its policies for flood damage to the commercial property.

FEMA answered the lawsuit and filed a third party complaint against Plywood and Merit, contending that they knowingly submitted false Proofs of Claim in violation of the False Claims Act. (As we will see later, Plywood's claims may not have been completely legitimate.) FEMA asked the court for a summary judgment dismissing Plywood's complaint. Plywood and Merit asked the court to dismiss FEMA's complaint.

FEMA argued that the damages Plywood claimed its property sustained as a result of the December 1992 storm were not covered by the SFIP. For this reason, it argued that the court should dismiss Plywood's claim. Relevant to FEMA's point, the SFIP makes an important exclusion to its coverage:

> PERILS EXCLUDED: The Insurer shall not be liable for loss [caused by] land sinkage, land subsidence, landslide, gradual erosion, or any other earth movement except such mudslides (i.e. mudflows) or erosion as is covered under the peril of flood.

Plywood claimed that damage to its property was a direct loss from a flood—and not specifically excluded from coverage. In support of this claim, Plywood relied on the expert opinion of Andrew Stein as to the causation of the damages to its property.

At his deposition, Stein confirmed that it was his opinion that, after the earth under the footings of the warehouse had been washed away, the footings of the foundation wall settled. This caused the cracking of the structure of the perimeter walls.

Plywood claimed that this testimony established that the damage to its property had been caused by earth movement resulting directly from the December 1992 storm. The SFIP is more precise, though. It excludes damages resulting from any earth movements other than those caused by "erosion as is covered under the peril of flood" or mudslide.

So, Plywood had to demonstrate that the damaging earth movement had been caused by flood-related erosion or mudslide in order to bring the damages within the scope of the SFIP.

Flood-related erosion, within the meaning of the SFIP, is defined as:

> The collapse or subsidence of land along the shore of a lake or other body of water as a result of erosion or undermining caused by waves or currents of water exceeding anticipated cyclical levels or suddenly caused by an unusually high water level in a natural body of water, accompanied by a severe storm, or by an unanticipated force of nature, such as flash flood or an abnormal tidal surge, or by some similarly unusual and unforeseeable event which results in flooding.

FEMA argued that the alleged damage to Plywood's property was not covered by the SFIP, since any water on the property came from an overflowing drain pipe—and not a natural body of water.

Plywood claimed that there was a natural body of water flowing from the Saddle River through its property—and that the December 1992 storm caused this body to overflow. In this claim, Plywood relied on the declaration of a local lawyer who stated that:

> On or about April 3, 1996, I drove to [the Plywood warehouse] and found the body of water located in front of the warehouse building ...I followed said body of water until it went underground [and reemerged], continuing on as an open brook... I followed said brook in my car to a point where it opened up from a tunnel and continued

> to enter into Saddle River... I went to the Bergen County Hall of Records, and found said brook on the tax maps...The body of water that I followed is labeled on the tax maps as a brook...and not as a drainage ditch.

So, Plywood claimed, its property was located "along the shore of [a] body of water" and the erosion of its land amounted to "erosion as is covered under the peril of flood" within the meaning of the SFIP.

The court recognized there might be some uncertainty about Plywood's claim—but that FEMA couldn't establish with any degree of certainty that the claim was bogus. It ruled:

> ...this Court cannot find as a matter of law, that the alleged damages to [Plywood]'s property are not covered by the SFIP.... For the reasons set forth above, FEMA's motion for summary judgment will be denied.

Next, it turned to the government's claim that Plywood and Merit Adjusters, Inc., had violated the False Claims Act. Specifically, the government argued that Plywood and Merit had knowingly submitted a false claim for payment upon their submission of the Proof of Loss.

Plywood and Merit asked the court to issue a summary judgment dismissing this charge.

As defined by the False Claims Act, a "claim" can be any request or demand for money or property which is made to "a contractor, grantee, or other recipient if the United States Government provides any portion of the money or property which is requested or demanded."

"Claims" within the meaning of the Act can take many forms. As the court hearing the Plywood case noted:

> A Proof of Loss claim submitted to FEMA for the collection of insurance benefits under an SFIP is clearly an "attempt to cause the Government to pay out sums of money[,]" and therefore, is a "claim" within the meaning of the Act.

The court then turned to the question of whether a reasonable fact-finder could find that the Proof of Loss submitted to FEMA was false or fraudulent and knowingly presented by Plywood and/or Merit.

The False Claims Act emphasizes that "no proof of specific intent to defraud is required," however, "[i]nnocent mistakes or negligence are not actionable under [the Act]." Plywood and Merit claimed the government had failed to produce sufficient evidence from which a fact-finder could conclude that they knowingly submitted a false claim.

But the government had produced the following evidence:

- An October 1992 letter to Morris Friedman from Marcus Associates, indicating that "the building as I am sure you know, is in disrepair, and will require a substantial investment on a new user's part to renovate/modernize it."
- The declaration of a former Plywood employee, stating that the vertical cracks on the upper left corner of the face of the building were present prior to the December 1992 storm and that "[a]s a general matter the building was not in good condition when operations stopped and the building was up for sale before the [storm]."
- Plywood's answers to FEMA's pretrial questions indicating that "[t]here was no damage to the masonry at the left corner of the premises prior to the flood of December 11, 1992[,]" and that "[t]here was no cracking of the left side rear wall and rear wall prior to the [storm]."
- A December 1995 letter to one of FEMA's attorneys from Plywood's attorney, amending Plywood's "answers to interrogatories to indicate that there was a minor crack located at the top of the front left side corner of the subject premises which pre-existed the [storm]."

This contradictory information at least suggested a false claim. And that was all it needed to do to proceed to trial. The court ruled that, because there was "a factual dispute which is both genuine and material as to whether the Proof of Loss contained information which was false or fraudulent," this claim would also go to trial.

Though Mother Nature has much greater power than man, intentional man-made disasters can be costly...and complicated.

CHAPTER FOURTEEN

Terrorism

Early Wednesday morning, April 19, 1995, a rented truck parked on the street in the front of the Alfred P. Murrah Federal Building in Oklahoma City. A few hours later, just after nine o'clock, the truck exploded—destroying most of the building in a cloud of fire and dust. Physical shock waves from the blast could be felt as far as thirty miles away.

Criminal investigators would later determine that the truck bomb had been constructed from several hundred pounds of fertilizer and non-electric igniters and blasting caps used in military demolition work. It was crude—but horribly effective.

Before the smoke had cleared completely, morgue workers had tagged 12 small pairs of feet. There belonged to children who were in a second-floor day-care center right above the spot where the bomb exploded. "It was really terrible," said a state politician, who'd been half a block away when the blast occurred. "Babies were crying and screaming, with blood and plaster and insulation on their bodies."

Eyewitnesses described the scene in fairly consistent—and thoroughly hellish—detail. "We can see people trapped, and we can't get to them," said Deputy Fire Chief Jon Hansen. "They're crying and screaming and weeping in there."

One doctor told a television news crew that he had to amputate a woman's right leg in order to get her out of the rubble. "These are wartime injuries," said the physician.

"What is it like?" said one firefighter. "It's like Beirut. It was a bomb, not an earthquake, not a tornado."

As days inched by after the explosion, the scene grew ever more dangerous. While the disaster response crews searched for survivors, workers from the morgue and from the federal Centers for Disease Control and

Prevention (CDC) stood by, dressed in white plastic body suits. They were present to monitor contamination from the decomposing bodies, which can emit a toxic bacterial gas. Firefighters removing the bodies wore disposable jumpsuits. After contact with corpses, they were sprayed with a commercial disinfectant.

In the days after the Oklahoma City explosion, telephone bomb threats led authorities to evacuate government buildings in New York; Detroit; Omaha, Neb.; Wilmington, Del.; Dallas; Fort Worth, Texas; Boise, Idaho; Portland, Ore.; Cincinnati; Dayton, Ohio; Steubenville, Ohio; Fresno, Calif.; East Palo Alto, Calif.; Riverside, Calif.; and Santa Ana, Calif.

Some people expected that the perpetrators of the Oklahoma City bombing to be agents of some foreign political group. However, the people responsible turned out to be native sons. Timothy McVeigh, a former soldier with right-wing leanings, and an alleged handful of accomplices planned and executed the crime.

Hoping to advance a political position that combined white supremacy with abject paranoia, McVeigh only served to make his beliefs even more repugnant—to a greater number of people—than they'd been before. As moronic as his mission may have been, McVeigh did lodge a wake-up call for many Americans: Terrorism was a bigger risk than most of them had thought.

Less than two years earlier, another bomb in a van had exploded in a parking garage under New York's World Trade Center. That attack killed six people and injured more than a thousand, crippling the twin 110-story towers and paralyzing Wall Street.

In that case, the perpetrators had been agents of a foreign group. Four minions of a cracked fundamentalist Islamic cleric detonated the bomb. With two incidents in relatively close succession, people—and insurance companies—started to rethink their opinions about domestic terrorism.

Still, despite the fears caused by the Oklahoma City and World Trade Center bombings, the greatest risk of terrorism loss occurs for most Americans when they travel abroad.

Increasingly, executives who travel abroad have kidnap and ransom (K&R) insurance policies through their employers. One asset of any organization is represented by its employees and its executive talent. Loss of such talent due to kidnapping is one—increasingly insurable—peril that proactive risk managers must address.

Underwriters such as Lloyd's of London provide K&R insurance. If you have employees who live or travel abroad, this coverage may need to be an essential addition to your insurance portfolio.

A curious but understandable condition is that of confidentiality: If it becomes known that an individual or a company has K&R insurance, the policy coverage automatically becomes void.

This is an interesting twist on the belief held by many that "having insurance only encourages claims."

Everyone fears the most rare and tragic of circumstances: the fatal terrorist attack. However, despite reports of terrorism, random crime and assaults pose the greatest threats to Americans abroad. Distinctly American clothing, jewelry, watches, corporate luggage tags, and loud speaking voices all identify candidates for violent crime.

Travelers tend to be most at risk at airports and in the vicinity of hotels, restaurants, and tourist sites.

Kidnappings of executives and their families have soared in several nations—mainly Colombia, Mexico, Brazil, and the Philippines. Most of these incidents ensnare well-to-do and middle-class locals, such as business owners, politicians, land owners, and bankers. Usually, they end safely once a ransom has been paid.

Perhaps a dozen such kidnappings a year involve American citizens, say security experts. Among foreigners visiting all locations, about 600 kidnappings have taken place since 1990, according to kidnap negotiation experts at Control Risks, Inc.

Cigna is one of several U.S. insurance companies that provide insurance coverage against the criminal calamities that may befall traveling executives. Other providers are Fireman's Fund, American International Group, and Chubb. Lloyd's of London, the venerable British institution, underwrites three-fourths of the world's kidnapping and ransom coverage. All told, reports Sedgwick, premiums for K&R insurance amounted to roughly $120 million in 1997, a 20 percent increase since 1993. Rates vary, but $5,000 will often cover several executives against limited risk. Blanket coverage in high-risk areas can cost $20,000 and up.

But, when it comes to terrorism risks, insurance is merely a backstop when preventive measures fail.

HOTTEST SPOTS FOR TERRORISM RISKS

Country	Incidents
1. Colombia	667
2. Algeria	380
3. Sri Lanka	268
4. Pakistan	209
5. India	192
6. France (Corsica-119)	132
7. Mexico	97
8. Spain	89
9. Burundi	85
10. Russia	78
11. U.K. (N. Ireland-61)	66
12. Peru	61
13. Philippines	61
14. Lebanon	47
15. Turkey	45
16. Bosnia-Herzegovinia	44
17. Venezuela	44
18. Albania	41
19. Tadzhikistan	40
20. Yugoslavia	38
Total	2,684

Source: Pinkerton Global Intelligence Services

In the spring of 1998, Pennsylvania-based IOA Re launched Strategic Underwriters International (SUI), a specialty insurer and reinsurer of kidnap & ransom and extortion coverage.

Kathleen Hutchinson, SUI's account executive, said her company has seen increased kidnapping activity around the world, but particularly in Colombia, where there is growing guerilla activity. "These people go out and kidnap people. It's how they make their living," she said, explaining that many kidnappers commit the crime for money.

Most Fortune 100 companies already carry insurance to cover terrorist's activities, Hutchinson said. SUI isn't looking to compete in this market; instead, it targets smaller companies that increasingly do business globally.

Teaching companies to protect themselves is just as important as insuring a potential loss, Hutchinson said. SUI provides loss consultants who help companies see where they are at risk and shows them how to protect themselves. They also show companies how to protect themselves from people who could plant bombs in their businesses. SUI also writes policies for families and individual tourists.

"If you're a U.S. company or a U.S. citizen you're perceived to have money," Hutchinson said. The motive is almost always profit, she said. "it could start out as a political statement and end up to be a ransom demand."

The risks are also increasing stateside, where extortion poses the biggest threat, Hutchinson said. "Here, you have more of an extortion threat than a kidnap threat. But what we have here in the U.S. that other countries do not have is the FBI, and they're very good at their job," she said.

Often, if someone is successful in getting money through kidnapping or extortion, the FBI nabs them before they can spend the money, she said. Political risk experts acknowledge that the lines between political terrorism, organized crime and drug and arms dealers are becoming increasingly blurred and hard to discern. As a result, identifying the source of threats to international companies and their employees is becoming more complicated.

Security experts argue that it's increasingly difficult to tell what kind of group is threatening who and why. "One of the problems is that all of the standard guidelines to identify these groups have gone. Since the end of the Cold War, the ideological basis and state backing (for terrorism) has gone. A lot of groups are involved with drugs or weapons dealing. The situation is much more complex, and it's very murky," said Alison Jameson, a European consultant in organized crime and political terrorism.

Even though the political risk insurance market might seem like the last place to expect a government-subsidized program...there is one. In addition to the private sector, the government-backed Overseas Private

Investment Corp. (OPIC) provides political risk insurance to U.S. companies in selected countries. OPIC wrote $16.5 billion in premiums during its 1996 fiscal year in political risk coverage.

Political risk coverage encompasses risks for political events, such as confiscation or nationalization of property by a foreign government, and contract risks, such as not being able to get money out of a foreign country, non-payment by a government or cancellation of an import/export license.

Also, policies cover losses from divesting operations in another country if it is required by U.S. law. Last—and most importantly—political risk covers property loss from wars, strikes and terrorism.

What's the U.S. government doing writing insurance for companies doing business abroad? Some insurance experts point out that the OPIC program is a leftover from the Cold War, when the government wanted to encourage businesses to expand in selected countries.

But others with experience in the market say that OPIC is really no different than NFIP. It's a faulty product of bureaucrats trying to direct public policy—with unintended consequences.

The summer of 1998 saw a lot of motion in the terrorism insurance markets. The previous spring's peace talks between the IRA and the British government seemed to calm violence in the U.K. Some of the London speciality insurance markets began to experiment with new forms of terrorism coverage.

In August 1998, Paul Bawcutt, Chairman of the London-based Risk & Insurance Research Group wrote in an opinion piece:

> ...[One] area where the industry has failed to respond to the needs of buyers is with terrorism risks. Some years ago, we were told that reinsurers were so disturbed about the increasing cost of property damage and business interruption claims arising out of terrorism in the United Kingdom that they would no longer provide any cover. As a result, Pool Re was formed to deal specifically with this risk exposure.
>
> The premiums quoted were extremely high, and have continued to be high despite a degree of competition from other markets.... Given the increasingly competitive and soft insurance market, it is amazing that

> this structure continues to exist, particularly as the gap between terrorism premiums and conventional premiums is wider and wider.... It's blatantly obvious that reinsurers should now be able to restore terrorism coverage within treaties, enable the primary companies to reinstate coverage and treat terrorism the same as they do other risks like arson, subsidence, earthquakes and floods. These natural disaster risks, in fact, produce much higher losses than terrorism ever has or is likely to in the future.

Also in August 1998, Wellington Underwriting PLC, a specialty London-based insurer, announced that it was launching an insurance policy to protect companies against biological terrorist attacks.

"This will appeal to anyone who feels that their business could be in danger," said Ben Garston, senior underwriter at Wellington. The insurance company already offered a range of political risk, war and terrorist products. But these only covered physical damage from fire and explosion and resultant loss of revenue—not for loss of revenue caused by chemical or other contamination.

"Furthermore, buildings rendered unusable for a considerable length of time may, while structurally intact, effectively become valueless," Garston said. "We will be working with major international brokers to sell [the coverage]. We'll provide coverage anywhere in the world."

And, still in August 1998, after attacks on U.S. embassies in Kenya and Tanzania and U.S. retaliatory attacks in Sudan and Afghanistan, travel agencies and terrorism experts were issuing advisories for American tourists overseas.

Federal and local authorities stepped up security measures in response to terrorist attacks in east Africa. Curiously, U.S. citizens didn't seem to be canceling overseas travel plans because of perceived threats.
The U.S. State Department issued an unusual worldwide caution that recommended travelers review their security arrangements, stay alert to changing conditions and exercise greater caution than usual.

"We had a lot of people scheduled to go to Africa shortly after the bombings who canceled their trips," said one San Diego-based travel agent. "Our rule of thumb is we'll cover cancellations for 30 days after a terrorist incident. We think that's a reasonable amount of time." He said that call volume jumped about 20 percent after the African bombings.

Pool Reinsurance Co. Ltd., the government-backed reinsurer of U.K. mainland terrorism risks, announced it would review premium rates in the wake of the historic Stormont Agreement signed in Northern Ireland on April 10. The agreement was supported by two public votes—one in Northern Ireland and one in Ireland—for a Northern Ireland assembly and potentially ended a conflict that had spilled onto the British mainland for decades.

Pool Re was set up in March 1993 after an Irish Republican Army bomb had ripped through London's financial district the previous April, resulting in almost $600 million in damage. In response to the IRA attack, insurers removed terrorism coverage from property programs and the government stepped in, authorizing the creation of Pool Re and acting as a reinsurer of last resort should claims exceed Pool Re's assets.

In the absence of terrorism claims in 1996 and 1997, Pool Re had already discounted premiums once in 1998—by 20 percent for properties in cities and 40 percent for properties elsewhere. The second round of discounts would lower premiums by as much as 80 percent.

According to Pool Re Chief Executive Leslie Lucas, the decision to reduce premiums so drastically was proposed to Treasury by the Pool Re board. At the same time, the board took the opportunity to simplify some of the aspects of Pool Re's rating system and bring its practices into line with the rest of the insurance market.

For example: Pool Re placed terrorism risks in one of four zones: central London; inner London and central business districts of specific large towns and cities; the rest of England, except for Devon and Cornwall; and the rest of Great Britain. Rates were different for each zone.

In October 1998, companies in Great Britain applauded a government announcement that terrorism premiums would be heavily discounted by the end of year. But many risk managers said that the insurance—sold on a stand-alone basis—should be reinstated into standard commercial property insurance policies.

The late 1998 discounts would also change that rate structure. The four categories would be streamlined into two rates: 0.015 percent as a multiple of the property value for the first two zones, and 0.003 percent for the other two.

An alternative terrorism insurance market, started in about 1994 to provide buyers with a choice of insurers and products, remained popular and showed little sign of crumbling at Pool Re's announcement.

"This has an impact on the bottom line because we have seen rates reduce very dramatically," said Phillip Perry, terrorism underwriter at Lloyd's Hiscox syndicate 33, part of Hiscox P.L.C. Reductions were anticipated, but not to this degree, he said. Even so, Hiscox's U.K. Terrorism Unit planned to continue to write terrorism coverage with rates lower than the Pool Re rate.

In addition, Hiscox offers coverage on a building-by-building basis. Pool Re, which as a tariff insurer provides only preset rates and terms, will cover only an entire property portfolio.

Commercial demand for terrorism insurance in England, Scotland and Wales remained steady despite 1998's peace agreement. Why? Terrorism had not abated. There were killings and bombings in Northern Ireland after the peace agreement was signed. Still, some Lloyd's underwriters offered coverage at rates between 10 percent and 20 percent lower than Pool Re.

In her statement to Parliament, Patricia Hewitt said:

> The discount will be withdrawn if, in the course of the year, significant new claims are notified to Pool Re. This would affect subsequent new or renewed policies.... Despite the relatively low level of terrorist activity on the mainland recently, experience has shown that businesses in Great Britain would be well-advised to maintain full insurance coverage against terrorist damage. This applies whether it is bought through the government-backed arrangements operated by Pool Re or through the alternative arrangements that have been appearing in the insurance market.

That same October 1998, a world away from Anglo-Irish peace talk, Colorado Governor Roy Romer called seven intentionally-set fires that destroyed a ski lodge and other buildings at the Vail Mountain ski resort an "act of terrorism."

The fires caused an estimated $12 million in damage, destroying the luxurious Two Elk restaurant, the Ski Patrol headquarters, a picnic spot and four chairlifts. They were started after the resort's owners had begun an 885-acre expansion that radical wildlife groups believed would make the area uninhabitable for endangered lynx.

"This is the worst terrorism that America faces—politically motivated violence," says one West Coast security expert. "In this sense, Timothy McVeigh blowing up the Federal building in Oklahoma City and these [environmentalists] who torched Vail are brothers in arms. And they're effective because they don't fit most Americans' stereotypical notion of a terrorist as a swarthy foreigner."

Once again, like earthquakes, floods and hurricanes, terrorism can happen—even here.

PART FIVE

Financing Catastrophe Losses

When a catastrophe strikes, people's first concern is for the health and safety of their family and friends. Once loved ones have been taken care of, the rebuilding process—and paying for it—begins. Insurance companies must satisfy many different obligations following a catastrophe and those obligations require money. To understand how insurers fund these losses, let's first look at a brief overview of insurance company finances.

When you suffer an insured loss, you usually contact your insurance agent or a claims services representative who takes care of settling your claim. The money to pay claims comes from the premiums we all pay and the investment income the insurance company earns on funds awaiting payout.

Fortunately for both us and the insurance company, most people do not file any claims during a given policy year, which leaves sufficient funds available for those who do have claims. In the unlikely event that an insurance company's claims and expenses exceed its premium and investment revenue, the insurance company will suffer a loss.

But a loss for the quarter (or the year) does not mean that the insurance company is insolvent. State regulators require insurance companies to keep additional funds on hand known as surplus so they can make it through extended periods of losses without going broke. Surplus—known outside the insurance business as owners' equity—is money placed at risk by the company's owners, who expect a profit in good times, but must tolerate a loss in times of unexpectedly high claims. Surplus provides insurance companies with a "cushion" against bad luck or poor performance. The larger the surplus, the greater the margin of safety against insolvency.

If an insurance company loses too much money, its surplus will be depleted and regulators will keep the company from writing any more insurance because there is no more "cushion" to protect policyholders against insolvency. Through continued financial reporting requirements, insurance regulators attempt to monitor financial conditions and protect the policyholder against insurance company default. As a result, insurance company failures are uncommon.

Another reason company failures seldom occur is the nature of most insurance claims. Consider a family that suffers a house fire that totally destroys their home. If their loss is an isolated event—and house fires usually are—the insurance company has no trouble coming up with the money from the premiums paid by the pool of policyholders.

Using a statistical concept known as the Law of Large Numbers, insurance company actuaries use historical loss data to calculate the expected number of homes that will burn during a typical year and the expected cost of rebuilding those homes. To this expected loss, they add some additional amount—called an expense loading—to cover administrative costs.

Finally, because the insurance company's owners face the chance that claims and expenses could exceed premiums resulting in a loss, a profit loading is added to give the firm's owners a profit as compensation for their risk of losing money. The expected loss added to the expense and profit loadings equal the premium charged. Using this statistically driven process, insurance companies collect enough premiums from each policyholder to pay for a normal flow of insurance claims, not to mention earn a profit.

In almost every type of insured event, claims occur infrequently and randomly. Losses are usually uncorrelated. Normally, everyone in the neighborhood does not suffer through a house fire at the same time. (The Chicago Fire of 1871 was different.) Given these characteristics, the pooling of exposures such as fire reduces the risk for each participant in the pool. By spreading each individual's risk across the entire pool, each individual policyholder bears a small portion of the pool's loss, which is far more predictable than bearing 100 percent of her own exposure. Because actuaries can predict the pool's losses with great accuracy, the individual's share of the pool's losses is quite close to actuarial predictions. This produces a risk reducing benefit from the pooling of risk.

Catastrophes are an exception to the benefits of pooling risk. When many policyholders suffer claims at the same time, the risk reducing function of pooling breaks down. Everyone in the neighborhood can't pitch in to help you with your fire loss if their house just burned down, too.

So how do insurance companies handle the massive waves of claims from a Hurricane Andrew or a Northridge Earthquake? Fortunately, thousands of financial professionals earn a living finding ways to maintain insurance company solvency throughout such a crisis. In this part of the book, we will examine the financial problems created by catastrophes along with ways—old and new—that insurance companies finance claims arising from catastrophic events.

The problems presented by catastrophe risk have a number of potential solutions, but those solutions are not without costs and the solutions have risks of their own. Whether we ask speculators, pension funds, reinsurers or the government to share in covering disaster costs, we can expect that someone will have to pay for rebuilding or face the prospect that some people will not recover from catastrophes.

Who should pay for recovery costs? That is a matter of some debate. Economic theory suggests two possible answers for payment of recovery: rebuilding costs should be borne either by those who place themselves and their property at risk (as an incentive to stay out of harm's way) or by those who benefit from recovery (as an incentive to pay for rebuilding). But the nature of insurance complicates the issue. Insurance is not funded after the fact; rather, insurance premiums are paid before claims arise. No one likes to pay for something that may never provide him or her with a benefit.

Should we tell everyone that no aid of any kind will be forthcoming in the event of a catastrophe? Such an approach sounds harsh, but may compel homeowners to move away from danger or prepare for disasters (e.g. buy adequate insurance) on their own. The dislocation costs and costs of preparation may be small in comparison to the costs of paying for a 1-in-250-year event.

New and innovative financing tools may spread the risk of disasters to those who are better able to tolerate such losses. But catastrophe losses are inevitable and spreading the risk does not make them go away. A decisive private/public plan for catastrophe cost allocation should be conceived before the next big catastrophe to achieve a reliable and equitable source of recovery funds.

CHAPTER FIFTEEN

Catastrophe Claims

A basic truth which emerged from the late 1980s and 1990s is that catastrophic losses are becoming increasingly common. Different observers attribute the increase to different causes—an increase in consumer awareness of disasters, power-hungry bureaucrats, risk-averse insurance companies. In the end, the cause doesn't matter so much. People think more about catastrophic losses than they used to, so a self-fulfilling prophecy occurs. More disasters are claimed by a growing chorus of interested parties.

The May 1994 federal court ruling *Rockland Federal Credit Union v. James L. Witt, FEMA, et al.* considered a common complication: a lender's interest in a property damaged during a natural disaster.

In September 1990, Rockland loaned Dianne Agostino $200,000—taking back a mortgage on her property located in Scituate, Massachusetts. Under the mortgage contract, Rockland retained the right to the proceeds of any insurance payment made to Agostino in the event the property was damaged or destroyed by "fire or other hazard."

FEMA issued a Standard Flood Insurance Policy (SFIP) to Natale and Dianne Agostino for the period from September 17, 1990, to September 17, 1991. The declaration page noted, among other things, Rockland as the lender on the insured property.

The Agostinos had other insurance, too. The Massachusetts Property Insurance Underwriting Association had issued a Dwelling Policy that excluded flood coverage. Although the flood policy didn't list Rockland as a named insured, it provided limited coverage to any mortgagee named in the declaration page for a period of "30 days after written notice to the mortgagee (or trustee) of termination of [the SFIP], and shall then terminate."

In early August 1991, FEMA mailed a renewal notice to the Agostinos.

The Agostinos did not respond and the policy lapsed on September 17, 1991. On September 27, FEMA mailed an expiration notice to the Agostinos and to Rockland. Because of the 30-day grace period, the Agostinos' policy would have continued in effect through October 27, 1991, if FEMA had received a renewal premium payment within that time period. It didn't.

In late October, a major north Atlantic storm front threatened coastal New England. The 200-mile-wide storm, which wasn't a hurricane and didn't start in the tropics, came ashore on October 30 with 20-foot waves and 70-mile-per-hour winds. It made headlines for the damage it did to then-President George Bush's Maine vacation home. It also did significant damage to the area around Scituate...and to the Agostinos' house.

The expiration of the policy would be the first major issue of dispute. But there would also be others.

In order to make a claim under the SFIP, the policyholder must notify FEMA "as soon as practicable" in the event of a flood loss. Then, the policyholder must send FEMA a Proof of Loss" within 60 days after the loss.

The SFIP outlines the specific content of the Proof of Loss. It is a legal statement that must be signed and sworn. It should note the date of the loss, the policyholder's interest in the property, the actual cash value of the damaged items, the names of any entity having a lien on the property—including any mortgagee—the amount of the claim allegedly due and certain details regarding any changes to the property and/or other insurance covering the property.

Although the Agostinos notified FEMA of their loss, there was no evidence that they submitted a Proof of Loss within 60 days of the storm smashing through Scituate. The Agostinos' attorney did send a letter to FEMA on November 13, but it didn't fit the description of a Proof of Loss laid out by the policy.

FEMA sent the Agostinos a letter dated November 25 that advised them in no uncertain terms:

> Your policy expired on September 17, 1991 and was not renewed. Therefore, there was no coverage in force on the date of the loss and no payment can be made to you.

FEMA also sent a copy of the November 25 letter to Rockland. It did this because, as a mortgagee listed on the Declarations page of the policy, Rockland had certain rights under the SFIP.

In the event that an SFIP policyholder fails to submit a Proof of Loss, a mortgagee may still protect its interest. The SFIP states:

> If the insured fails to render Proof of Loss, the named mortgagee (or trustee) upon notice, shall render proof of loss in the form herein specified within 60 days thereafter and shall be subject to the provisions of this policy relating to appraisal and time of payment and of bringing suit.

So, "upon notice" that the policyholder had failed to supply proof of loss, Rockland had 60 days to submit its own Proof of Loss. The key issue of dispute was what constituted "notice" to Rockland and triggered the start of the 60-day period.

FEMA argued that Rockland had notice through the September 27 and November 25 letters. Rockland countered that it did not have notice until its receipt of a much later letter, dated April 23, 1992.

On April 2, 1992, Rockland had sent FEMA a letter entitled "Mortgagee's Notice of Loss." In that letter, Rockland's lawyers had referred to the 30-day grace period for a mortgagee in effect at the time of the big storm. Reserving its rights to decline the claim later, FEMA had responded to Rockland's attorneys that it would consider the claim "provided that the applicable terms and conditions of the policy are met." The letter further requested that Rockland's lawyers submit the amount of the mortgagee's interest on the date of the loss.

This request would later become yet another point of dispute. Rockland's attorneys didn't submit the requested information until June 24, 1992. In that response, Rockland's lawyers sent FEMA the November 1991 notice of loss from the Agostinos, the April 1992 notice of loss from Rockland and a signed and sworn affidavit detailing Rockland's interest in the property. The affidavit stated that, on October 30, 1991, the Agostinos had owed Rockland $205,848.70 under the mortgage. Rockland argued that the June 24 letter constituted its proof of loss under the SFIP.

On July 22, 1992, FEMA informed Rockland's attorneys that it would not make a payment to Rockland, as mortgagee, under the SFIP. FEMA explained that, when written notice of the cancellation was forwarded to Rockland, the SFIP remained in force for Rockland's benefit for only 30 days. Because FEMA had sent a carbon copy of its November 1991 denial letter to Rockland, the lender's April 1992 notice of loss was untimely.

Rockland responded by suing everyone—FEMA, the Massachusetts Property Insurance Underwriting Association and Lloyd's of London. It sought a declaration as to which of three insurance policies covered property damage to the Agostino property.

The September 27, 1991, notice from FEMA constituted the requisite "written notice to the mortgagee" of the policy's termination. Rockland received that notice on October 7. So, depending on whether the 30-day period began to run when FEMA mailed the expiration notice or when Rockland received it, the SFIP expired either on October 27 or November 6, 1991.

The court settled the question:

> ...for purposes of FEMA's motion for summary judgment, this court will assume...that the latter construction applies, i.e., that the SFIP was in effect only for the benefit of Rockland up to and including November 6, 1991. Accordingly, Rockland's interest was covered under the SFIP at the time of the October 30, 1991 storm.

So, the dispute moved to the question of whether Rockland had given FEMA notice of loss in a timely manner. According to FEMA, Rockland had been informed of the Agostinos' failure to render their proof of loss on two occasions. First, on October 7, 1991, Rockland had received FEMA's expiration notice. Second, on November 25, FEMA notified the Agostinos that it would not be processing their claim—and sent a carbon copy of that letter to Rockland.

According to Rockland, formal notice from FEMA didn't come until the agency's April 23, 1992 letter. So, Rockland argued that its June 24, 1992 proof of loss was filed within 60 days.

The court decided that the chronology was not as complicated—or as lengthy—as Rockland's argument was making it sound. By letter dated November 13, 1991, the Agostinos had submitted a notice of loss. By letter dated November 25, FEMA had unequivocally denied the

Agostinos' claim because the policy had expired on September 17. Rockland had received a carbon copy of the November 25 letter.

As a result, the court decided:

> No reasonable person could interpret the November 25, 1991 letter as anything but an indication that the Agostinos would not be filing a Proof of Loss. In [that] letter, FEMA rejected the Agostinos' attempt to file a notice of loss. The next step, i.e., filing a Proof of Loss, would therefore be futile.... Therefore, Rockland was on notice that the Agostinos would not be filing a Proof of Loss in or around late November 1991. The 60-day period expired no later than early February 1992.

So, Rockland's June 1992 Proof of Loss had not been filed in a timely manner.

Rockland had also tried to argue that, because FEMA agreed to consider its claims in April 1992, the Proof of Loss must have been filed in a timely manner. Under this theory, FEMA's request for claim information from Rockland effectively extended the period.

The court disagreed, noting:

> FEMA expressly reserved its rights and defenses in the letter thereby precluding any reasonable reliance on the letter on the part of Rockland. The court allowed FEMA's motion for summary judgment, dismissing Rockland's claims.

As is often the case, FEMA had prevailed.

Losses in the '90s: Bigger than Ever

The risks posed by natural disasters in the U.S. have increased significantly in recent years. This increased risk reflects itself to some extent by the increase in insured losses caused by natural disasters over the last decade. But those losses pale in comparison to the disasters that many experts believe could occur in the near future.

Prior to 1989, catastrophe insurance losses averaged less than $2 billion per year (in 1995 dollars). This figure jumped to more than $10 billion per year since 1989, with losses peaking in 1992 at $25 billion. According to American Insurance Services Group's (AISG) Property Claims Services unit, insured losses from natural disasters totaled $75 billion in the six-year period between 1989 and 1995. This figure dwarfs the $51 billion in losses (adjusted for inflation) for the 38-year period between 1950 and 1988. This kind of increase is alarming.

Several disasters in the 1990s—Hurricane Hugo in 1989 ($4.2 billion in insured losses), Hurricane Andrew in 1992 ($15.5 billion), and the Northridge Earthquake in 1994 ($12.5 billion)—helped to awaken the insurance industry and public officials to the increased risk of catastrophe losses. If these natural events had struck even more densely populated areas, however, the insured and uninsured losses would have been several times higher.

Catastrophe risk has increased for two primary reasons. First, climate and geological changes have increased the severity and frequency of earthquakes and hurricanes. Meteorologists believe we are entering a period of greatly increased hurricane activity, and geologists expect at least a couple of major earthquakes in the next decade. Second, population growth and economic development in high-risk coastal areas have increased dramatically. Historically, insurers have accommodated this growth and development by expanding insurance coverage in high-risk areas. Of course, this has increased insurers' exposure to catastrophic losses.

These factors have combined to greatly heighten the likelihood of one or more economically devastating events in large population centers. A 1996 study by the Insurance Services Office indicated that more than one-third of insurers could be bankrupted by a $50 billion catastrophe, depending on the nature and location of the event.

In the past two decades, the increase in weather volatility has heightened the difficulty in predicting catastrophic property losses. Such climatic volatility is often associated with global climate change. Again, this may be more a matter of volatility than overall impact. Some experts believe that a number of critical trends in natural disasters actually point downward. However, the core problem is that catastrophe losses from weather are becoming less predictable, and there is insufficient preparation for a truly severe event.

As climate becomes more volatile, actuarial models have become unreliable, which increases the risk of incorrect prediction and insurance pricing. For example, one model might predict five hurricanes over a five-year period, with average associated losses of $3 billion. Another, equally reliable model might predict 10 hurricanes during the same period, with losses of about $2 billion each. If the underlying risks were automobile insurance claims, a good actuary would probably take an average of the two sources' opinions to create his own estimate. But estimates from the major modeling firms (Applied Insurance Research, Risk Management Solutions, EQE, and others) vary widely; there is so much uncertainty that actuaries have little reliable information upon which to base their estimates.

The actual extent of the risk still isn't clear. In Florida, homeowners insurers have stirred consumer ire by proposing hefty rate hikes based on computer models. Pointing to their computer models' figures, insurers have filed for substantial rate increases to cover potential hurricane losses. Vows Bill Nelson, the state's insurance commissioner: "I will not let the consumers of Florida become hostage to a computer."

Some scientists also question catastrophe (cat) models, arguing that the past disaster patterns on which they are based may be a poor guide to the future. But recognized experts, such as Colorado State University professor Bill Gray, have observed weather pattern shifts that may cause more hurricanes and other bad storms that confirm what the models are saying. Gray has been right before...can both Gray and the models be wrong?

Earthquake models don't fare much better. Geologists cannot predict with any degree of certainty when and how severe the next earthquake will be. With few significant earthquakes from which to draw data, modelers must use extrapolation and interpolation to estimate the extent of insured losses in the wake of a powerful tremor. But the Northridge quake provided scientists with enough data to know that a severe event in a populated location could have devastating financial consequences for the insurance industry.

The only "silver lining" to come from Andrew and Northridge may have been a heightened awareness of the potential losses from catastrophes. With this heightened awareness, the insurance market has been changed forever, most likely in a way that will increase the financial survivability of most insurers during the next catastrophe.

CHAPTER SIXTEEN

Insurance, Reinsurance and Self-Insurance

Some regional property insurance markets grapple continually with severe problems in financing catastrophe risk. These issues seem small, however, compared to the exposure that uninsured and underinsured property represents. In the end, many catastrophe risks are simply too difficult to insure. The result is diminished availability and high price of property coverage in areas subject to natural disasters.

There are two main causes of these insurance market problems. First is the newly revised estimate for the "actuarial cost" of catastrophe risk. This is the estimated annual average loss from catastrophes. Since Andrew and Northridge, actuarial estimates of the potential cost of the next catastrophe have skyrocketed. Premiums should reflect these new estimates; otherwise, insurance companies would be offering coverage "below cost." Second, and perhaps more important, is the greater severity of the disasters observed in recent years.

Given the magnitude of these events, the sums required to fund catastrophic claims can be neither readily obtained at reasonable cost nor accumulated over time (for tax reasons). These conditions make insurance a product that is costly and difficult to supply in at-risk areas.

For many insurers, the heightened severity of the next disaster is compounded by the concentration of insurance policies in high-risk areas. An insurer facing such a situation has only two alternatives. It can reduce its exposure in high-risk areas and/or increase its reinsurance to cover a greater portion of its losses. However, regulations and other factors constrain an insurer's ability to decrease its market share at will. Further, insurers cannot buy sufficient reinsurance at a price they can afford to pay to reduce their exposure to a safe level.

Pointing out that it is policyholders that must ultimately pay the cost of reinsurance protection, State Farm executive Vincent Trosino recently opined that there was not enough reinsurance available for State Farm's needs at a price that the homeowners insurance market will bear. State Farm is so large that there may not be enough catastrophe reinsurance capacity, period.

Researchers at Conning & Co., a private insurance investment and research concern based in Hartford, Conn., say the industry is largely responsible for creating its own man-made disaster. The fundamental problem, according to the Conning study, is that the basic homeowners insurance policy has exploded out of control. While competing amongst themselves for market share, the researchers say, insurance companies have been expanding benefits and taking on additional risk without corresponding premium increases.

The huge disasters that laid waste to parts of Florida, southern California and a few other places merely directed attention to a problem that has been developing for years. Indeed, major property/casualty insurance companies have not just suffered recently; they have lost money on their policies in all but one of the last 16 years, ignoring investment income. Of course, investment income cannot be ignored; underwriting losses, which do not include investment results, may simply reflect extremely competitive market conditions rather than poor management.

But management decisions to compete so aggressively may render the industry more vulnerable to catastrophe risk. Perhaps the largest single factor in creating the financial problems, according to Conning's Claude Fongemie, has been a shift in the late 1970s from selling policies that simply covered the market value of homes and their contents to ones that provide for the full cost of replacing the home and everything in it.

"When catastrophes did strike, the [claim] settlements decimated the insurers who had written the coverages," said Fongemie. "The cure is to improve the insurance-to-value equation and bring benefits back in line with premiums."

Because of escalating costs for building supplies and rising labor rates, Fongemie says, replacement costs can far exceed a home's market value. In addition, with a replacement policy, the wear and tear on a 10-year-old couch is disregarded since the insurance company pays for a new one.

Since the mid-1980s, Fongemie estimates that the cost of replacing a home and its contents rather than paying for them at market value has added as much as 60 percent to insurer claim costs. In contrast, insurance premiums have declined. Fongemie calculated that in 1984 the cost of $100,000 worth of coverage was $350. Eleven years later, he estimates the premium at $210, a 40 percent decrease, in spite of rising claims costs.

Competition through expanded coverage may be worse than cutting prices, though the result is the same: slimmer profit margins and premiums that do not reflect the exposures insurers face. We cannot expect insurers to protect their policyholders if they cannot charge premiums adequate enough to cover claims and purchase sufficient reinsurance to diversify their risk.

Some experts believe that approximately 75 percent of all homeowners have inadequate coverage because their insurance coverage is based on such things as mortgage balances or market values. Many of these homeowners fail to upgrade their policies regularly to reflect such physical improvements as porches and decks, kitchen and bathroom enhancements and finished basements that would affect home replacement costs.

Often, the insurance valuation problem arises because many insurers still rely on antiquated, quick and easy square-footage methods of calculation compared with new, more sophisticated methods of estimating based on advanced technology and computerization.

The consequences? Policyholders underpay or insurers pay to replace improvements for which they never charged sufficient premiums.

Clearly, some insurance coverages have been underpriced (and others still are), but insurers may have overreacted to the perception of greater risk. Rather than adjusting policy terms incrementally, conducting inspections and carrying out relatively small rate increases spread across the entire population, the industry has raised prices drastically and beat a hasty retreat in places like Florida and other coastal areas to avoid exposure. This may address the fairness issue by not penalizing policyholders in lower risk areas, but creates more acute problems in high-risk areas.

Has the industry overreacted? The Conning research suggests that with different pricing and benefits, the companies might have been able to withstand the disasters without such drastic reductions in availability and without sharply increasing premiums and deductibles. But State Farm, the largest U.S. homeowners insurer, has doubled its premium for many policyholders in south Florida, and Allstate requires some homeowners in Florida to carry a $5,000 deductible for windstorm losses.

Managing insurance company catastrophe risk is important, but insurers may have done better to expand rather than contract. Until Hurricane Georges in September 1998, insurers have enjoyed very healthy profits in the Florida homeowners market with few catastrophe claims.

Private insurers also argue that government should create a national reinsurance facility to maintain industry solvency when catastrophes occur. "What's needed is a way to smooth out the huge hits," said Gary Grant, a vice president and actuary at State Farm. Government pools traditionally have provided coverage to ease "availability crises" when the private market breaks down.

But, as we'll see later, government usually cannot provide an equitable long-term solution—if they could, the private market may not have abandoned such exposures in the first place.

Reinsurance

In August 1992, Hurricane Andrew caused an unprecedented level of destruction. Andrew was one of the most devastating natural catastrophes ever recorded but it also led to a wave of financial catastrophes. The hurricane affected almost every major insurance company in the United States. Behind the scenes was a little-known but important group of companies—known as reinsurers—who suffered as much or more than insurers from the effects of Andrew.

Reinsurers provide a backup layer of protection for insurance companies to prevent insurers' losses from spiraling beyond their ability to pay. While reinsurance contracts can take many forms, the most common form of reinsurance for catastrophe risk is the excess of loss contract. Under excess of loss reinsurance, the primary insurance company must absorb a certain level of losses before the reinsurance protection begins to pay.

For example, ABC insurance company may choose to purchase $500 million of excess of loss reinsurance that becomes effective once ABC's losses reach $1 billion. In reinsurance jargon, ABC purchased $500 million of coverage, excess of $1 billion. Unless losses exceed $1 billion, the reinsurer will not have to pay. The reinsurer must pay for all losses over $1 billion, with a maximum payout of $500 million. If losses exceed $1.5 billion, the reinsurance coverage will be exhausted at $500 million and ABC will have to absorb any losses over $1.5 billion, in addition to the first $1 billion of losses.

Although uncommon, reinsurance company failures do occur. Reinsurance buyers must monitor the financial condition of reinsurers to avoid going unpaid when a catastrophe strikes and overwhelms a reinsurer's resources. Insurers depend on rating agencies such as Standard and Poor's and A.M. Best to provide information about a reinsurer's ability to pay under difficult conditions.

The availability of reinsurance is crucial to the provision of homeowners insurance in areas exposed to catastrophes. Without reinsurance, insurance companies offering policies to the public face virtually unlimited losses. After Hurricane Andrew, the departure of reinsurers caused catastrophe reinsurance capacity to drop by more than 30 percent.

The average U.S. catastrophe reinsurance program before Hurricane Andrew totaled $144.3 million for a typical primary insurance company. Immediately after Andrew, the average program capacity dropped to $93.7 million—and carried much higher premiums. What's worse, some insurance companies could not buy enough catastrophe reinsurance at any price.

The decrease in catastrophe reinsurance supply following Andrew led to changes in the reinsurance marketplace. Lloyd's of London syndicates had traditionally stepped in to offer coverage during periods such as this but the Lloyd's market was still reeling from financial problems of its own in the early 1990s. Instead, a number of Bermuda-based specialty reinsurance companies emerged to become a major force in the property catastrophe reinsurance market.

In just over eighteen months, over $4 billion of capital was infused into Bermuda companies formed for the purpose of writing property catastrophe reinsurance. Companies such as Mid Ocean, Cat Limited, and Renaissance Re sprang up to capitalize on the panic prices paid by desperate insurance companies seeking reinsurance protection. Investors in the companies included some large investment banks and securities firms, including Goldman Sachs, Morgan Stanley, and J.P. Morgan.

Their foresight quickly paid off. In 1994, Bermuda catastrophe reinsurance companies averaged a combined operating profit ratio of 40 percent and an average 15 percent return on equity. Moreover, this performance took place during a year that witnessed almost $19 billion in worldwide catastrophe losses.

By taking on pieces of exposure (and premiums) from different types of risks from all over the world, Bermuda's catastrophe reinsurers took advantage of a diversified portfolio of risks. In some cases, these reinsurance companies purchase reinsurance for their own books of business. These transactions, called "retrocessions," provide partial protection for the reinsurers' surplus during periods of high losses. This kind of diversification prevents any single event from putting the reinsurance companies out of business.

Bermuda's development as a world center for reinsurance occurred for one reason: Bermuda has no corporate income taxes. The tax-free status of Bermuda-based insurers such as Exel's XL Mid Ocean Reinsurance, Renaissance Re, and ACE's Cat Limited allows these companies to build their capital quickly (without the drag of taxes) and provide enormous amounts of catastrophe reinsurance capacity without the threat of insolvency.

Without the reinsurance coverage available from these companies, many primary insurance companies would have to raise premiums, cut the availability of insurance or both.

While tax considerations may appear inconsequential, many U.S. executives in the industry are calling for tax reforms to allow domestic insurers to develop their own catastrophe reserves. Under current U.S. law, a property insurance company can deduct only losses that have already occurred as a business expense.

While these deductions may also include an estimate of what will be paid out for reported and incurred-but-not-reported claims, an insurer cannot deduct the estimated expense of an earthquake or hurricane that may occur in ten years. Therefore, insurance companies that want to build a reserve for future events must do so on a fully taxable basis.

In a speech to financial experts, United Services Automobile Association (USAA) President and CEO Robert Herres called for tax reforms whereby private insurance companies could build industry catastrophe reserves tax-free up to the $25 billion level, a level he believes is adequate for the next severe event.

He estimated that this would take ten years and cost the U.S. Treasury approximately $450 million in lost tax revenue. While critics believe that offering such an inducement opens up opportunities for others to ask for similar tax breaks, his proposal may make sense if the U.S. insurance industry is to operate through a major catastrophe without waves of insolvencies and Federal government assistance.

Despite the problems of the early 1990s, current market conditions for reinsurance actually favor the buyer. Driven down by increasing competition and few catastrophes since 1994, reinsurance prices (known as rates-on-line) have declined to the point where property catastrophe reinsurers actually hope a major disaster will occur so reinsurance prices will increase. With such an event, reinsurers hope competitors will be swept out of the market by a megacatastrophe, allowing survivors to charge a relatively high price for the coverage they offer.

Despite reinsurers' complaints about low prices, many primary insurance companies still say they cannot afford the reinsurance coverage since their own customers are unwilling to pay adequate premiums. Consequently, many insurers face a socially unacceptable—albeit hidden and incalculable—level of risk from catastrophes. Unfortunately, the reinsurers are likely to get their way when the next storm or earthquake hits in the wrong place.

Self-Insurance and Loss Mitigation

One way to "prefund" catastrophe costs is to prevent them in the first place through loss mitigation efforts and expenditures. Unfortunately, the failure of market forces and public policy to encourage cost-effective hazard mitigation has increased the potential severity of catastrophic losses.

Many owners do not see it in their interest to reduce the vulnerability of their property to damage from natural disasters. There are many reasons for inadequate loss mitigation efforts and expenditures, including:

- lack of knowledge or underestimation of the exposure to loss and the benefits of mitigation;
- lack of insurance premium discounts for mitigation because of regulatory constraints on rates;
- tax deductions for unmitigated and uninsured disaster losses;
- inadequate enforcement of building codes;
- lack of financing for mitigation expenditures; and
- expectations of government financial assistance in the event of a disaster.

The lack of mitigation makes it more difficult and expensive for insurers, reinsurance companies and financial markets to assume catastrophe risk.

Mitigation has become a more important issue since Hurricane Andrew hit Florida in 1992 and the Northridge quake rocked southern California in 1994. Specifically, there is heightened interest in building codes. Stringent building codes and earthquake "retrofits" can decrease or eliminate building damage during a storm or earthquake.

Aerial photographs of the south Florida area following Andrew show dramatic differences among subdivisions constructed by different contractors and under different codes. Current Florida codes call for homes to withstand 110 mile-per-hour winds, though budget cuts have reduced building inspector enforcement efforts. Evidence from the Northridge earthquake indicates that retrofits generally reduced the level of losses where they were employed.

Hurricane Alicia and Hurricane Diana struck two different areas in 1984. According to the Insurance Information Institute (III), though the hurricanes were of similar magnitude, differing levels of building code enforcement accounted for a wide disparity in losses. Alicia caused $675 million in losses in Texas where codes are loosely enforced, but Diana resulted in only $36 million in the Carolinas where codes command more respect.

In May 1997, experts from the insurance industry and interested organizations emphasized the importance of efforts to mitigate the effects of catastrophes on the public and property during the Property Claim Services' Annual Catastrophe Conference. Paul Devlin, counsel and director of land use planning for the Insurance Institute for Property Loss Reduction (IIPLR), stressed the potential positive impact of mitigation.

"Effective mitigation efforts can have a tremendous impact," he said. "Even a slight reduction in losses can mean $5 billion to $10 billion in savings to the [insurance] industry."

Conrad Kawulok, vice president of the National Roofing Contractors Association, outlined steps to reduce catastrophe losses: "We must increase financial incentives for insureds to help mitigation efforts, educate consumers about the costs versus the performance of building materials, and develop and foster industry relationships." Roofing construction and building materials quality may determine homeowners windstorm losses more than any other single factor.

According to the U.S. Office of Technology Assessment (OTA), Congress funded the National Earthquake Hazards Reduction Program (NEHRP) in 1977 to explore quake mitigation technology and has allocated funds every year since that time to continue earthquake loss mitigation research. But OTA staffers believe that insurance premiums must reflect the risk reduction of earthquake mitigation. Otherwise, homeowners will not bother.

Fortunately, the California Earthquake Authority (CEA) uses some of its premium income to offer home inspections and low interest loans to homeowners who retrofit their homes with loss mitigation technology. But many homeowners are foregoing CEA coverage altogether and using the premiums saved to implement their own mitigation plans.

Mitigation doesn't have to be complex. It can be as simple as urging insurers to work with policyholders to have them do simple things such as putting away lawn furniture that can become projectiles in high winds, trimming trees and spending about $200 to tie down roofs.

More complex methods of mitigation would include states implementing stricter building codes and offering tax or premium incentives for retrofitting structures to withstand the storms, says South Carolina insurance regulator Edward Jedziniak.

South Carolina allows insurers to use catastrophe models in rate-making, but the underwriter must show how any increases would be phased in with incentives, Jedziniak said. "If you want to catastrophe model, that's OK. If you want to raise the rates to reflect the risk, that's OK. But in the same manner, reduce the rate when people mitigate."

James Lee Witt said local communities and individual homeowners had to be the ones to initiate flood mitigation efforts, such as elevations and buyout programs, to break the disaster cycle. "Mitigation is a local issue," Witt said. "It should be a local issue. It should come from the local level up." Witt said FEMA has worked with local communities around the country to buy out 20,000 repetitive flood-loss structures since the massive Mississippi River flood of 1993. Both federal and local funds were used for the buyouts.

Witt said it only makes sense for local and state governments to prepare for disasters and take practical steps that can reduce their impact, in terms of economic losses and the threat to the population. "We need to spend money on prevention," he said. "It will cut costs and it will save lives.... Mitigation is a long-term effort, not a short-term solution, but it is a long-term investment that will pay off."

CHAPTER SEVENTEEN

Government Intervention

The government disaster aid program of last resort is run indirectly by the IRS. Tax write-offs make up one important tool for dealing with the financial impact of catastrophe losses. The general rule is that you can deduct the uninsured portion of a "casualty loss" from your income tax obligation for that year. But the write-off doesn't put cash in your pocket to replace lost property...and even this standby approach comes with some pretty heavy legal caveats.

The November 1997 United States Tax Court decision *George P. Brown v. IRS* highlights a few of these.

Brown worked as a bus driver for the Metropolitan Dade County Transit Agency. He rented a house in the South Miami area, where he lived with his family until September 1992—when he and his wife separated. Soon after his marriage ended, Brown's house was destroyed by Hurricane Andrew's 120 mile-per-hour winds.

At the time of loss, Brown had no renter's insurance and lost nearly all his personal property. He ended up taking the loss as a deduction from his 1992 income tax. He maximized his deduction by claiming head-of-household status and aggressively estimating the value of the personal possessions he lost. The tactic seemed to work—for a while.

In 1997, the Commissioner of Internal Revenue determined a deficiency in Brown's federal income tax for 1992 in the amount of $2,040. According to the IRS, there were problems involving Brown's household filing status and casualty loss deduction. The matter was automatically sent to the Tax Court for a ruling. The court considered each of the issues raised by the IRS.

The first issue was whether Brown had been entitled to claim head of household filing status for 1992. In the statutory notice of deficiency, the IRS determined that Brown's proper filing status for 1992 was married filing separate. (An individual may be considered a head of a household if, and only if, such individual is not married at the close of his taxable year.) Brown testified that he and his wife were never legally separated but that they lived apart from September 1992 until 1996. Since he was not legally separated and his wife was still living with him during July and August 1992, the tax court ruled that Brown was married at the close of his 1992 taxable year. Accordingly, Brown was not entitled to claim head of household filing status for 1992.

The second issue was whether Brown was entitled to a casualty loss deduction. He had claimed a casualty loss in the amount of $33,321 on his 1992 amended return. After accounting for certain limitations, he changed the amount of the deduction to $28,099. But he wasn't thorough enough in recasting his estimates.

The Tax Court noted:

> Section 165(h)(1) provides that any casualty loss deduction of an individual is allowed only to the extent that the amount of the loss arising from each casualty exceeds $100. Section 165(h)(2) further limits the deduction to the amount that the aggregate of the losses for the taxable year, in excess of the section 165(h)(1) limitation of $100 per casualty, exceeds 10 percent of the individual's adjusted gross income for the taxable year.

From this basis, the proper measure of the amount of the loss sustained is the difference between the fair market value of the property immediately before and after the catastrophe; and it can't exceed its depreciated value.

Brown's adjusted gross income for 1992 was $51,215. Therefore, he was entitled to a casualty loss deduction only if he could prove that he sustained a loss in excess of $5,222. (Ten percent of his adjusted gross income, plus the $100 deductible.)

He submitted several photographs as evidence of the damage caused by Hurricane Andrew. Based on these photos, the tax court was convinced that Brown sustained a casualty loss during 1992. However, he failed to substantiate the amount of the loss claimed on his return and submitted no receipts showing the value of his damaged property.

Brown had compiled a list of items that were destroyed by Hurricane

Andrew; the list contained his own estimate of their value. But this was a shaky foundation on which to build a claim. At trial, things got even murkier. He testified that several items on the list actually belonged to his landlord and that much of the property was several years old when it was destroyed. Finally, Brown did not include on the list the automobiles claimed on his amended return as a loss.

The court fell back on the letter of the law and wrote:

> In the event that a taxpayer establishes that he has incurred a deductible loss, but is unable to substantiate the precise amount of the loss, we may estimate the amount of the deductible loss, bearing heavily against the taxpayer whose inexactitude in substantiating the amount of the loss is of his own making.

After reviewing the list and considering his testimony, the court estimated his loss from the hurricane to be $7,062. It concluded:

> After taking into account the section 165(h) limitations, [Brown's] allowable casualty loss deduction is $1,840. Since [Brown] has not claimed any other itemized deductions, we hold that he is only entitled to the standard deduction for an individual filing as married filing separate, which is greater than his allowable casualty loss deduction.

The moral of the story: If you are going to count on a tax deduction as any part of your disaster recovery plan, make sure you keep scrupulous notes about what you own and how much you paid for everything.

Other government support plans are more direct than IRS tax breaks...and for this reason they anger some parties. The May 1998 federal appeals court decision *Vesta Fire Insurance Corp. et al. v. State of Florida* considered the case of an insurance company that didn't want to cooperate with the state's Joint Underwriting Association (JUA).

After Hurricane Andrew hit Florida in 1992, insurance companies frantically rushed to lower their exposure to hurricane damages. To prevent insurance from becoming completely unavailable to consumers, the Florida legislature passed several statutes. These included:

- A "Moratorium Statute," which prohibited the nonrenewal and cancellation of residential insurance policies for reasons related to the risk of hurricane damage. The Moratorium Statute was passed as temporary legislation.
- The "Moratorium Phaseout Statute," which allowed limited cancel-

lation and nonrenewal of residential policies. The Moratorium Phaseout Statute provided that, in a twelve-month period, no insurer could cancel or nonrenew more than 5 percent of its residential policies in Florida or more than 10 percent of its residential policies in a single Florida county. This phaseout was interpreted by the Department of Insurance—despite another statute permitting the total withdrawal after a 45-day notice—as prohibiting an insurer's total withdrawal from doing business in the State of Florida.

• Legislation requiring insurers to pay annual premiums to the Florida Hurricane Catastrophe Fund. This fund is intended to provide reinsurance to insurance companies doing business in Florida. The reinsurance provides protection to companies which, following a hurricane, are unable to pay fully on their policies.

Vesta sued, representing a group of insurance companies that wanted out of Florida. They argued that the Moratorium Phaseout Statute violated several provisions of the United States Constitution, including:

• the Taking Clause of the Fifth Amendment;
• Vesta's Due Process rights under the Fourteenth Amendment; and
• the Contract Clause.

The trial court hearing the case didn't see a strong connection between the regulatory actions and Vesta's constitutional claims. It ruled for the state and ordered the insurance companies to abide by the moratorium legislation.

The insurance companies appealed...and the appeals court gave their argument more detailed consideration. Noting that "only the Moratorium Phaseout Statute directly implicates the Constitution," the court noted:

> The required contribution to the fund, absent the Moratorium Phaseout Statute, is a constitutional exercise of the State of Florida's police power. Thus, the constitutionality of the Moratorium Phaseout Statute is the focus of [this] opinion.

The appeals court first turned to the Taking Clause of the Fifth Amendment, which states, in relevant part, "nor shall private property be taken for public use, without just compensation." This amendment was designed to bar the Government from forcing some people alone to bear public burdens which should be borne by the public as a whole.

The insurance companies alleged substantial financial losses as a result of being unable to withdraw from the Florida insurance market, coupled with the forced contributions to the Catastrophe Fund. This statutory scheme, they argued, resulted in a taking of their "property" without just compensation in violation of the Fifth Amendment.

The appeals court noted that the Supreme Court has recognized three factors that should be considered to identify a regulatory taking:

- the economic impact of the challenged rule, regulation, or statute on the plaintiff;
- the extent to which the regulation interferes with a company's right to expect a reasonable return on investment; and
- the nature of the challenged action.

Vesta and other insurance companies argued that the district court had failed to consider these factors properly. The appeals court agreed. The insurance companies pointed to their economic loss in the Florida market and some $1 million in premiums they'd paid to the Catastrophe Fund as negative economic impacts. They also argued that the nature of the Moratorium Phaseout Statute—specifically, the potential for another extension—required them to stay in the Florida insurance market indefinitely.

At the trial stage, the state and JUA had relied heavily on their assertion that the moratorium would end in 1996. But at the appeal, which was heard in 1998, the moratorium was still in place—and was scheduled to remain in place until June 1999. So, Vesta's original argument held more weight.

The state and JUA were left to argue that the possibility for rate increases counterbalanced any negative economic impact of the moratorium.

However, Vesta and the other insurers had made several applications for rate increases—and they'd all been denied. Following the language of the Supreme Court rulings, the insurance companies also claimed that the limitations on their withdrawal from the Florida market had interfered with their investment-backed expectations. The district court hadn't addressed this factor.

Vesta argued that, whatever regulation it may have anticipated when it had entered the Florida market, it could not anticipate that withdrawal from that market—should additional regulation become too burdensome—would be prohibited.

Next, the court considered the Contract Clause of the United States Constitution, which provides that "[n]o State shall... pass any... Law impairing the Obligation of Contracts."

Three factors must be considered when a court evaluates a claim that the Contract Clause has been violated:

- whether the law substantially impairs a contractual relationship;
- whether there is a significant and legitimate public purpose for the law; and
- whether the adjustments of rights and responsibilities of the contracting parties are based upon reasonable conditions and are of an appropriate nature.

It concluded that Vesta had made a sufficient showing that the Florida legislation had substantially impaired the contracts between the insurance companies and their insureds.

Finally, Vesta argued that the nature of the government actions in the Florida insurance market supported its claim that the government was taking its assets without compensation. The insurance companies contended that the compulsory nature of the legislation—by itself—resulted in a taking. The appeals court noted that:

> ...all government regulation is compulsory in nature. But the nature of the state's interest is critical in determining whether a taking has occurred. When important public interests are served, a taking is less likely to have occurred.

The appeals court understood the urgency of the state's position—and even allowed that it might win its fight with Vesta. But the case would have to go to trial. Specifically, the court wrote:

> After Hurricane Andrew, several insurance companies became insolvent, unable to pay their policies. Other companies sought to withdraw altogether from the Florida insurance market. This withdrawal could have had serious negative effects on Florida's real estate market and on the economy of the State. The moratorium was intended as a stabilizing force in the market and was within the State of Florida's police power.

However, the good intentions of the state didn't mean that its actions were legally defensible. There were too many unknowns—including the economic impact of the moratorium and Vesta's reasonable expectations—to support the lower court's summary judgment. The appeals court noted that the moritorium probably did interfere with Vesta's ability to enter and enforce contracts. Specifically, the court wrote:

> Insurance provides coverage of a specified risk for a specified time. At the end of that time, insurance companies reevaluate the risk and decide whether they wish to remain the insurers of that risk. Under the Moratorium Phaseout, Plaintiffs are forced to continue contractual relationships that otherwise, could be rightfully terminated.

If the post-Hurricane Andrew legislation created a substantial impairment to Vesta's contracts, the state would have to prove "a significant and legitimate public purpose behind the regulation." Then again, the state had demonstrated a legitimate public purpose: protection and stabilization of the Florida economy, particularly the real estate market. In all, the contract interference claim was murkier than the taking claim.

The appeals court finally concluded that the lower court's summary judgment for the state was inappropriate. However, the moratorium did not unconstitutionally interfere with existing insurance contracts. The split decision came down slightly on the insurance companies' side—they'd have another opportunity to make their case to getting out of the Florida insurance market. The outcome has yet to be determined.

Proposals for Government Help

Payouts in the wake of Hurricane Andrew and the Northridge earthquake alone caused the failure of over a dozen insurance companies and triggered a need for new kinds of reinsurance and risk transfer that will shore up a potentially exhausted insurance system when the next "big one" occurs. Not surprisingly, many insurers also have called for federal assistance.

But politicians and economists alike believe a government safety net would be a mistake over the long haul, said Kevin Murdock, assistant professor of strategic management at Stanford Graduate School of Business, who has taken a close look at the U.S. insurance system. A government bailout program would likely leave taxpayers footing the bill for poorly managed insurance companies. Murdock and research partner

Christopher Lewis believe the insurance fix is a job primarily for the private sector to handle, with government playing only a supporting role. To that end, Murdock and Lewis have devised a model for risk management and distribution that would help insurers shoulder their burden when the next megacatastrophe hits. Their proposal, parts of which are now under consideration by Congress, recommends a hybrid form of public and private reinsurance.

Murdock and Lewis' research considers three key problems confronting insurers.

First, they identify an abundance of housing development in relatively unsafe areas. "Think of development patterns 30 years ago and what they are today," said Murdock. "We've increased building on the Florida coast and near the San Andreas Fault." There has been a 69 percent increase just in insured coastal property values, to $3.1 trillion, since 1988. That has created new social risks—and costs. The building boom over the last few decades coincided with a period of relatively low incidence of natural disasters—until recently. Following the recent string of calamities, however, the cost of building with poor construction or in risky locations is just now being realized.

Second, the solution for handling the fallout from natural disasters does not create incentives to reduce costs. For example, the government's compassionate policy allows uninsured homeowners to receive low-cost loans or grants to rebuild. Insured homeowners receive nothing.

Third, the current market for disaster insurance has not worked well because it doesn't fit into either of two standard mechanisms for handling risk: an insurance model or a market model. "The insurance industry is built around the pooling model, so it's not designed to handle these big, infrequent risks," said Murdock.

Murdock and Lewis' proposal creates tradable reinsurance contracts—financial instruments that can be traded in open markets, much like contracts for oil and grain futures. The government would kick-start the market by initially underwriting a quarter of all contracts and then slowly phasing out its participation.

The government's role would guarantee the initial availability of these reinsurance contracts so that large insurers and reinsurers could develop the systems to manage natural disaster risks using these contracts. Then private investors, such as investment banks, could carve a lucrative market out of the new financial vehicles, eventually eliminating the need for government participation. Murdock and Lewis envision the reinsurance contracts laying off risk for insurers only after very large disasters, where damage exceeds $25 billion.

The Murdock and Lewis proposal expands on similar types of transactions taking place in the private market as well as a bill that has made it out of committee in Congress. The Natural Disaster Protection and Insurance Act—and other proposals like it—would provide federally backed reinsurance for catastrophic losses. In addition to reducing "free rider" reliance on the Federal Government in times of catastrophe, a Federal reinsurance facility would ensure that homeowners insurance is more affordable and accessible, while protecting the private insurance sector from possible insolvency.

Under one recent proposal introduced by New York Republican Congressman Rick Lazio, the U.S. Treasury would be authorized to issue annual reinsurance contracts to eligible state insurance pools to cover residential losses that occur in 1-in-100 year events. Primary insurers or state insurance pools, such as Florida's Hurricane Catastrophe Fund, would be given the opportunity to purchase reinsurance contracts for certain disastrous events from the Treasury Department through an auction.

Income from the auction would be reserved in a fund to be tapped if a single hurricane, earthquake, volcanic eruption or tsunami caused more than $10 billion in losses. Payments from the fund would then be made to contract holders with valid claims for the next $25 billion in losses. Primary insurers would then be able to offer coverage with the confidence that some type of reinsurance would be available, and that the reinsurer—the U.S. Treasury in this case—would not default.

Lazio believes that while restoring stability within the reinsurance industry is an integral part of disaster relief, relieving some of the burden on the federal government is just as important. His bill would permit the federal government to reinsure primary insurers, such as Allstate or State Farm, through the state pools. Taxpayers would not pay for the program, at least directly. Insurers would pay premiums to the state pools, which pass along these premiums through the Treasury's reinsurance auction.

Insurers would pass their costs along to customers, through rate filings with state insurance commissioners. This legislation failed to make it through Congress during the 1998 session.

Many consumer groups oppose federal intervention. "These guys screwed up," said Mary Griffin, an insurance specialist at Consumers Union in Washington, "and they want the government to come and save them from themselves."

Consumer groups believe insurance companies can afford to spend more on claims than they take in from policies in part because insurers receive investment income on funds awaiting payout. But pro-consumer activism may reduce insurers' and investors' willingness to place their funds at risk without adequate return or government support. Many of these groups support flat rate pricing in which both high and low risks pay similar prices on the grounds of "fairness."

Ultimately, individuals or institutions that impose risk on others should pay for it—or the insurance market as a whole may suffer. In testimony before Congress, Robert Klein, Associate Professor and Director, Center for Risk Management and Insurance Research at Georgia State University, pointed out the dangers of public policy that subsidizes high risk policyholders at the expense of others.

When low-risk policyholders observe that they can obtain protection elsewhere at a lower cost, they will leave the insurance pool, which causes the pool to shrink. The pool then becomes populated with high-risk policyholders and no one left to subsidize them. This is known as adverse selection. Also, many of the high risks left in the pool will live in one geographical area, leaving the pool vulnerable to a catastrophe. Klein advocated a coordinated public and private solution to the problem of catastrophe risk.

Those who support federal intervention believe that "federal insurance" would reduce the amount Congress must spend case-by-case for disasters such as the recent flooding in North Dakota. Rather than just handing out money, programs such as the National Flood Insurance Program (NFIP) collect something from those who expect help during flood losses.

If NFIP's losses exceed the program's resources, FEMA has the authority to borrow funds from the U.S. Treasury. But it must pay back the loan with interest out of future premiums, meaning the program is expected to be self-sufficient. This is a far cry from "something for nothing."

Most reinsurers said they back a federal reinsurance facility. "There is reinsurance available, but only up to a certain level. What this bill does nicely is complement what is out there," said Francis Bouchard, Director of Federal Affairs for the Reinsurance Association of America, a trade group.

The California Earthquake Authority

Perhaps the most publicized state disaster legislation in recent years is the California Earthquake Authority (CEA), a state-managed insurance pool that provides residential earthquake policies. The pool is privately financed by participating insurers who made an initial capital contribution according to market share. Theoretically, the fund will be able to pay out at least $10.5 billion after an earthquake. The creation of the CEA hinged on an IRS exemption from federal income tax that allows a tax-free reserve to be built up for disaster recovery.

Part of the CEA's funding capacity ($1.5 billion) was supposed to come from institutional investors via a catastrophe bond issue, originally referred to as Earthquake Risk Bonds (ERB). Before coming to market, however, the entire cat bond layer was replaced by National Indemnity, Berkshire Hathaway's "super-cat" reinsurer, which offered a price that was slightly lower than the ERB. U.S. super-investor Warren Buffet, Berkshire Hathaway's Chairman, has stated that he expects cat bonds ultimately to cause financial hardship for the unsuspecting, but obviously he is prepared to take on that kind of risk for his own account.

The CEA's original $10.5 billion (plus accumulated premiums) in capacity comes from the following sources (in order of payment, should losses reach those levels):

- First, losses are paid from accumulated premiums from policyholders;
- Next, losses are paid from $1 billion contributed by insurers when CEA began operations;
- Next, losses are paid from $3 billion infusion from participating insurers;
- Next, losses are paid from $2 billion in reinsurance contracts;

• Next, losses are paid from $1 billion CEA line of credit;
• Next, losses are paid from $1.5 billion in reinsurance from Warren Buffet;
• Finally, losses are paid from $2 billion in additional assessments against insurers (they can add a surcharge to CEA policies to recover assessments).

Source: California Earthquake Authority

During late 1996, the CEA was activated and participating companies were required to contribute to the CEA's initial $1 billion capitalization. The contributing companies can offer CEA earthquake policies, but are prohibited from offering their own earthquake insurance policies to prevent "cherry-picking." ("Cherry picking," also known as "cream skimming," would result when insurance companies take the most profitable earthquake policies for themselves, while forwarding less attractive business on to the CEA.)

Earthquake policies offered by the CEA take a "mini-policy" form that provides dwelling coverage with a 15 percent deductible, and caps contents coverage at $5,000 and living expense coverage at $1,500.

Because of the risk-sharing features of the CEA and the improved regulatory environment, California's largest insurers—State Farm, Allstate and Farmers—began writing new homeowners insurance again after a period of refusing new business. They had refused to write new policies due to a California requirement that they offer earthquake coverage along with every homeowners policy. Since these companies did not want any additional earthquake exposure, they did not write any new policies. With the advent of the CEA coverage, these companies could write new business without taking on quake risk.

Since commencing operations in late 1996, the CEA has fallen short of expectations. Sales of earthquake insurance are reported to be lower than they were prior to the CEA's creation. The CEA's lackluster performance has been linked to the minimal coverage its policies offer and its prohibition against installment premiums—which would make quake coverage more affordable. In order to attract more customers, the CEA recently announced a change to allow installment premium payments.

Fortunately for both California residents and the CEA, there have been no significant claims and CEA has been able to keep most of its premiums, net of expenses and reinsurance premiums. The accumulation of funds along with interest adds to the CEA's ability to fund the next disaster.

Florida's Windstorm Pools

In the wake of Hurricane Andrew, Florida's homeowners insurance market was in a shambles. Insurers reevaluated their exposure to hurricane risk and initiated plans to cut the number of policies while increasing rates. Allstate announced plans to nonrenew over one-third of its existing policyholder base, eliminate new writings and file for a 41 percent increase in premiums. Other insurers advanced similar plans, but Florida lawmakers would not tolerate such drastic action. In addition, Insurance Commissioner Bill Nelson (an elected official) took a hard-line position against insurers that attempted to make drastic reductions in their Florida coastline exposure.

Florida limited non-renewals to 5 percent per year while most rate increase approvals amounted to only a fraction of the size requested. But the pressure on the Florida insurance market still increased since few insurers wanted to make commitments in light of the "new" exposure.

To relieve some of that pressure, the Florida legislature created a state run reinsurance facility in 1993 known as the Florida Hurricane Catastrophe Fund (FHCF). The FHCF—or "Cat Fund"—offers reinsurance coverage to participating insurers for a single event windstorm in Florida that the National Hurricane Center classifies as a hurricane. While this arrangement made insurers less uneasy, it did not keep insurers from wanting to leave.

During the period from 1993 to 1996, two state-run insurance pools, the Florida Windstorm Underwriting Association (FWUA) and the Florida Residential Property and Casualty Joint Underwriting Association, otherwise know as the JUA, became much more active participants in the provision of Florida homeowners insurance.

Many coastal states have state programs called "beach and windstorm plans" to cover beachfront property against hurricane damage. The FWUA's mission was to provide protection in a very limited area, but the situation called for much more. Subsidized by private insurance companies, the FWUA grew to over 120,000 policies by 1996.

The JUA is Florida's version of a residual market plan, a mechanism for covering policyholders denied coverage through the voluntary insurance market. Since JUA-type plans usually operate at a loss (because of artificially low premiums), they must assess private insurers for losses according to their pro-rata share of the voluntary market.

The Florida Residential JUA was created to relieve the insurance availability crisis. Because insurers were slowly withdrawing from the market, the JUA eventually became the second largest insurance company behind State Farm. But legislators knew that their tinkering with the private insurance market could not persist in an economically tolerable way.

During 1996, Florida's regulators accelerated efforts to stabilize its homeowners insurance market and legislators passed several bills to ease the availability crisis. Regulators streamlined their approval process for new companies entering the Florida market, offered incentives for private insurers to assume homeowners policies from the state-run JUA facility and granted more "reasonable" rate increases and coverage limitations to private insurers.

The FHCF continues to provide some reinsurance protection for 292 companies writing homeowners insurance in Florida. In addition, Florida officials recently retained an investment banker to explore a multibillion-dollar bond issue to prefund claim payments following the next costly catastrophe.

Insurance Commissioner Bill Nelson and his staff shrank the high-priced JUA insurance pool from nearly one million policies in 1996 to fewer than 300,000 within two years. Nearly all the remaining policies were in hurricane-prone southern Florida. But the other, more specialized, statewide insurer of last resort—the windstorm pool—ballooned. So, in 1998, the total risk to the two pools was higher than at the JUA's peak in 1996.

Nelson said he wants to shrink the industry-controlled windstorm pool as well, preferably through legislative changes. "If I can't get the votes to do it, ultimately the market will do it," Nelson said. "As the market improves and (insurers) start getting greedy again, going after each other to keep their market share, it's going to create the right climate."

Nelson's vehicle for "depopulating" the JUA was to give insurers a $100-per-policy bounty to take policies out of the state fund. The strategy increased competition, adding about 25 new insurers to the state. Critics, however, voiced doubts about the viability of these fledgling "take-out companies" because many hadn't been tested by a major storm.

Hawaii Hurricane Relief Fund

Although 1992's Hurricane Andrew and 1989's Hurricane Hugo rank as the top two U.S. windstorms in terms of financial losses, Hurricane Iniki, which hit Hawaii in 1992, caused over $1.6 billion in insured losses, and devastated Hawaii's private insurance market. Consequently, state authorities established the Hawaii Hurricane Relief Fund (HHRF) as a public insurance pool that sells hurricane risk policies.

Under the plan, private insurers are allowed to sell homeowners insurance with an exclusion that eliminates coverage for hurricanes. Homeowners that purchase a policy with the exclusion must seek hurricane coverage through the HHRF if they want the coverage or if their bank requires it.

The HHRF is designed to fill the gap left by private insurers who abandoned the market following Iniki, but its financing sources make it clear that private insurers and policyholders will ultimately foot the bill for disaster claims. The HHRF pool's total capacity of $1.7 billion is funded through a combination of deductibles, assessments on insurers, reinsurance purchased directly by the HHRF (using funds from premium and mortgage taxes), and a line of credit to be repaid through surcharges on future policies. If losses total more than $1.7 billion, claims will be paid on a pro rata basis. The HHRF replaced an earlier stop gap measure that extended the state's existing lava-hazard pool to include policyholders with hurricane exposure.

State Guaranty Funds

Following the Depression period of the early 1930s, Congress created the Federal Deposit Insurance Corporation (FDIC) and the Federal Savings and Loan Insurance Corporation (FSLIC) to avoid a repeat of the losses caused by failed financial institutions. Unlike banks, insurance companies are regulated by the states—an action to protect insurance policyholders against insurance company failures was considered a state issue. The state mechanism for protecting policyholders against insurance company default became known as the State Guaranty Fund.

While insurance company failures have been few and far between, the collapse of the Baldwin United Life Insurance Company in the 1970s accelerated the development of state guaranty funds for both property/ liability insurance and life/health insurance. Following recommendations from the National Association of Insurance Commissioners (NAIC), many states began to create state guaranty funds *en masse* in the 1970s and today all states have such a safety net for policyholders.

While state legislatures are free to adopt their own plans covering the losses of an insolvent insurance company, most state guaranty funds offer generous—albeit limited—protection for property owners who file claims against an insurance company that becomes unable to meet its obligations. In most states, property owners can expect to receive full payment for claims up to $300,000. Unfortunately, collecting this amount can take years, particularly for larger, more complicated insolvencies.

In some cases, solvent companies assume the assets and liabilities of the insolvent company and rescue their policyholders without guaranty fund intervention. While the acquiring firm may have to cover losses beyond the value of the insolvent firm's assets, many insurance companies view the acquisition as both a good will gesture as well as an opportunity to acquire a large group of new customers without the usual customer acquisition costs.

Unfortunately, some insolvent companies cannot be sold and are liquidated under state control. When state regulators place an insurer in liquidation and they determine that there is a deficit, regulators make assessments on all solvent companies writing similar business in their state according to their market share.

For example, suppose XYZ Insurance Company of Illinois fails, leaving behind unpaid policyholder claims of $100 million in Illinois (after assets have been exhausted). If State Farm holds 21 percent of the homeowners insurance market in Illinois, State Farm will receive an assessment notice for $21 million, its pro rata share of XYZ's losses. Depending on the state, insurers may be able to use some or all of their premium tax obligations (about 2 percent of premiums in most states) over an extended period of time to offset their assessments. This effectively transfers at least a portion of the insolvency costs to the state. Insurers and policyholders will pick up the remainder of the tab through outright losses for the company's owners and increased premiums for policyholders.

While state guaranty funds serve a legitimate and important purpose, the safety net created by guaranty funds sends the wrong signal to both insurance companies and policyholders. With guaranty funds, insurance companies do not need to worry about most of their policyholders in the event of catastrophe since the guaranty fund will cover them. Consequently, why should insurance company executives pay for extensive reinsurance protection? Policyholders might want them to purchase that protection, but knowing that the guaranty fund will protect them, why would policyholders want the extra expense included in their premium? Furthermore, companies who operate responsibly are the ones who must pay for the mistakes of their insolvent competitors—hardly an optimal set of incentives.

In 1987—perhaps the worst year for state guaranty funds—assessments on property/liability companies still amounted to only 0.005 percent of premiums. But state guaranty funds create incentives to operate in a risky fashion, leaving solvent insurers to clean up the mess. Is this fair? Clearly not, but it may take a colossal loss to bring reforms to a system that has not yet received the attention that it deserves.

Summary

Several of the issues considered in this chapter came to a point in the Homeowners' Insurance Availability Act of 1997, which would have created Federal reinsurance for state disaster programs. This self-funded facility would have protected these programs against relatively rare but extremely damaging natural disasters, primarily earthquakes and hurricanes.

This federal reinsurance backstop would provide a layer of protection above what state insurance programs like the CEA and the Hawaii Hurricane Relief Fund, and state reinsurance programs like the FHCF, currently provide. The bill also would provide states with the opportunity to auction Federal reinsurance directly to insurers and reinsurers within the state. Federal reinsurance coverage would not begin for any state until insured residential losses exceeded that state's retention.

Premiums collected from each state program would be actuarially-based. They would be set by the new National Commission on Catastrophe Risks and Insurance Loss Costs, and would be at least two times the state's average annual expected loss, plus expenses. The Loss Costs

Commission would also set an actuarially-determined reserve, or minimum price for reinsurance sold through the state auctions.

For both the backstop over state programs and the auction, Federal liability was capped at $25 billion per year after a four-year phase-in period. There is also a provision that if due to losses in prior years the program is running at a deficit, the limit available in subsequent years will not exceed what can be paid off by the programs premiums within twenty years.

CHAPTER EIGHTEEN

Catastrophe Models and Financing Tools

During Hurricane Andrew, reinsurers sustained losses on virtually every account they had underwritten. Many reinsurance companies either folded or stopped doing business in catastrophic risks. Turmoil in the reinsurance market caused problems for homeowners since reinsurers provide financial stability and consistency to the primary insurance markets.

Stunned by the natural disasters of the last decade, property insurers turned to computer models for guidance in underwriting. The variety of software programs on the market today project the loss potential from earthquakes, hurricanes and other catastrophes by analyzing historical data and loss experience.

The models simulate hazards, calculate damages at insured sites and estimate property and business interruption losses across a portfolio of sites. The models have become increasingly sophisticated, enabling analysis of exposures within ZIP codes and according to latitudes and longitudes. So powerful is their potential, the technology will influence public policy—illustrated by the intense debate among insurers, regulators and consumers over issues of data quality and applications.

Underwriters have varying degrees of confidence in these computer models. Some use the programs to evaluate their overall portfolio. Others tap them to set property insurance rates in specific regions. Clearly, they are an important tool in decision making, but not a substitute for existing underwriting techniques.

Some state insurance regulators criticize computer models as tools carriers can manipulate to pass on staggering rate hikes to consumers. Other state regulators view the models as tools for evaluating the risk exposures of carriers and their solvency. Reinsurers are paying an ever-larger share of catastrophic losses and rely on commercial software programs to help them evaluate the catastrophe risk of reinsurance submissions and hedge their bets with retrocession. Some reinsurers are developing proprietary models.

There are three parts to any such model. The first is the collection of data about potential events and the meteorological and seismic descriptions of these. A simulated hurricane, for example, is specified by a storm track and the most important meteorological characteristics of the storm along this path. Examples of these characteristics are its forward velocity, central pressure differential and radius of maximum winds. For an earthquake they are the type of fault involved, the segment of the fault which ruptures, and the magnitude of this rupture. For both earthquake and hurricane events, the models estimate the probability of each event occurring during a year.

The second part of a catastrophe model is a database of the properties that could be damaged by the event. Typically this is a detailed database that includes, among other things, the property and contents values, the materials used to construct the building and the deductible and policy limit of the insurance on the structure.

The final part of such a model estimates the total damage to properties based on their location and type of construction and on the characteristics of the simulated earthquake or hurricane, and then applies the insurance coverages, policy limits and deductibles to arrive at the insured losses to each structure. These are aggregated to produce industry loss totals for each event.

Catastrophe models are by no means perfect, but they are the best tools we have for estimating expected annual losses in the insurance industry. Models are not intended to estimate damage to a particular structure for a single event, but instead average damage from many events. By averaging anticipated damages over thousands of structures, models can reasonably estimate the effects of an individual storm or earthquake.

Because we are finally looking at averages of averages, models are the most effective tools for determining appropriate rates. While there is still some risk that model parameters have been chosen incorrectly, a reinsurer can adequately protect itself by adding on a profit loading. This gives the reinsurer a margin of safety in its coverage pricing decisions.

Catastrophe models for property risk are beginning to serve a vital role in public policy. For example, they highlight the importance of adopting and enforcing building codes for property in earthquake—and windstorm-prone regions.

Models for casualty risks can serve a similar role. A large scale movement of the San Andreas fault or another quake in the New Madrid area will have a ripple effect throughout the United States. Models can define the financial fallout. Insights gained can inspire or focus public policy initiatives to mitigate economic and social consequences of a disaster.

Some model designers recognize the potential. EQE International Inc. developed an injury-projection component in the earthquake product the firm built for the California Department of Emergency Services. Other model designers are studying options for prototype catastrophe models. They are far from ready for commercial applications.

Certainly, creating catastrophe models for casualty lines—perhaps by expanding existing models for property lines—will require a significant investment of time, money and people. Data demands are enormous, just as they are with models for property lines. Accuracy is essential, and it is not easily accomplished. In the realm of workers' comp, for instance, records must identify the number of employees at a site, the number of shifts worked, the number of people per shift, the collapse hazards of buildings and the loss associated with minor, severe and very severe injuries.

Insurers can play a role in the development of catastrophe models for casualty lines by encouraging a dialogue between the model designers and the scientists who work in the insurance industry. They have been forging relationships as they examine and validate catastrophe models for property lines built on civil engineering, seismology, statistics and economics. On the strength of those relationships, they can do the same for casualty lines.

Insurance regulators support catastrophe modeling but would like to see underwriters exercise some restraint when using the models to set rates. The controversial catastrophe models, which insurers and reinsurers are increasingly using to help determine rates, drew criticism and praise during a half-day seminar at the Chartered Property Casualty Underwiters (CPCU) Society's annual meeting in Dallas during September 1997.

Regulators from South Carolina and Florida made it clear that while catastrophe models have a place in rate-making, they won't allow the models to be the last word in how much is charged for property coverage.

One Florida regulator hoped to put to rest the notion that his state has no faith in catastrophe modeling simply because the state challenged the models' reliability. "There is a myth out there that Florida does not acknowledge catastrophe modeling for hurricanes," said Kevin M. McCarty, assistant director of insurer services at the Florida Department of Insurance. "That is simply not true."

In fact, Florida regulators rely on modeling to derive rates for the state's own hurricane catastrophe fund. But regulators in the state have also been somewhat critical of modeling, challenging one method in Florida's Division of Administrative Hearings earlier this year. The suit charged that a model approved by the Florida Commission on Hurricane Loss Projection Methodology would undercut the Department's authority in approving or rejecting rates. An administrative law judge dismissed the challenge in September.

That doesn't stop Florida regulators from looking closely at each individual filing, whether or not the insurer submitting it used modeling to come up with rates. The higher rates insurers calculate using models may not be high enough.

Scientists have indicated that climatic changes as a result of global warming will result in more hurricanes. And, some scientists claim that fact is not adequately reflected in catastrophe models. "They are far more scientific and accurate than the alternative," said Rade T. Musulin, VP and actuary for Florida Farm Bureau Insurance Cos. in Gainesville, Florida.

Before modeling, insurers' rate-setting methods did not incorporate factors such as variations of losses by geographic area, demographic shifts and changes in weather patterns.

New Financial Tools

Faced with the prospect of limited—and expensive—reinsurance coverage, insurance companies had two choices: hold all of the risk themselves or look for other ways to pass some of the risk on to someone else. Choosing the latter, insurance companies, securities exchanges and investment banks began the development of instruments now known as Alternative Risk Transfer (ART) products or insurance derivatives.

These innovations bring the insurance industry closer to the securities industry in structure and substance. Wall Street, with trillions of dollars in the public markets, has positioned itself to provide capital solutions to insurers seeking greater capacity and lower costs than traditional catastrophe reinsurance protection. New financial instruments that can be used to hedge or transfer catastrophe risk appear on an almost daily basis.

Although many people have come to view the word "derivative" in a negative light, derivatives stand out as one of the world's great risk management tools. The size of the U.S. derivative securities markets, with about $3 billion traded per day, avoids the major difficulty of thin markets in which reinsurance prices rise after a catastrophe, precisely when capital is needed most. Because the derivatives market is both large and liquid, insurance and reinsurance markets can lay off substantial amounts of risk without overwhelming the market's capacity or affecting prices.

Although reinsurance has existed for centuries, methods of converting insurance risk into tradable securities have been developed only since 1990. Perhaps the first effort towards insurance risk securitization (conversion into tradable securities) was the introduction of the Catastrophe Futures Contract at the Chicago Board of Trade in 1992. While the product never really caught on, investors became more aware of insurance risk as a tradable commodity.

Richard Sandor, considered by many to be the "Father of Financial Futures," believes that insurance risk is no different than any other type of risk traded on U.S. futures exchanges. While most types of insurance risk can be reduced through pooling, the correlation of catastrophe risk across policies does not lend itself to the risk reducing function of pooling. Like commodity price risk or interest rate risk, catastrophe insurance risk cannot be reduced through pooling or diversification; it can only be transferred to others.

In an article in the *Journal of Applied Corporate Finance*, Sandor points out that the insurance industry, including the reinsurers, have about

$250 billion of surplus available to cover an estimated $30 trillion worth of U.S. property exposure. Clearly, any sizable catastrophe would leave the insurance and reinsurance companies vulnerable to a follow-on second or third event. In contrast, Sandor estimates that the capital markets possess approximately $20-25 trillion of capital, depending on market conditions.

Furthermore, normal fluctuations in the markets on a daily basis amount to more than just about any conceivable catastrophe. Insurers need surplus—funds to pay for unexpectedly large claims—to protect policyholders. If the capital markets can provide catastrophe coverage amounting to only 1 percent of the capital market's total capitalization, catastrophe risk bearing capacity would soar. Therefore, the capital markets may be the most logical place to look for solutions to the problems posed by catastrophe risk.

Catastrophe Bonds

One of the most important developments in catastrophe funding is the catastrophe bond, sometimes known as an "act of God bond." Insurance companies sell these bonds to investors that qualify for "private placement" securities and are traded by dealers in the over-the-counter bond market. (Don't look for prices in the newspaper—the bonds do not trade actively and are not traded on an exchange.) Unlike typical bonds, which represent the issuer's promise to pay principal and interest without condition, cat bonds represent an insurer's conditional promise to pay all of the principal and interest, provided that certain losses do not exceed a specified level.

United Services Automobile Association (USAA), a multi-line insurance company serving military families, was not the first to issue cat bonds, but USAA's two offerings (1997 and 1998) are the largest and best known issues. In the first step of the transactions, USAA created an offshore special-purpose reinsurer called Residential Re that would provide $500 million of reinsurance coverage after USAA's coastal losses exceed $1 billion.

To fund the reinsurance coverage, Residential Re then sold $500 million worth of one year cat bonds to investors and placed the proceeds in a trust that invests in interest bearing U.S. Treasury securities. Bondholders understand that they will receive their principal back only if USAA's windstorm catastrophe losses do not exceed $1 billion. The U.S. Treasury securities are liquidated either to pay for losses if necessary or pay bondholders back if losses don't reach the trigger point.

In exchange for bearing USAA's risk, Residential Re receives a reinsurance premium from USAA and pays bondholders an interest rate reflecting the cost of capital and the possibility that the bonds may default.

Although the structure of the 1997 and 1998 transactions were slightly different, the success of the 1997 deal attracted aggressive interest in the 1998 offering, which reduced the interest rate that Residential Re paid to investors. In turn, this reduced the reinsurance premium that USAA paid to Residential Re. As a result of the two cat bond issues, USAA has established itself as an innovative catastrophe financier while creating a ready market for its catastrophe risk outside of the reinsurance arena.

Other companies, including ACE, St. Paul, Swiss Re, and Tokio Fire and Marine have issued cat bonds in a variety of innovative structures that depend on measurements of industry losses, company specific losses and the severity of earthquakes.

Similar to cat bonds, contingent surplus notes provide insurers with capital in the event of a catastrophe. Arkwright Mutual, a specialty insurer of highly protected risks, issued $100 million in 30-year contingent surplus notes in 1996, following Nationwide's $400 million contingent surplus note issue in 1995.

In both cases, proceeds raised from the bond issuance were placed in a trust for use in the event of a catastrophe. If utilized, the funds held in trust would be replaced by an IOU in the form of "surplus notes" issued by the mutual insurer.

By issuing surplus notes, which are treated as surplus for regulatory purposes, the insurer can continue to operate despite suffering significant losses.

The catch? Contingent surplus notes carry higher than normal interest rates to reflect the possibility that investors will not get paid. Insurance regulators have the power to prevent insurers from making payments on surplus notes if the payments would threaten the insurer's ability to pay claims.

Selected Events in Innovative Catastrophe Risk Financing

Year	Event
1992	Catastrophe Futures Introduced at Chicago Board of Trade
1995	Chicago Board of Trade Introduces Options on PCS Cat Index
1996	Aon Introduces Proprietary CatEPut(r) Product with RLI Insurance
1997	USAA Sells $477 million of Cat Bonds Tied to Hurricane Risk
1997	Tokio Fire and Marine Sells Cat Bonds Tied to Tokyo Earthquake Risk
1997	Bermuda Commodities Exchange Lists Options on Guy Carpenter Index
1998	USAA Again Sells Cat Bonds, but Bonds Carry Lower Risk Spread
1998	Exel/Mid Ocean Swaps $200 million of Property Cat Exposure

This securitization of risk may not have to wait for a firming market to gain popularity, though. When Cat Bonds were introduced, they were overpriced for insurers by design. Since then, almost every one that's been issued has been more competitive. By the late 1990s, the prices looked similar to open-market catastrophe reinsurance.

In a venture into the capital markets, American Re has formed American Re Capital Markets, through which the company will provide clients opportunities to mitigate risk in the financial markets. Initially, the company would focus on the weather derivatives market, protecting both buyers and sellers of weather-dependent products and services against significant fluctuations in weather conditions.

The weather derivative market began heating up in the late 1990s, when large utility companies and companies that sell energy became concerned about warmer winters and cooler summers.

These companies started trading temperature risk via contracts that obligate one party to pay the other if the aggregate temperature in a particular city is less or greater than a set point.

"It's an interesting marketplace. Reinsurance companies all underwrite earthquake and hurricane risk every day, and the data to price that risk is very sparse compared to the data involving temperature risk. From a pure underwriting perspective, this is very logical for us," one risk manager said.

The beauty of Cat Bonds or any other form of insurance risk security is that it can be customized to fit the needs of both buyers and sellers of catastrophe risk. However, customization makes trading more difficult since traders must understand the particulars of each offering rather than specializing in just a few liquid, standardized instruments.

At least for now, Cat Bonds are unlikely to be actively traded in the secondary market. Rather, buyers will hold them to maturity as part of an overall portfolio diversification strategy.

Catastrophe Options

Catastrophe options are perhaps the oldest form of Alternative Risk Transfer currently available. In general, option contracts allow holders to buy or sell an underlying asset or index at a specified price on or before the option's expiration date. In layman's terms, option holders can benefit when the value of an asset or index (i.e., insurance industry losses) rises or falls. Insurance companies need a financial instrument that gains value when catastrophe losses increase. Cat options do just that.

The Chicago Board of Trade (CBOT) launched its PCS (Property Claims Services) catastrophe insurance options in September 1995. PCS options gain and lose value based on measurements of industrywide catastrophe losses on both a national and a regional basis. The options enable insurers to access new catastrophe capacity, gain better geographic spread and hedge their retention levels in addition to existing reinsurance contracts. They are primarily traded as "call spreads," similar to reinsurance layers, with values based on industry loss estimates quantified in PCS's national and regional catastrophe-loss indices. PCS options also offer speculators a chance to "bet on the weather."

PCS options experienced heavy trading levels after Hurricane Fran hit the North Carolina coast in 1996, and as Hurricane George approached the U.S. in September 1998. Trading activity has been confined to reinsurers and large commercial insurers, such as Travelers/Aetna Property Casualty Corp. and U.S. Fidelity & Guaranty Group seeking to spread risk. The PCS contract still faces market acceptance challenges; insurers are reluctant to pursue untested, nontraditional methods of risk transfer and are concerned about regulatory constraints that do not fully recognize the use of derivative products as hedging instruments.

But PCS options offer a place for insurance risk buyers and sellers to meet and agree upon a price. Because the contracts are guaranteed by the CBOT, there is much less risk of default than a traditional reinsurance contract.

This factor alone may attract buyers who need protection against "the mother of all catastrophes," during which many reinsurers could get wiped out. Furthermore, the CBOT cat options may be the only form of catastrophe protection available the day after a disaster like Hurricane Andrew has stunned the industry.

In March 1997, the CBOT gained competition for its PCS Cat options contract. The Bermuda Commodities Exchange and reinsurance broker Guy Carpenter & Company, Inc. announced a new index that measures the insured damage to homeowner properties in the U.S. caused by atmospheric perils such as hurricanes, tornadoes, and winter storms.

The Guy Carpenter Catastrophe Index serves as the reference index for option contracts that are traded on the Bermuda Commodities Exchange (BCE), as well as for off-exchange contracts between insurers, reinsurers, and investors. Guy Carpenter's Indexco subsidiary publishes the index on a quarterly basis. Bruce Thomas, CEO of Indexco, says, "Until now there has been an enormous gap between the needs of insurers and investors that has effectively prevented the securitization of catastrophe risk. The Guy Carpenter Catastrophe Index bridges the requirements of both groups for a significant subset of catastrophe exposure."

Like the PCS contracts, contracts based on the Guy Carpenter Catastrophe Index will help supplement traditional reinsurance. Although the Guy Carpenter Catastrophe Index should correlate well with the atmospheric loss experience of companies with large concentrations of homeowner insurance, there will always be some element of basis risk. Basis risk is the difference between the risk being hedged and the instrument used to hedge it. Use of industrywide indexes to hedge insurance risk may have a strong relationship with a specific company's losses, but this relationship will not be perfect. In other words, the index option contracts will not be a perfect hedge.

The BCE/Indexco offering reduces this gap through the use of loss measurements all the way down to specific ZIP codes, but some basis risk remains. In this respect, reinsurance has an advantage since reinsurance contracts are tailored to an insurer's exact needs.

Both PCS and the BCE/Indexco contracts provide a general hedging tool for insurers and reinsurers, but the liquidity necessary for large scale hedging has not yet materialized. Perhaps the lack of interest stems from a relatively soft—low price—market for reinsurance. Indexco's 1997 figures reflected a very tame year for catastrophe losses. Perhaps with more damage, interest in cat options will increase as both insurers and speculators seek protection and profit.

Insurance broker Aon and specialty insurer RLI Corporation recently introduced another form of alternative risk financing: Catastrophe Equity Puts. Using Aon's proprietary CatEPut© product, RLI can supplement its traditional reinsurance program with a sale of securities to its reinsurer at a pre-negotiated rate in the event of a catastrophe loss. The three-year program, which allows RLI to sell (put) convertible preferred shares to its reinsurer once its reinsurance capacity is exhausted, is designed to protect RLI's surplus.

In the event the options are exercised, its reinsurer (Centre Re) becomes part owner of RLI in exchange for a capital infusion. This sort of transaction enhances RLI's ability to stay in business after a catastrophe.

Swaps

A lesser-known strategy of exchanging catastrophe exposure is the swap transaction. Under a swap agreement, two parties agree to pay each other well-defined cash flows under certain conditions. Swaps have long been a part of the credit and currency markets.

Under a catastrophe swap, the insurance company agrees to pay a group of investors (the swap counterparty) a floating interest rate plus a risk premium in exchange for investors' commitment to pay a sum of money following a catastrophe. The interest rate on the investors' money at risk exceeds rates paid in the capital markets to reflect the possibility that the investor could lose the entire contractual amount in the event of a catastrophe. The interest rate amounts to a premium; but, although swap transactions operate much like reinsurance programs, they are classified as swaps to avoid the regulatory scrutiny and premium taxes associated with traditional reinsurance contracts.

According to the London-based *Risk Financier* newsletter, total worldwide catastrophe risk swap activity has exceeded $680 million since 1995. Swap volume is sure to increase as market participants become more comfortable with the transactions and nature of the risks.

Another risk financing vehicle is the Catastrophe Risk Exchange, or Catex. This facility is licensed to act as a reinsurance intermediary to trade catastrophe risks among insurers and reinsurers. Although not currently active, Catex will give companies the ability to swap and diversify exposures regionally and by cause of loss to reduce overall exposure concentration.

Betting on the Weather

The depth and capacity of the $20 trillion capital markets naturally attract financial institutions that want to transfer large risks quickly and at low cost. Insurers need access to large amounts of capital under certain, unusual conditions (i.e., after a catastrophe). Therefore, insurers are willing participants (sellers of risk) in the emerging market for securitized insurance risk. This, of course, assumes that they can find willing buyers of risk for a reasonable price.

But who would want to take on this catastrophe risk? The answer is, quite simply, any individual or institution that wants more diversification for his or its portfolio. As investors become more comfortable with owning securities with payments that are contingent on catastrophic losses, demand for insurance risk securities will grow because portfolio managers need assets that are uncorrelated with their existing holdings.

Under the Capital Asset Pricing Model (CAPM) and other standard portfolio theories, optimal portfolio management requires that managers seek out investments that provide their portfolio with a higher return at a given level of risk (return volatility) or that reduce risk for a given level of return. Since catastrophes are uncorrelated with most other investments (most stocks, bonds, etc.), insurance risk securities reduce overall portfolio risk.

Virtually everyone agrees with the theoretical benefit of insurance risk securities and transactions. The returns on these securities combined with their zero-beta return characteristic (returns that are uncorrelated with returns on other securities) makes these instruments attractive to many investment managers. Unfortunately, there is not a sufficiently large market for any of these instruments to call them an unqualified success yet.

Some experts believe that the true test of the market for cat bonds and options will be the next megacatastrophe. Now that the fledgling market has provided nice returns for several years, interest in these markets appears to be growing.

But will the unlucky investors holding these securities during the next disaster choose to buy similar securities after being burned for the first time? Perhaps not, but others probably will when the market price for risk rises to a point where it becomes attractive.

Insurers hope that investors will step forward to offer catastrophic risk capacity after the next big one, if only to keep the reinsurance companies from taking advantage of a bad situation.

Many industry observers speculate on the role capital markets will play in the catastrophe risk market, but leading analysts from the insurance rating firm A.M. Best believe it is inevitable that property catastrophe risks will be bundled or securitized into an asset class unto itself—only time will tell if they are right.

CONCLUSION

Throughout this book, we've looked at the ways catastrophes—natural and man made—can affect people and their wallets. Without exception, we are all exposed to the effects of catastrophes, directly or indirectly. Miraculously, we usually withstand these forces much larger than ourselves without personal injury, but we face the financial challenges left in the wake of these catastrophic events.

Catastrophic events call for a combination of loss mitigation, insurance coverage and government assistance to protect property interests. But many people in high-risk areas forego flood insurance or earthquake coverage only to suffer the financial consequences. Government policy should encourage people to do the right thing—to take care of themselves.

But even doing the right thing—purchasing insurance coverage and vigorously pursuing a claim—may not be enough. Consider the May 1994 federal court decision *Norman and Helena Brownyard v. Maryland Casualty Co. and Valiant Insurance Co.,* which dealt with one of the basic claims-paying tactics that comes into play when a natural disaster causes a lot of property damage.

The Brownyard's home in Mount Pleasant, South Carolina was insured by Valiant when, in 1989, Hurricane Hugo did major damage to the Carolina coast. Once Hugo had done its worst, the Brownyards were left with an awful mess. They ended up claiming losses of $322,306—a lot for that part of the state.

In May 1990, Valiant paid $6,374 to the Brownyards in partial payment of the claim. But, immediately after this very small initial payment, problems started. Specifically, "a dispute ensued over the cause and extent of damage to the Brownyard home." In layman's terms: Valiant suspected that the Brownyards were padding...or outright fabricating...claimed losses.

Gene Silver, an adjuster for Maryland Casualty Co.—the company that handled adjustment of the claims for policies issued by Valiant—assumed handling of the claim. But, the adjuster merely got caught in the crossfire between two angry parties. After almost a year of "numerous conflicts and repeated difficulty," Maryland Casualty suggested the parties enter into arbitration proceedings.

Although the Brownyards' were reluctant at first, they agreed after Maryland personnel assured them that arbitration would be an expeditious method that could probably dispose of the dispute within 60 to 90 days. Probably. It took another couple of months—until late September 1991—for an arbitration agreement to be signed.

In April 1992, attorneys for both sides met with Will Evans, the arbitrator, in an effort to explore the settlement. Evans mentioned his plan to hire an independent contractor as a consultant if the settlement discussions should fail. Immediately after the meeting, the Brownyards made a settlement proposal. Valiant's attorney said he would consult with his clients to determine whether the proposal was acceptable.

Over the next two months, the Brownyards' attorney repeatedly tried to find out the insurers' reaction to the offer—but he couldn't get a response. Finally, in June, the Brownyards' attorney wrote to the insurers' attorney; he stated that, unless his clients received a meaningful response soon, they would contact the arbitrator and ask him to proceed immediately. The insurers' lawyer responded, in part:

> I am sorry for the apparent lack of interest on my client's behalf, but Gene [Silver, the adjuster] has not been in the office and then apparently went on vacation. Obviously, you must do what is in the best interest of your client....

A few weeks later, the Brownyards' attorney sent a second letter requesting a response to the settlement proposal. Again, the insurers failed to respond.

Soon after that, Evans wrote to both sides advising that he was ready to proceed and asking for written authorization to secure the services of the consultant. The Brownyards' attorney sent its written authorization. The insurers, once again, failed to respond. The arbitrator was powerless to force the insurers to respond.

On September 11, 1992, just ten days before the statute of limitations was to run on the claim, the Brownyards filed suit against Maryland Casualty.

Their complaint alleged, in part, that the insurers were purposefully unresponsive and delayed their claim. They also alleged that the insurers refused to cooperate in the arbitration proceedings and engaged in a "pattern of conscious footdragging," to an extent that Valiant and Maryland can be said to have waived any right they had to arbitrate the claim.

The Brownyards claimed significant prejudice from the insurers' refusal to participate or further the arbitration or settlement in a reasonable, timely, and meaningful way—preventing repairs from being carried out to their property. Lastly, since the insurers refused to renew their policy in 1992, the Brownyards had to get insurance with another company at a significantly higher cost—and without any contents coverage "because of the current, unrepaired condition of their home."

The insurers denied the allegations and asserted that the Brownyards were bound to the arbitration agreement that they had signed in 1991. They asked the court to dismiss the Brownyards' case. The court denied the motion.

Some insurance people take a sporting attitude to the games that companies will sometimes play in delaying claims. This is obviously not something that shows up in television commercials, but it is a reality of the business. Tying claims up in arbitration is a favorite tactic—and it's not necessarily illegal. But the way that Valiant and Maryland Casualty were handling the Brownyard case seemed to bordering on the reckless.

In April 1993, Maryland Casualty—which seemed to understand the facts of the case were beginning to turn in the Brownyards' favor—asked the court to send the dispute back to arbitration. The court denied this motion finding that "further discovery would be required to establish whether actual prejudice exists in this case." The insurance companies should have started getting nervous...and, probably, settled the case at this point. But they kept playing tough. A little while later, they asked the court—again—to send the dispute back to arbitration.

The court wasn't amused. It rejected the insurance companies' arguments, concluding:

> ...the insurers ignored repeated telephone calls and letters concerning the settlement offer, and failed to tender any counter-proposal. Such behavior...manifested an attitude of total noncompliance with good faith resolution of the case.

The court ruled that Valiant and Maryland Casualty had waived their right to pursue an arbitration forum. The case would have to go to trial. Finally, the insurance companies got the hint that they were flirting with major problems from the court. A trial wasn't likely to go well for them...so, they settled the case on quiet terms with the Brownyards.

Says one insurance litigator who reviewed the case:

> I can't for the life of me understand what these [insurance companies] thought they were doing. It sounds like the adjuster convinced the claims people that something weird was going on with the claim and then couldn't put together any evidence to back up his theory. ...But, then again, this isn't so unusual. Some companies will pick out borderline cases and drag out the settlement to the eve of trial. It's like a Darwin test. They figure that if the claim is really bogus, it will shrivel up in the meantime.

Getting government out of the business of encouraging people to put their property in harm's way should be part of a national strategy for dealing with natural disasters.

That was one clear message during a one-day conference on insurance regulation sponsored by the Competitive Enterprise Institute in Washington during April 1998. The CEI is a Washington-based think tank that promotes free market economics and limited government.

The questioning of some government catastrophe policies came not from a CEI officer but from Robert Klein, associate professor of risk management and insurance and director of the Center for Risk Management and Insurance Research at Georgia State University in Atlanta. Klein made it clear that while private markets work best when those who determine the risk pay the full cost and reap the full benefits from their actions, he thinks there are times when private markets aren't always the best choice.

Klein also pointed out that catastrophe exposure has grown over recent years, even as recent natural disasters—notably 1992's Hurricane Andrew—have awakened insurers to the nature of the risks they face. Climate change, continued coastal development and a lack of mitigation have all exacerbated risk, he said. Insurance markets have tightened but still are not in "sustainable equilibrium," he added.

"Excessive risk not only threatens insurers, it threatens all of us," because catastrophe costs ultimately could be passed on to taxpayers, said Klein. He suggested a number of policy initiatives that could help mitigate catastrophe exposure. These include:

- eliminating direct government subsidies to rebuild uninsured structures;
- eliminating tax subsidies for uninsured losses;
- allowing tax-favored insurer catastrophe reserves;
- restructuring state catastrophe financing mechanisms, which Klein said now are flawed because of inadequate rates and "cross subsidies" that encourage excessive risk-taking;
- focusing on predisaster planning and mitigation;
- facilitating more catastrophe reinsurance;
- increasing research, information and public education on catastrophe risk management;
- establishing an interim federal catastrophe reinsurance mechanism;
- easing state insurance regulatory restrictions by allowing insurers to increase prices, to develop innovative policies, to underwrite policies that consider mitigation, and to reduce exposures when individual insurers are overexposed.

"We have not seen the likes of a $50 billion to $100 billion catastrophe yet," said Ross Davidson, with San Antonio-based USAA. Disasters of that magnitude could send some insurers spiraling into insolvency; lead consumers to stop loan payments and cash out life insurance policies, retirement accounts and other savings; and create tremendous pressures on the public sector, he said. The result could "shake our economic, social and political foundations."

Davidson advocates the creation of a "policyholder safety reserve" to deal with catastrophe proposals. Under the USAA proposal, a voluntary catastrophe reserve would be set up, under which insurers would accumulate tax-deductible reserves. Insurers would accumulate reserves at their own pace, but the amount they could put up would be capped according to their individual exposures. Income on the reserves would be tax-sheltered until the reserve reached the cap. The reserve would be used to offset domestic losses from a list of named perils that "exceed a simple, high-level trigger," he said.

An entirely new approach to natural disaster coverage—one that balances mitigation, response, insurance, risk securitization and building standards enforcement—is necessary to eliminate the persistent and significant cross-subsidies in the present system, according to a prominent insurance analyst.

J. Robert Hunter, director of insurance for the Washington-based Consumer Federation of America, said that some states are big winners and others are big losers under the current system.

He said that while North Dakota and California receive a net subsidy under the current disaster relief system of $100 or more per household, the District of Columbia, New Jersey and Connecticut have to pay $50 per household or more to support other jurisdictions.

Indeed, he told a press briefing, the current system probably should not be called a "system" at all. "This is not a system," Hunter said. "This is a tragedy."

Releasing a new report on the impact of federal disaster relief, Hunter said that the current system is actually a prescription for disaster, rather than a prescription for avoiding disaster. He said that only the National Flood Insurance Program has required that safe building standards are in place. And there are no national windstorm or earthquake standards.

In addition, he said, there is no national enforcement of any standards that are in place. This, Hunter said, is of major importance. "Studies after Hurricane Andrew indicated that, had the standards in place in Florida been enforced, damage would have been reduced by 40 percent," he said.

Hunter added, however, that insurance companies also bear significant blame for recent problems in disaster-prone markets, such as Florida. Indeed, he said, prior to the recent spate of disasters, insurers rushed to write all risks, including catastrophic risks.

"In great measure, the insurers brought trouble onto themselves by careless writing, not paying enough attention to proper spread of catastrophic risk," Hunter said.

Following Hurricane Andrew and other disasters, many insurance companies severely restricted their writings in disaster-prone areas.

It now appears that the insurance market overreacted but the market is righting itself. Not only is a great deal of new catastrophe reinsurance available but new risk-financing mechanisms—such as securitization—are being used to add capacity. Hunter noted that insurance industry-backed initiatives—first through the Earthquake Project and then through its successor organization, the Natural Disaster Coalition—tried to establish a federal role in the disaster insurance market.

However, these efforts were geared less towards a real solution to the problem and more towards a guarantee to bad out private insurance interests if a large event occurred. "Wisely, Congress never acted on the bills put forth by either the Earthquake Project or its successor organization," he said.

In addition, he said, there must be a cost-benefit analysis, including an answer to the question of when the taxpayer can get off the hook. As for mitigation, Hunter asked, what are the standards and who will enforce them? Should there be federal minimum standards that state and local officials will be required to enforce in order to qualify for insurance or reinsurance?

Eugene Lecomte, a past president of the Insurance Institute for Property Loss Reduction in Boston said that, in 1996, natural disasters caused $21.3 billion in economic losses around the planet. About $9 billion in insurance claims—mostly in the United States—were filed as a result. Lecomte said insurers do not need to know conclusively that incidents of catastrophic weather are symptoms of human-induced climate change before they act.

"Global climate change is one of the elements that could be causing the problems," he said. "There's nothing that we can do as a society to stop hurricanes. There's nothing we can do to stop tornadoes or earthquakes. But there is something we can do to get people out of harm's way, and to mitigate or reduce the losses."

Some of his solutions sound like those advocated by professional environmentalists. "We've got to be smarter about where we live," said Lecomte, whose institute is a nonprofit corporation devoted to reducing deaths, injuries and property losses from natural disasters. "You don't build your house in the water, you build it back from the water. You don't build at the river's edge, you build back from the river. You give the rivers and the oceans and the coastlines room to live and breathe, and act as nature intended them to do."

But the allure of waterfont property—and the all-to-easily-purchased coverage—perpetuates the problem.

The January 1993 federal appeals court decision *Robert and Ann Foster v. FEMA* dealt directly with the way that the system deals with the risks associated with a home in a coastal resort area. This case sums up all that's out of whack about disaster response in the U.S.

Although the case focuses on some technical details (or maybe *because* it focuses on technical details) it also illustrates some of the big picture issues we've considered.

On August 1985, the Fosters bought an ocean-side house in Nags Head, North Carolina. On the date of purchase, they also bought an SFIP from Omaha Property and Casualty. As is always the case, the policy was issued pursuant to the National Flood Insurance Act and was for a one-year term, expiring in August 1986. At the end of that term, the Fosters renewed the policy for one more year.

But, at the end of the second term, the Fosters were in the middle of selling the house, so they let the flood insurance lapse. When the sale fell through, the Fosters renewed the policy on September 16, 1987, making the policy effective through September 16, 1988. Once again, in 1988, the Fosters let the policy lapse due to a pending sale of the house. And, once again, the sale fell through. So, the Fosters renewed the flood policy yet again, this time making it effective through September 28, 1989.

Trouble was brewing, though—and it would explain why the Fosters were having so much trouble selling the house. In April 1989, the town of Nags Head condemned the Fosters' house. It had been damaged by flood waters caused by various coastal storms during the previous few years.

To be more specific:

> A representative of the Department of Natural Resources and Community Development, Division of Coastal Management for the State of North Carolina, issued a Certification of Imminent Collapse for Oceanfront Structures on August 18, 1989. The property was inspected on October 6, 1989 and torn down on October 31, 1989.

After certification of their property, the Fosters submitted a claim to their flood insurer for Upton-Jones benefits. However, FEMA denied coverage on the ground that the flood insurance contract had not been in continuous effect for two years prior to the date of certification.

The Fosters didn't spend much time debating with FEMA. They just filed a lawsuit. The federal court hearing the case didn't see much to their claim. It noted that the Fosters had failed to comply with the two-year provision of the Upton-Jones Amendment and went on to note:

> The amendment was enacted to create a system whereby owners of structures on land subject to imminent collapse "as a result of erosion or undermining caused by waves or currents of water exceeding anticipated cyclical levels" could have an authorized state or local agency certify that the structure was subject to imminent collapse and collect benefits for the relocation or demolition of the structure. However, the benefits were not intended to expand the coverage of the SFIP, but were intended to assist in lowering the high insurance costs involved with ocean and lake-side erosion. The amendment was designed to facilitate that objective by giving owners an incentive to relocate the structure before it actually collapsed, thereby saving the flood insurance program the total replacement cost of the structure.

But there were even more complexities. Flood insurance law goes through modifications on a fairly regular basis. In 1987, the SFIP provided that if FEMA did not receive the renewal application and premium prior to the expiration date of the policy, the policy terminated. Robert Foster admitted that the flood insurance policy had expired in September 1988 and that he did not renew it until almost two weeks later. The Fosters' policy contained the language:

> This policy shall not be renewed and the coverage provided by it shall not continue into any successive policy term unless the premium payment for any successive policy term is received by us at the NFIP, prior to the expiration date of this policy.

So, the break in Foster's coverage would be fatal to his claim for benefits—except for some amendments to the SFIP that took effect in May and June 1988.

In May 1988, FEMA published amendments to the SFIP in the Federal Register that altered its renewal section. The new policy stated:

> This policy shall not be renewed and the coverage provided by it shall not continue into any successive policy term unless the renewal premium payment is received by us within 30 days of the expiration date of this policy.... If the renewal premium payment is mailed by certified mail to us prior to the expiration date, it shall be deemed to have been received within the required 30 days.

The Fosters' policy also stated:

> While this policy is in force, should we have adopted any forms, endorsements, rules or regulations by which this policy could be broadened or extended for your benefit by endorsement or substitution of policy form, then, such matters shall be considered to be incorporated in this policy without additional premium charge and shall inure to your benefit as though such endorsement or substitution of policy form had been made....

At the time that the Fosters' place was torn down, the law said that—to make the kind of claim they were making—an SFIP had to have been in place on June 1988 and for two consecutive years before the condemning of the insured property.

The Fosters argued that the flood insurance law should be read as requiring satisfaction of either of two conditions before making a claim like theirs. This was a very...loose...reading of the law. It suggested that merely having flood insurance on or before June 1988 would satisfy the statute, regardless of continuity of coverage.

FEMA conceded that the Fosters were covered by an SFIP in June 1988. However, in order to satisfy the statute, they had to meet several conditions—including keeping the policy in force for at least two years before the claim. FEMA argued that dropping the conditions would allow homeowners who had flood insurance to let their policies lapse until the structure was near collapse and then renew the policy for a quick windfall. This, FEMA argued, subverted congressional intent.

After analysis of the statute and its purposes, the court concluded "that FEMA's interpretation best advances the goals set forth by Congress. Requiring the Fosters to satisfy both subsection (i) and subsection (ii) comports with Congress' intent that homeowners have two years of continuous coverage prior to certification in order to collect Upton-Jones benefits."

The court issued a summary judgment for FEMA and dismissed the Fosters' suit. They appealed.

According to the appeals court, the liberalization clause of the May 1988 amendment applied to the Fosters, rendering the 1988 break in coverage inapplicable to the case. But the rest of the decision turned against the Fosters. The appeals court ruled:

> Nevertheless, even if the 1988 break in coverage is not a lapse for legal purposes, the lapse in 1987 is fatal to their claim for benefits because it occurred when the Fosters failed to renew their policy on August 5, 1987. This lapse occurred before the 1988 amendments to the SFIP and therefore was a lapse under the existing terms of the Fosters' policy. The Fosters renewed the policy on September 16, 1987, which is less than two years prior to the August 18, 1989 certification. Therefore, the Fosters fail to satisfy subsection (ii).

The appeals court analyzed the law—with all of its changes—the same way the lower court had. In effect, it chastised the Fosters: If they were going to own a house on the Carolina coast, they were being foolish to make a practice of letting their flood insurance lapse.

FEMA sometimes seems to wield its economic power in an arrogant manner. This is especially true when it comes to the central role that NFIP plays in influencing local building codes and development patterns.

An August 1994 decision by the United States District Court in Key West highlighted the effects—some controversial—that NFIP has on development. With the insurance program running consistent taxpayer-subsidized deficits, it's surprising there aren't more politically-charged lawsuits like *Florida Key Deer et al., v. Wallace Stickney.*

The endangered Florida Key Deer is a geographically isolated subspecies of the Virginia white-tailed deer known to occur only on the islands of the Lower Keys within Monroe County, Florida. Standing less than 30 inches tall, the Key deer evolved as a distinct subspecies because of its restriction to a fragile island ecosystem with limited resources. The entire population of the endangered species was about 400.

Big Pine Key is the core of the Key Deer range, approximately two-thirds of the total population inhabit Big Pine Key and the adjacent No-Name Key during some part of the year. The court accepted as fact that

"The Key Deer may not be able to recover as a species without protection of adequate habitat on Big Pine Key." Residential development on the Key made this unlikely—and NFIP enabled the development on the small island.

Of course, the deer didn't call in the lawyers. They were represented by several environmentalist groups—the National Wildlife Federation, Florida Wildlife Federation, and Defenders of Wildlife. (Wallace Stickney, the defendant, was the head of FEMA when the case started.)

The environmentalist groups wanted the court to order changes in the way FEMA administers NFIP. They argued that NFIP encouraged new development that harmed endangered species of deer...and that it broke federal law by failing to consult with the United States Fish and Wildlife Service (USFWS) before issuing NFIP policies for development of the small islands where the Key Deer live.

FEMA, on the other hand, argued that environmentalist groups had no standing to sue over the operation of NFIP. The court sided with the environmentalists:

> [The groups] need not prove conclusively that there is a direct cause and effect relationship between the availability of federal flood insurance and development, or that federal flood insurance is a major cause of the development that causes harm to the Key Deer. Rather, [they] must only make a showing that there is a "substantial likelihood" that the injury is "fairly traceable" to [FEMA's] act or omission, and a "substantial likelihood" that the relief requested will redress the injury claimed.... The evidence presented in this case clearly demonstrates that there is more than a substantial likelihood of cause and effect between federal flood insurance and new development, especially where...FEMA provides the only commercially available flood insurance in Key Deer habitat.

The groups had met their burden of demonstrating a substantial likelihood that a causal relationship existed between the availability of flood insurance and the rate or amount of new development. In the context of their claim relating to FEMA's procedural violation, they only had to show that FEMA has failed to initiate consultation as required by the Endangered Species Act.

Monroe County, Florida—the last remaining habitat of the Key Deer—

had adopted land-use ordinances so that it could receive the benefits of NFIP. There was no other source of generally available commercial or residential flood insurance in the Florida Keys other than federal flood insurance issued by FEMA.

The USFWS had determined that the greatest threat to the continued existence of the Key Deer is human encroachment—specifically, the direct loss and/or restriction of available habitat as a result of developmental pressure. Secondary factors associated with development, including road kills, were equally detrimental to the Key Deer's survival.

The USFWS was in competition with private development for land acquisition for Key deer recovery. At the time of the court ruling, approximately 1,409 acres on Big Pine Key were publicly owned and contained in a Key Deer Refuge. Approximately 4,027 acres—some 60 percent of Key deer habitat on Big Pine Key—were vacant, private lands slated for future development.

Putting a fine point on the conflict, the USFWS had made numerous factual and policy determinations, based on the best professional judgment of experts on its staff and a review of available information, that implementation of the NFIP by FEMA would facilitate and encourage new development in undeveloped areas on Big Pine Key.

In August 1984, the Associate Solicitor of the United States Department of Interior (USFWS's parent department) issued an official policy determination on the issue of whether the consultation requirements of the Endangered Species Act apply to the issuance of federal flood insurance under the NFIP.

In finding that FEMA was obligated to initiate formal consultation if the NFIP may affect an endangered species, the Associate Solicitor stated:

> ...in making its decisions on whether to determine eligibility for particular communities to participate in the flood insurance program, FEMA must follow the provisions of the National Flood Insurance Act, and it must also insure that its actions that indirectly or directly authorize or subsidize construction or acquisition in flood plain areas are not likely to jeopardize listed species or result in the destruction or adverse modification of critical habitat. The implicit approval of construction or acquisition and the issuance of flood insurance to make available needed financing for such projects clearly involve the

> de facto authorization of such actions by FEMA; "but for" the all pervasive activities of FEMA, development in flood plains would probably not take place.

So, the Department of the Interior had determined that the Endangered Species Act applied to FEMA's implementation of NFIP. Having determined this, the USFWS formally requested FEMA to initiate consultation pursuant to the ESA. In correspondence from the USFWS to FEMA dated August 11, 1989, the USFWS stated:

> It is our belief that FEMA's issuance of flood insurance [in Monroe County] encourages development to occur in Key Deer habitat. Without Federal flood insurance, development would be much less attractive. Unregulated development is not compatible with Key Deer survival. FEMA's responsibility under the ESA requires that [FEMA's] actions be reviewed relative to impacts on threatened and endangered species. The Fish and Wildlife Service feels that FEMA has not fulfilled its requirements under the Act.

In his response, FEMA's Associate General Counsel summarized his agency's position on its obligations under the ESA:

> It is FEMA's position that the [ESA] does not apply to the National Flood Insurance Program at all.... [b]ecause FEMA does not authorize, fund or carry out any actions that in any way expressly jeopardize endangered species, [ESA] does not apply to FEMA.

After exchange of correspondence, the USFWS Field Supervisor handling the matter referred it to the Assistant Regional Director for further action. In that process, the Field Supervisor stated:

> Attached is a copy of the letter I recently received from [FEMA] in response to my request for...consultation of the impact of the [NFIP] on the endangered Key Deer. As you see, FEMA contends that the Endangered Species Act "...does not apply to the National Flood Insurance Program at all" and that my request for consultation is "... clearly without merit."
>
> ...At this point, I have done all I can do. I don't believe another letter from me is appropriate as they have stated their interpretation of the law. This matter should be referred to our Solicitor's office for response to FEMA. I encourage you to raise this at the Regional or Washington Office level as I firmly believe the NFIP as managed under FEMA [requires] consultation.

Clearly, this bureaucratic paper trail made FEMA's position weak. The agency argued—lamely—that it doesn't threaten endangered species directly and if it didn't sell NFIP coverage someone else would. The only difference would be that the someone else would be a commercial insurance company charging a lot more in premiums.

The court rejected this argument soundly, writing:

> As long as FEMA is actually providing federal insurance, irrespective of whether some other private company was willing to provide private insurance, the USFWS would still require FEMA to consult. ...it is immaterial that some level of development would still occur if no flood insurance was available in Key Deer habitat. ...[FEMA] has no authority to deny [the USFWS] request, and must enter into consultation.

Worse still for FEMA, in a series of regulatory hearings, the USFWS had provided witnesses to support its argument. Its expert witness—a seasoned participant in land development in Monroe County—testified that the availability of federal flood insurance in Monroe County had a definite effect on the rate or amount of development on Big Pine Key.

Developers had to meet minimum building criteria imposed by FEMA in order to obtain building permits. Banks and lending institutions required flood insurance before they would provide financing. So, the availability of flood insurance affected building regulations and the availability of institutional financing. If federal flood insurance were replaced with private flood insurance at higher annual premiums, as little as 40 percent higher, there would be less development in the area.

Another witness—this one, a long-time resident of Big Pine Key—testified from her own personal knowledge regarding the requirements of obtaining federal flood insurance as a precondition to obtaining a construction loan for new development in Big Pine Key. She said that she had lived on Big Pine Key for 17 years and owned two properties there. Her bank required her to secure flood insurance as a prerequisite to obtaining a construction loan. Without bank financing, she would not have been able to build her home; without federal flood insurance, the bank would not have provided the financing.

With all this documentation stacking up against FEMA, the court in the Key Deer case was ready to come down hard:

> Congress has recognized that the availability of federal financial assistance, including federal flood insurance, is often the "determining factor" in the use, location, acquisition and development in floodprone areas, and has specifically made such assistance contingent on participation in the NFIP. [The Endangered Species Act] imposes an affirmative obligation on all federal agencies to "utilize their authorities in furtherance of the purposes of [the ESA] by carrying out programs for the conservation of endangered species and threatened species." FEMA...is therefore in violation of that provision of the ESA. Indeed, FEMA has refused to consult with the USFWS even after formal request to do so. FEMA's actions, and inaction, violate the ESA.

In short, FEMA couldn't exercise the influence it did on local governments and development regulators—and then try to minimize that influence when in relation to obligations that it had to other government agencies. As FEMA critics like to point out, in behaving this way the subsidized agency resembles a spoiled child.

The court concluded that FEMA had to honor its obligation under the ESA to consult with the USFWS regarding the effect of the NFIP within the habitat of the Key Deer. Judge Michael Moore wrote:

> Consultation between the action agency and the USFWS is designed to answer such critical questions as whether the project or activity may proceed as planned, whether it should be halted, whether it should be modified to avoid impacts on a given species, or whether these impacts should be accepted and an exemption granted permitting the project to proceed. The process is designed to facilitate the resolution or prevention of potential conflicts between programs and endangered species conservation early in the process.

So, FEMA was ordered to consult with the USFWS on the Big Pine Key matter within 30 days. It was an embarrassing rebuke to an arrogant agency. Disaster response, as a field, could do with more of this kind of rebuke.

Despite the missteps of government and the insurance industry, the system works fairly well. But it could work better. Government should be in the business of helping those who have at least tried to help themselves.

Specifically, FEMA should not provide multiple bail outs for people who build in the path of floods, wildfires or any other recurring disaster. The private insurance industry must bear the losses of their own bad decisions. But the taxpayers are powerless to stop the madness of high-risk development encouraged by loss-making government assistance programs.

In time of crisis, government should lend a helping hand—not issue hand outs. Only when people must take responsibility for their own actions can we truly expect them to be reasonably ready when disaster strikes.

APPENDIX ONE

General Disaster Preparation

Every family, organization and business should have a crisis management plan prepared in advance of any natural disaster. A crisis management plan should include the following elements:

- ☐ Security. Visible security is a deterrent to theft, violence and other problems. Look critically at the safety of the location and position of your house, office, hotel room, etc. What kind of crimes or dangerous activities occur normally in the area? Will anything about the area (its location on an evacuation route, etc) change noticeably before, during or after a disaster?

- ☐ Compliance with laws. Review the most recent fire, safety and health rules or guidelines for your home or office. Get copies of any safety or health inspections. Make sure any structures or modifications meet zoning guidelines.

- ☐ Insurance. Be sure you have appropriate property and liability insurance coverage in place. Review your policies to ensure that you have all the coverage that you think you do for water damage, earthquakes, etc.

- ☐ Information gathering. Determine the number of people likely to be in your home or office. Assess how many people with disabilities will be attending and whether any special setups, equipment or personnel will be required.

- ☐ Contact lists. Gather the names and telephone numbers of all emergency contacts, and have the list readily available.

❑ Point person. Assign one employee or family member to be the "point person" for coordinating the crisis management plan, and name an alternate. Identify the roles other people will play.

❑ Communication equipment. Walkie-talkies, cellular phones or pagers should be available to family members or key employees.

❑ Prepare your property:
- ❑ install insulation, weather stripping, etc.;
- ❑ shield windows and glass;
- ❑ secure loose items.

❑ Set up emergency heating equipment: fireplace with wood or coal or camp stove with fuel. (Know the proper usage and provide proper ventilation.)

❑ Insulate pipes with layers of insulation or newspaper wrapped with plastic.

APPENDIX TWO

In Case of Loss

The provisions set out in the Standard Flood Insurance Plan are highly specific, and FEMA will expect you to adhere to them strictly. The following is a list of the necessary requirements in case of an SFIP loss—it is a good program to use any time a disaster strikes.

1. Notify us in writing as soon as practicable;
2. As soon as reasonably possible, separate the damaged and undamaged property, putting it in the best possible order so that we may examine it; and
3. Within 60 days after the loss send us a proof of loss, which is your statement as to the amount you are claiming under the policy signed and sworn to by you and furnishing us with the following information.

a. The date and time of the loss;
b. A brief explanation of how the loss happened;
c. Your interest in the property damaged (for example, "owner") and the interests, if any, of others in the damaged property;
d. The actual cash value of each damaged item of insured property after depreciation is deducted from the cost of replacement of the property...;
e. Names of mortgagees or anyone else having a lien, charge or claim against the insured property;
f. Details as to any other contracts of insurance covering the property, whether valid or not;
g. Details of any changes in ownership, use, occupancy, location or possession of the insured property since the policy was issued;
h. Details as to who occupied any insured building at the time of loss and for what purpose; and
i. The amount you claim is due under this policy to cover the loss, including statements concerning:
(i) The limits of coverage stated in the policy; and
(ii) The cost to repair or replace the damaged property (whatever costs less).

Business Interruption Coverage

FEMA is very clear about the steps that must be taken to recover for business interruption. In order to get paid you must prove that:

- ❑ the property sustained damage that is covered under the policy and that the damage was caused by a covered cause of loss;
- ❑ there was an interruption to the business which was caused by the property damage;
- ❑ there was an actual loss of business income during the period of time necessary to restore the business; and
- ❑ the loss of income was caused by the interruption of the business and not by some other factor or factors.

FEMA's Duty to Inform

According to the Stafford Act and other federal regulations, FEMA is required to provide anyone who applies for asssistance with the following information:

- ❑ all forms of such assistance available;
- ❑ any specific criteria which must be met to qualify for each type of assistance that is available;
- ❑ any limitations which apply to each type of assistance; and
- ❑ the address and telephone number of offices responsible for responding.

APPENDIX THREE

Dealing with Contractors

People emerging from a natural disaster are often beseiged with offers and solicitations from contractors—both licensed and not—to do home or office repairs. If the repairs needed are minor, hand-shake deals may work. But, if the repairs are significant and if they are going to be claimed on an insurance policy, the buyer should proceed more carefully. Among the recommended precautions:

- ❑ Plan carefully what you want done on paper in both words and drawings.
- ❑ Deal only with licensed contractors. Ask to see their license with another form of identification.
- ❑ Get at least three bids. Don't just use whomever your insurance adjuster recommends.
- ❑ Ask for and check references of other work the contractor has done.
- ❑ Get evidence of workers' compensation and liability insurance.
- ❑ Don't let your contractor take care of filing insurance papers. Do it yourself.
- ❑ Get a written contract with the contractor's number on it. Verbal promises are not enough.

- ❑ Don't pay cash. Don't let the payments get ahead of the work completed. Also, by law, a down payment cannot exceed 10 percent of the contract price or $1,000, whichever is less.

- ❑ Remember, you have a right to cancel a contract within three business days from the time you sign it.

- ❑ Never sign a blank contract or one with blank spaces.

- ❑ Keep a copy of the signed contract.

Other construction-related scams include people selling construction supplies at inflated prices or posing as FEMA staff—but charging money to process claims. Specifically, these theives may include:

- ❑ People trying to sell plastic sheeting or tarps from FEMA, or people offering to install plastic sheeting. FEMA DOES NOT CHARGE for plastic sheeting. FEMA DOES NOT CHARGE to install plastic sheeting.

- ❑ People charging a fee to help residents apply for processing applications for FEMA grants and SBA loans.

- ❑ Inspectors who claim to work for FEMA, but want to charge cash fees for inspecting property.

APPENDIX FOUR

Loss Mitigation

The severity of catastrophic losses has increased due to failure to encourage cost-effective hazard mitigation. The reasons are many, but include:

- lack of knowledge or underestimation of the exposure to loss and the benefits of mitigation;
- lack of insurance premium discounts for mitigation because of regulatory constraints on rates;
- tax deductions for unmitigated and uninsured disaster losses;
- inadequate enforcement of building codes;
- lack of financing for mitigation expenditures; and
- expectations of government financial assistance in the event of a disaster.

Policy Changes and Catastrophic Losses

Public policy initiatives can—and do—help mitigate catastrophe exposure. These include:

- eliminating direct government subsidies to rebuild uninsured structures;
- eliminating tax subsidies for uninsured losses;
- allowing tax-favored insurer catastrophe reserves;
- restructuring state catastrophe financing mechanisms, which are flawed because of inadequate rates and "cross subsidies" that encourage excessive risk-taking;

• focusing on predisaster planning and mitigation;

• facilitating more catastrophe reinsurance;

• increasing research, information and public education on catastrophe risk management;

• establishing an interim federal catastrophe reinsurance mechanism;

• easing state insurance regulatory restrictions by allowing insurers to increase prices, to develop innovative policies, to underwrite policies that consider mitigation, and to reduce exposures when individual insurers are overexposed.

APPENDIX FIVE

Winter Weather Driving Tips

Project SafeSide: Keeping You Ahead of the Storm is a partnership program between The Weather Channel and the American Red Cross to equip Americans with the skills necessary to survive the most deadly weather events. The following are winter weather safety tips offered by Project SafeSide for people who have to drive during harsh winter weather.

- ❑ If you must drive:
  - ❑ let someone know where you are driving and what route you plan to take;
  - ❑ keep your gas tank full for emergency use and to prevent the fuel line from freezing;
  - ❑ travel with a disaster supply kit in your car trunk, including blankets.

- ❑ If you get stuck while driving:
  - ❑ stay with your car—do not try to walk to safety;
  - ❑ tie a brightly colored cloth to your antenna and raise it high for rescuers to see;
  - ❑ start the car every hour for about 10 minutes using the heater;
  - ❑ make sure the exhaust pipe is clear so fumes won't back up in the car;
  - ❑ leave the overhead light on when engine is running so that you can be seen.

For more winter weather safety information from Project SafeSide, and to develop a Family Disaster Plan, access the websites of The Weather Channel, at www.weather.com/safeside, or the Red Cross at www.redcross.org/disaster/safety, or DisasterRelief.org.

APPENDIX SIX

Catastrophe Losses

The insurance industry considers an event that causes more than $25 million in damages a catastrophe. The loss estimates below represent anticipated insured loss on an industry-wide basis.

Estimated Losses from US Catastrophes

Year	Number of Catastrophes	Payments (Billions)
1982	33	$1.5
1983	33	2.3
1984	26	1.6
1985	34	2.8
1986	26	0.9
1987	24	0.9
1988	32	1.4
1989	34	7.6
1990	32	2.8
1991	36	4.7
1992	36	23.0
1993	36	5.6
1994	38	17.0
1995	34	8.3
1996	41	7.4
1997	25	2.6

Each loss estimate reflects the total pure loss insurance payment for personal and commercial property lines of insurance. The estimate does not include loss involving uninsured property, including uninsured publicly owned property and utilities, agriculture, aircraft and property insured under the National Flood Insurance Program or Write-Your-Own Program. The estimates also exclude loss adjustment expense.)

Source: American Insurance Services Group, Property Claims Services Division

APPENDIX SEVEN

The 10 Most Costly U.S. Catastrophes

Date	Catastrophe	Est. Insured Loss (Mil)
August 1992	Hurricane Andrew (Florida)	$15,500
January 1994	Northridge Earthquake (California)	12,500
Sept. 1989	Hurricane Hugo (Mid-Atlantic states)	4,195
Sept. 1998	Hurricane Georges (Florida, Gulf Coast)	2,500
October 1995	Hurricane Opal (Florida)	2,100
March 1993	20-State Winter Storm (Midwest)	1,750
October 1991	Oakland/Berkeley Fires (California)	1,700
Sept. 1996	Hurricane Fran (Eastern Seaboard)	1,600
Sept. 1992	Hurricane Iniki (Hawaii)	1,600
May 1995	Flood/Wind/Hail (Texas, New Mexico)	1,135

Source: Property Claims Services, a unit of AISG, Inc.

APPENDIX EIGHT

Defining Flood

According to FEMA's Standard Flood Insurance Policy, a *flood* is defined as:

> (a) A general and temporary condition of partial or complete inundation of normally dry land areas from:
> 1) The overflow of inland or tidal waters.
> 2) The unusual and rapid accumulation or runoff of surface waters from any source.
> 3) Mudslides (i.e. mudflows) which are proximately caused by flooding as defined in subparagraph A-2 above and are akin to a river of liquid and flowing mud on the surfaces of normally dry land areas, as when earth carried by a current of water and deposited along the path of the current.
>
> (b) The collapse or subsidence of land along the shore of a lake or other body of water as a result of erosion or undermining caused by waves or currents of water exceeding the cyclical levels which result in flooding as defined in A-1 above.

APPENDIX NINE

Major U.S. Earthquakes

Year	Location	Estimated Losses (Millions of 1994 Dollars)
1886	Charleston, SC	n/a
1906	San Francisco, CA	$6,000
1925	Santa Barbara, CA	60
1933	Long Beach, CA	540
1935	Helena, MT	40
1946	Aleutian Islands, AK	200
1949	Puget Sound, WA	220
1952	Kern County, CA	350
1952	Bakersfield, CA	60
1964	Anchorage, AK	2,280
1965	Puget Sound, WA	70
1971	San Fernando, CA	1,700
1975	Hawaii	n/a
1979	Imperial Valley, CA	60
1983	Coalinga, CA	50
1987	Whittier Narrows, CA	450
1989	Loma Prieta, CA	6,870
1992	Petrolia, CA	70
1993	Scotts Mills, OR	30
1994	Northridge, CA	20,000

Source: Office of Technology Assessment

APPENDIX TEN

Fire Information

The 10 Most Costly Fires in U.S. History

Date	Event	Estimated Loss ($M 1995)
April 1906	San Francisco Earthquake/Fire	$ 5,915
October 1871	Great Chicago Fire	2,129
October 1991	Oakland-Berkeley Tunnel Fires	1,678
November 1872	Great Boston Fire	951
October 1989	Polyolefin Plant/Pasadena, TX	923
February 1904	Baltimore Conflagration	545
April/May 1992	Los Angeles Riots	616
October 1993	Laguna Wildfires/Orange Co., CA	557
December 1995	Massachusetts Textile Mills	500
February 1942	USS Lafayette	496

Source: National Fire Protection Association; Property/Casualty Insurance Fact Book

Santa Ana Winds

The Santa Ana winds which blow in to southern California from Mexico in the fall, bring with it warm, dry desert air. However, it also is the cause of devastating wildfires. Characteristics of Santa Ana Winds are:

1. Hot: The sinking movement of the high-pressure system wind causes it to warm; air temperatures increase 5.5 degrees for every 1,000 feet it descends. Moving across the hot deserts of Nevada and eastern California adds to the warming effect.

2. Fast: Wind gains speed as it squeezes through the narrow mountain passes and canyons of the San Gabriel and San Bernardino Mountains.

3. Dry: The sinking air motion can cause humidity levels to drop to single digit levels.

The following weather conditions contribute to the Santa Ana Effect:

1. Low Pressure: A low-pressure area with counterclockwise winds develops off or along the California coast.

2. Jet Stream: Powerful Santa Ana winds need a strong jet stream over Southern California. The jet stream is what guides storms, and its position and strength vary.

3. High-Pressure: The cold, dense air from an Alaskan storm helps create a high-pressure system centering roughly over the northern Utah- Nevada border. For strong Santa Ana Winds, the high-pressure system must exist for a greater vertical depth over California, extending from about 18,000 feet above sea level to the ground.

4. Cold Front: Cool air from a cold front moves from the Gulf of Alaska into the Great Basin states.

5. Air Circulation: Air circulating clockwise in the high-pressure system moves west toward Southern California, becoming the northeasterly winds called Santa Anas.

Sources: James Murakami, Meteorologist at UCLA Atmospheric Science Department; National Weather Service.

Wildfire Risk Factors

The National Fire Protection Association has identified three critical factors in assessing risk and replacement value in areas exposed to wildfire risk. Those primary factors are:

- Fuel—This factor considers whether an area is covered in grass, trees or dense brush, giving an indication of how intensely that area will burn.

- Slope—This factor identifies whether a risk is located on a steep grade. Slope can affect how quickly a wildfire may spread and can be a significant factor in reconstruction costs;

- Access—This factor identifies whether a risk is located on a dead-end, winding or narrow road that fire trucks may have trouble negotiating.

APPENDIX ELEVEN

Y2K Claim Trigger Points

The Y2K problem has initiated some heated debates over the "triggers" of coverage for liability claims. And the answer appears to lie at either end of a chronological continuum:

• the moment of actual physical injury or the manifestation of physical injury; or

• the moment of the installation of the causative software or the sale of the product incorporating the software, which in most instances will be some years earlier.

In considering the trigger of coverage for Y2K liability claims based on some physical injury or damage, it is useful to group the resulting claims into two categories:

• incidental-injury claims, that is, injury or damage to third parties that has occurred as a result of and collateral to a Y2K failure; and

• intrinsic-failure claims such as a product's inability to perform its intended function because of a Y2K glitch in the governing software.

As if the so-called Y2K problem wasn't bad enough, there are problems that made its potential impact even worse. These included:

• The leap year problem. 2000 is a leap year—with an extra day in February—and 1900 was not. So, even the date numbers are wrong after the 59th day of 2000.

• The null set problem. Some programs are designed to read "99" as shorthand for the logical concept of nothing (as opposed to the number 0). This is what logicians call "no data" or "null set."

• The re-initialization of system date in some Global Positioning System ("GPS") transceivers have a date error in them that will reset August 22, 1999 to January 6, 1980.

Y2K and the Federal Government

The Y2K glitch creats a number of problems for the federal government, among the most worrisome are:

• IRS tax systems could be unable to process returns, which could jeopardize the collection of revenue and the entire tax processing system.

• Payments to veterans with service-connected disabilities could be severely delayed because the Veterans Affairs' compensation and pension system either halts or produces checks that are so erroneous the system must be shut down and the checks processed manually.

• Federal systems used to track student education loans could produce erroneous information on loan status, such as indicating that an unpaid loan had been satisfied.

APPENDIX TWELVE

Terrorism

Terrorism has become increasingly common—and increasingly insurable in recent years. The following chart shows the hottest spots in the world for terrorist activities.

Country	Incidents
1. Colombia	667
2. Algeria	380
3. Sri Lanka	268
4. Pakistan	209
5. India	192
6. France/Corsica	132/119
7. Mexico	97
8. Spain	89
9. Burundi	85
10. Russia	78
11. U.K./N. Ireland	66/61
12. Peru	61
13. Philippines	61
14. Lebanon	47
15. Turkey	45
16. Bosnia-Herzegovinia	44
17. Venezuela	44
18. Albania	41
19. Tadzhikistan	40
20. Yugoslavia	38

Total 2,684
(Numbers include kidnappings, murder and theft)
Source: Pinkerton Global Intelligence Services

Terrorism Avoidance Tips

Most people face the greatest risk of suffering a loss related to terrorism when they travel—especially abroad. The following are a few basic tips for minimizing the risk of kidnapping or other terrorist activity:

• Stay in touch. Make your itinerary available to a handful of discrete friends or colleagues; keep them posted.
• Locate places of refuge. Know in advance where to find hospitals, doctors, police stations, and embassies or consulates of the United States or friendly countries.
• Safety in numbers. Avoid traveling alone. If solitary travel is absolutely necessary, at least skip unplanned side trips to locations where security is doubtful.
• Stay flexible. If exposed to travel risks for an extended period, avoid predictable patterns of behavior. Vary routes between work and residence. Dine in different locations.
• Identify trouble spots. Both the Bureau of Consular Affairs and the Overseas Advisory Council publish travel advisories. Pinkerton Global Intelligence Services, in Arlington, Virginia; Kroll Associates, in New York; and Control Risks Group, in Washington, D.C., supply updates on worldwide criminal activity, political tensions, and terrorism. Brigham Young University, in Salt Lake City, produces a cultural and political guide series for nearly every nation.

The U.S. State Department issues travel warnings about countries and regions that it believes are not safe for civilian travel. The following is an example of these warnings:

1. WARNING: THE UNITED STATES DEPARTMENT OF STATE WARNS U.S. CITIZENS TO AVOID TRAVEL TO ALGERIA. TERRORISTS HAVE ATTACKED PORTS, TRAINS, AND AIRPORTS. THE LEVEL OF RISK FOR FOREIGNERS IS EXTREMELY HIGH.
2. FOR AMERICANS WHO DECIDE TO BE IN ALGERIA DESPITE THIS WARNING, THE DEPARTMENT URGES THAT THEY EXERCISE MAXIMUM CAUTION, INCLUDING THE FOLLOWING MEASURES: AVOID USE OF REGULARLY-SCHEDULED COMMERCIAL FLIGHTS; BE MET OR ACCOMPANIED BY ARMED GUARDS UPON ARRIVAL OR DEPARTURE AT AIRPORTS; AND HAVE SUBSTANTIAL ARMED PROTECTION WHILE TRAVELING OVERLAND, AT WORK SITES, AND AT ACCOMMODATIONS. U.S. EMBASSY PERSONNEL TAKE THESE PRECAUTIONS.
3. MOST TERRORIST ATTACKS IN ALGERIA HAVE BEEN CONCENTRATED IN THE NORTH OF THE COUNTRY. THERE HAVE BEEN FEWER TERRORIST INCIDENTS IN THE DESERT REGION SOUTH OF THE SAHARAN ATLAS MOUNTAINS. U.S. OIL COMPANIES OPERATING IN THIS

REGION HAVE EXPERIENCED NO RECENT ATTACKS. THESE COMPANIES NONETHELESS PRACTICE THE MAXIMUM SECURITY MEASURES DESCRIBED ABOVE.

...5. ENTRY REQUIREMENTS: PASSPORTS AND VISAS ARE REQUIRED FOR U.S. CITIZENS TRAVELING TO ALGERIA. ALGERIAN EMBASSIES MAY NOT GIVE VISAS TO PERSONS WHOSE PASSPORTS INDICATE TRAVEL TO ISRAEL.

...7. AREAS OF INSTABILITY: POLITICAL, SOCIAL, AND ECONOMIC PROBLEMS HAVE CREATED AN ENVIRONMENT IN WHICH ACTS OF TERRORISM ARE REGULARLY PERPETRATED. A STATE OF EMERGENCY HAS BEEN IN EFFECT SINCE EARLY 1992. SINCE SEPTEMBER 1993, TERRORIST ACTIONS AGAINST FOREIGNERS HAVE RESULTED IN THE DEATHS OF MORE THAN 120 FOREIGNERS. THOUSANDS OF ALGERIANS FROM ALL WALKS OF LIFE AND CLASSES OF ALGERIAN SOCIETY, INCLUDING WOMEN AND CHILDREN AND RETIREES, HAVE BEEN AND CONTINUE TO BE VICIOUSLY ASSASSINATED. CAR BOMBINGS, SHOOT-OUTS BETWEEN GOVERNMENT FORCES AND ARMED GROUPS, AND OTHER VIOLENCE OFTEN OCCUR. IN THE LOCALITIES IN WHICH LARGE NUMBER OF AMERICAN EXPATRIATES RESIDE, ALGERIAN MILITARY AND OTHER SECURITY PERSONNEL OFFER GENERALLY ADEQUATE PROTECTION, BUT IN MANY OTHER LOCALITIES, ESPECIALLY IN REMOTE HAMLETS AND THE POORER SECTIONS OF URBAN AREAS, PROTECTION IS NOT ASSURED.

8. ALTHOUGH THE GOVERNMENT OF ALGERIA HAS DISCONTINUED A LATE-NIGHT CURFEW IN THE CENTRAL AREA AROUND ALGIERS, IT CONTINUES TO MAINTAIN ROADBLOCKS AT MANY MAJOR INTERSECTIONS. SECURITY PERSONNEL AT ROADBLOCKS AND INTERSECTIONS EXPECT FULL COOPERATION. IN RESPONSE, TERRORIST GROUPS OCCASIONALLY PUT UP FALSE ROADBLOCKS AS AMBUSHES.

9. BANDITRY AND ASSAULT INVOLVING FOREIGNERS OFTEN OCCUR IN THE FAR SOUTHERN REGION OF ALGERIA NEAR THE BORDER WITH NIGER. BANDITS HAVE ROBBED, ASSAULTED, KIDNAPPED, AND KILLED TRAVELERS IN ALGERIA SOUTH OF TAMANRASSET.

...11. TERRORIST ACTIVITIES: SLIGHTLY MORE THAN 120 FOREIGNERS HAVE BEEN KIDNAPPED AND MURDERED

IN ALGERIA SINCE SEPTEMBER 1993, SOMETIMES IN ASSAULTS INVOLVING DOZENS OF ATTACKERS. FOR EXAMPLE, IN L99-, A GROUP OF SEVEN CATHOLIC MONKS (NONE U.S. CITIZENS) RESIDING SOME 300 MILES SOUTHWEST OF ALGIERS WERE TAKEN HOSTAGE AND DECAPITATED BY A GROUP OF TERRORISTS WITH WHOM THE MONKS HAD HAD PREVIOUS PEACEFUL CONTACT. TERRORISTS HAVE THREATENED TO KILL ALL FOREIGNERS WHO DO NOT LEAVE ALGERIA. IN RESPONSE TO THESE THREATS, THE U.S. GOVERNMENT HAS SUBSTANTIALLY REDUCED THE NUMBER OF U.S. GOVERNMENT PERSONNEL IN ALGERIA. DEPENDENTS OF U.S. GOVERNMENT PERSONNEL MAY NOT ACCOMPANY EMPLOYEES TO ALGERIA. AN AIR FRANCE FLIGHT WAS HIJACKED AT ALGIERS AIRPORT ON DECEMBER 24, 1994, BY HEAVILY ARMED TERRORISTS WHO THREATENED TO BLOW UP THE AIRCRAFT. THE U.S. EMBASSY AT ALGIERS HAS SPECIFICALLY IDENTIFIED PORTS, TRAINS, AND AIRLINE TERMINALS AS TERRORIST TARGETS AND WARNS AGAINST TRAVELING ON REGULARLY SCHEDULED COMMERCIAL TRANSPORT. EMBASSY PERSONNEL HAVE SUSPENDED THEIR USE OF REGULARLY SCHEDULED COMMERCIAL FLIGHTS.

13. INFORMATION ON CRIME: THE CRIME RATE IN ALGERIA IS MODERATELY HIGH, AND IS INCREASING. SERIOUS CRIMES HAVE BEEN REPORTED IN WHICH ARMED MEN POSING AS POLICE OFFICERS HAVE ENTERED HOMES OF OCCUPANTS, HELD THEM AT GUNPOINT, AND ROBBED THEM. ARMED CARJACKING IS ALSO A SERIOUS PROBLEM. PETTY THEFT AND HOME BURGLARY OCCUR FREQUENTLY. THEFT OF CONTENTS AND PARTS FROM PARKED CARS, PICKPOCKETING, THEFT ON TRAINS AND BUSES, THEFT OF ANYTHING LEFT IN A HOTEL ROOM, AND PURSE SNATCHING ARE COMMON. MOST RESIDENCES OF FOREIGNERS ARE PROTECTED BY ALARMS, GRILLS, WATCHDOGS, AND/OR GUARDS. THE LOSS OR THEFT OF A U.S. PASSPORT ABROAD SHOULD BE REPORTED TO LOCAL POLICE AND THE NEAREST U.S. EMBASSY OR CONSULATE.

INDEX